VALUE-ADDED PROCESSES IN INFORMATION SYSTEMS

COMMUNICATION AND INFORMATION SCIENCE

A series of monographs, treatises, and texts
Edited by
MELVIN J. VOIGT
University of California, San Diego

Recent Titles:

Alan Baughcum and Gerald Faulhaber • Telecommunications Access and Public Policy
Mary Cassata and Thomas Skill • Life on Daytime Television
Herbert Dordick, Helen Bradley, & Burt Nanus • The Emerging Network Marketplace
William Dutton & Kenneth Kraemer • Modeling as Negotiating
Glen Fisher • American Communication in a Global Society
Oscar Gandy, Jr., Paul Espinosa, & Janusz Ordover • Proceedings from the Tenth Annual Telecommunications Policy Research Conference
Edmund Glenn • Man and Mankind: Conflict and Communication Between Cultures
Gerald Goldhaber, Harry Dennis III, Gary Richetto, & Osmo Wiio • Information Strategies
Bradley Greenberg, Michael Burgoon, Judee Burgoon, & Felipe Korzenny • Mexican Americans and the Mass Media
Heather Hudson • When Telephones Reach the Village
Robert Landau, James Bair, & Jean Siegman • Emerging Office Systems
James Larson • Television's Window on the World
John Lawrence • The Electronic Scholar
Kenneth Mackenzie • Organizational Design
Armand Mattelart and Hector Schmucler • Communication and Information Technologies
Robert Meadow • Politics as Communication
Vincent Mosco • Broadcasting in the United States
Vincent Mosco • Policy Research in Telecommunications: Proceedings from the Eleventh Annual Telecommunications Policy Research Conference
Vincent Mosco • Pushbutton Fantasies
Kaarle Nordenstreng • The Mass Media Declaration of UNESCO
Kaarle Nordenstreng & Herbert Schiller • National Sovereignty and International Communication
Harry Otway & Malcolm Peltu • New Office Technology
Everett Rogers & Francis Balle • The Media Revolution in America and in Western Europe
Dan Schiller • Telematics and Government
Herbert Schiller • Information and the Crisis Economy
Herbert Schiller • Who Knows: Information in the Age of the Fortune 500
Jorge Schnitman • Film Industries in Latin America
Indu Singh • Telecommunications in the Year 2000
Jennifer Daryl Slack • Communication Technologies and Society
Keith Stamm • Newspaper Use and Community Ties
Robert Taylor • Value-Added Processes in Information Systems
Sari Thomas • Studies in Mass Media and Technology, Volumes 1–3
Barry Truax • Acoustic Communication
Georgette Wang and Wimal Dissanayake • Continuity and Change in Communication Systems

In Preparation:

Sara Douglas • Labor's New Voice: Unions and the Mass Media
Fred Fejes • Imperialism, Media, and the Good Neighbor
Howard Fredericks • Cuban-American Radio Wars
W. J. Howell, Jr. • World Broadcasting in the Age of the Satellite
David Paletz • Political Communication Research
Lea Stewart & Stella Ting-Toomey • Communication, Gender, and Sex Roles in Diverse Interaction Contexts
Tran Van Dinh • Communication and Diplomacy in a Changing World
Tran Van Dinh • Independence, Liberation, Revolution
Frank Webster & Kevin Robins • Information Technology: A Luddite Analysis

VALUE-ADDED PROCESSES IN INFORMATION SYSTEMS

Robert S. Taylor

Syracuse University

ABLEX PUBLISHING CORPORATION
NORWOOD, NEW JERSEY

Printed in the United States of America.

Library of Congress Cataloging-in-Publication Data

Taylor, Robert S. (Robert Saxton)
Value-added processes in information systems.

(Communication and information science)
Bibliography: p.
Includes index.
1. Information storage and retrieval systems.
2. Information science. I. Title. II. Series.
Z699.T33 1985 025'.04 85-18677
ISBN 0-89391-273-5

Ablex Publishing Corporation
355 Chestnut Street
Norwood, New Jersey 07648

CONTENTS

PREFACE

Though one might say that this book is the culmination of years of experience, writing, teaching, and thinking about the information field, that would not be quite correct. The word "culmination" has a certain finality about it, as though I have succeeded in finding The Word. No such luck. This book is rather an early presentation of a way of thinking about the field of information (studies, science, systems, transfer, practice). It may be incomplete. It may even be superficial, in the sense that the field is so vast that only surfaces can be described. In a day of specialists, I am a generalist. I believe that specialization only makes sense if it has a frame of reference within which pieces can be fitted together and can build on each other. In this context, I think the value-added approach to be a useful and valid frame of reference for the description and rationalization of diverse types of information systems. This book discusses why I think this is so.

The literature is vast: information science, axiology, value analysis, systems theory and applications, computer applications, management science, systems analysis, librarianship, economics of information, cost-benefit analysis, to name but a few of the areas of concern. I obviously could not cover these domains in any formal sense. I had to be "uninhibitedly eclectic," in the felicitous phrasing of Janis and Mann (1977, p. xvi). Scanning, selectivity, serendipity, and the suggestions of colleagues were the principal determinants of this eclecticism. Many pieces, not included in the references and stretching back twenty years or more, have had impact. Undoubtedly, a well-read and critical reader will find lacunae.

A break in the circle, however, had to be made sometime, somewhere. I felt that the organizing power of the value-added approach was too important, indeed too interesting, to languish waiting for the nirvana of perfect form and expression. I have supplied a rough description and a beginning synthesis. There may be ambiguities, even inconsistencies. There are some outrageous statements, which, it is hoped, might generate a few empirically testable hypotheses. The approach needs peer criticism, a filling-in of the structure, empirical testing, and then, perhaps, resynthesis.

This is an ecumenical book, a synthesis of what it is we as information people do. Indeed, I start from the praxis of information provision which finds its expression in such seemingly diverse activities as management information systems, information analysis centers, and libraries. These activities make up our reality, a reality we have not been able to describe very well. The book is also about the use of information. In focusing on the use of information, we can look across systems at similarities, rather than at differences caused by varying technologies, disciplinary traditions, and a need to protect a turf. It is disheartening, however, to see the number of studies on information use (in the thousands) and to realize that they have had very little effect on the design and operation of information-providing systems. Nor have they—and this is even more disheartening—really told us very much about the actual use of information. This book therefore constructs a frame of reference for ordering what we know about information use environments, and what we might be able to find out given care, hard thinking, and some luck. It is in this mixture, this interface between the praxis of information provision and the use of information that the value of information will be determined. It is in this negotiating space between system and user that the determinants of value, the benefits and the costs of information use will be ascertained if not calculated. This book discusses ways those processes might be isolated and studied.

If there is bias here—and I am sure there is—it comes from my own background in librarianship and document-based systems. But these biases have been tempered and perhaps illuminated by a variety of expanding experiences in information retrieval, data processing, curriculum design for the information sciences, research in question negotiation and information seeking, new college design, educational management, teaching, and the development of a new professional program in information resources management. In a previous incarnation, I was a newspaper reporter and an intelligence agent, pursuits which seemed to have something to do with the analysis and communication of information. Two new graduate professional courses which I offered at Syracuse University were especially useful in testing ideas and in forcing organized approaches to the concerns of this book: IST 501, The Information Environment; and IST 684, Concepts of Information Resources Management. Seven years of student critiques, evaluations, and papers were invaluable in forcing better definition and structure on some of the ideas expressed in this book.

There were a number of people associated in various ways with the advent of this book. I wish to acknowledge the help of the National Science Foundation who provided support from 1981 to 1983 so that the value-added approach could be developed and tested in the context of abstracting and indexing operations. I am especially indebted to Karen Levitan and Helene Ebenfeld of NSF for their insights and encouragement. I wish to thank M. Lynne Neufeld and Martha Cornog of the National Federation of Abstracting and Information Services for their invaluable help in the project. Parts of the NSF project report are reflected in Chapters Two, Three, Four, and Six. I wish especially to acknowledge the research assistance of Susan MacMullin of the Environmental Protection Agency whose contributions to the project were considerable. The important section on problem dimensions and information traits in Chapter Three is her work. Donna Tarbania, now of the Diebold Research Group, evaluated and influenced the content of Chapters Eight and Nine on decision contexts and productivity. For many suggestions and insights, I am indebted to Dean Evelyn Daniel and to Professors Marta Dosa, Leigh Estabrook, and Mona Farid of the School of Information Studies at Syracuse University.

The results of helpful discussions with Forrest Woody Horton of Washington, D.C. are threaded throughout the book. Comments by Martha West of Information West of Los Altos, California, on information analysis are reflected in Chapter

Seven. Discussions with Charles McClure of the University of Oklahoma influenced Chapters Eight and Nine. At early stages of work, I was the fortunate recipient of helpful comment from Charles Bourne of Lockheed DIALOG, Arthus Elias of BIOSIS, Lois Granick of Psychological Abstracts, Colin Mick of Palo Alto, California, J.H. Westbrook of General Electric, and Ronald Wigington of Chemical Abstracts.

All of these people and many more have had effect on the development of this book. The form and content, however, remains my own, a responsibility I cheerfully accept in exchange for the opportunity for discussion and insight.

As a person who does not compose well at a keyboard—neither typewriter nor computer terminal—I wish to acknowledge with thanks the text editing and computer input abilities of Audrey Burian. A final note of thanks: This book would not have been possible without the support and good humor of Leni Taylor. I thank her.

Robert S. Taylor
Syracuse, New York
June 1984

Acknowledgments

Texts from several papers, written by the author about the value-added model and published during the past four years, have been incorporated, sometimes without change, in various parts of the book. They are not specifically cited. Grateful acknowledgment is made to the following publishers for permission to make use of these copyrighted papers.

1. Crane, Russak & Co., Inc., for MacMullin and Taylor. ''Problems Dimensions and Information Traits,'' *The Information Society, 3*(1), 91–111. This appears in Chapter Three.

2. John Wiley & Sons, Inc., for Taylor. ''Value-Added Processes in the Information Life Cycle,'' *Journal of the American Society for Information Science, 33*(5), 341–346 (1982). Parts of this appear in Chapters One, Two, and Three.

3. Butterworth Scientific, London, for Taylor. ''Information and Productivity: On Defining Output.'' I: *Social Science Information Studies, 2,* 131–138 (1982): II: *Social Science Information Studies,4,* 31–41 (1984). These appear in Chapter Nine.

4. Knowledge Industry Publications, publishers of the *Proceedings of the Annual Meetings* for the American Society for Information Science, for the following papers by Taylor: ''Information and Productivity: Definitions and Relationships,'' Vol. 17 (1980), 236–238, which appears in Chapter Nine: ''On Defining Organizational Information Environments,'' Vol. 18 (1981), 129–131, which appears in Chapter Three; ''Benefits and Costs of Information Use,'' Vol. 19 (1982), 296–297, which appears in Chapter Three; ''Value-Added Processes in Information Analysis,'' Vol. 21 (1984), a brief summary of Chapter Seven.

5. The Institute of Industrial Research and Standards, Dublin, Ireland, for Taylor, ''Organizational Information Environments,'' in G.P. Sweeney (Ed.). *Information and the Transformation of Society,* North-Holland Publishing Co., 1982: 309–322, which appears in Chapter Three.

6. North-Holland Publishing Co. for Taylor, ''Value-Added Processes in Document-Based Systems: Abstracting and Indexing Services,'' *Information Services and Use, 4*(3), 127–146 (June 1984), an extensive summary of Chapter Six.

Grateful acknowledgment is also made to the following publishers for permission to reprint copyrighted material: to Harper & Row Publishers, Inc. for permission to reprint excerpts from *Management: Tasks, Responsibilities, Practices* by Peter F. Drucker, copyright 1973, 1974 by Peter F. Drucker; to The Free Press for permission to reprint excerpts from *Decision Making: A Psychological Analysis of Conflict, Choice, and Commitment,* by Irving L. Janis and Leon Mann, 1977; from Learned Information, Inc. for permission to reprint excerpts from Charles T. Meadow ''Matching Users and User Languages in Information Retrieval'' in *Online*

Review, Vol. 5, 1981; from the American Association for the Advancement of Science for permission to reprint an excerpt from C. Eisenhart ''Expression of the Uncertainties of Final Results'' in *Science,* Vol. 160, 14 June 1968; to *Administrative Science Quarterly* for permission to reprint excerpts from M.S. Feldman and J.G. March, ''Information in Organizations as Signal and Symbol'', Vol. 26, 1981; to the Institute of Electrical and Electronic Engineers, Inc. for permission to reprint excerpts from D.S. Frischmuth and T.J. Allen, ''A Model for the Evaluation of Technical Problem Solving'' in *IEEE Transactions for Engineering Management,* 1969; to the Open Court Publishing Company for permission to reprint an excerpt from R. Frondizi, *What is Value?,* second edition, copyright 1971; to the *Harvard Business Review* for permission to reprint excerpts from J.P. Kotter, ''What Effective General Managers Really Do'', Vol. 60, 1982; to Prentice-Hall, Inc. for permission to reprint excerpts from James Martin, *An End-User's Guide To Data Base,* copyright 1981 and to reprint excerpts from Henry Mintzberg, *The Structuring of Organizations,* copyright 1979; to the Enoch Pratt Public Library for permission to reprint excerpts from Lowell Martin, *Adults and the Pratt Library: A Question of the Quality of Life,* copyright 1974; to *Technology Review* for permission to reprint excerpts from M.B. Packer, ''Measuring the Intangible in Productivity'', Vol. 86, 1983; to John Wiley and Sons, Inc. for permission to reprint an excerpt from R.W. Swanson, ''Performing Evaluation Studies in Information Science'' in the *Journal of the American Society for Information Science,* Vol. 26, 1975, and for excerpts from J. H. Westbrook, ''Materials Standards and Specifications'' in Kirk Othmer, *Encyclopedia of Chemical Technology,* third edition, Vol. 15, 1981; to Hutchinson Publishing Group Limited for permission to reprint excerpts from E.G. Wood, *Added Value,* copyright 1978.

Chapter One

BACKGROUND EXPLORATIONS AND ASSUMPTIONS

There are several threads that form the warp and woof of this book. This introductory chapter identifies a few of the strands, and describes them briefly, emphasizing the author's arguments and assumptions. The author believes that the reader is best served by some initial understanding of the landscape as seen by the author and by being aware of the major themes.

First of all, there is one basic tenet which frames and informs the book. That is that information transfer is an intensely human process—both in those formalized activities we call systems and in the use and uses of information, the output of those systems. It is a book about the practice of information: how we as a society, and more specifically how we as a profession organize, structure, and provide users with data, information, and knowledge. Despite the mumblings about the human use of information and the assessment of needs over the past several decades, as a profession we have gradually allowed the technology, especially the computer, to dominate our planning and indeed to dictate the shape, mode of use, and even the content of information systems. This should not be misunderstood. This book is not a diatribe against information technology. The author is not a Luddite, waiting to throw glitches into the computer or surreptitiously to insert bugs into the software. The author is rather a skeptical optimist who believes that the human frame of reference must inform and structure information system design. The late Rene Dubos (1973, p. 382) stated the approach eloquently:

> The real prophets of doom . . . are not those who criticize technological civilization, but those who accept domination of the machine. The optimists in contrast are those who deeply believe that the human person has always been, in William James's phrase, "the starting point of new effects."

We start from the human context and pose three questions:

1. What does an information system do for human beings to justify its cost?
2. Can we relate the system costs (value added in the economist's terms) to the user enhancements added by the system (value added in the context of this book)?
3. What will be the cost in time, effort, and money that users, sitting in particular

environments with particular problems, must invest to obtain useful information from any particular system?

These questions are explored, in a variety of guises and settings, and, it is hoped, clarified in this book.

TWO FUNDAMENTAL APPROACHES

Two approaches are fundamental to the argument of this book. First we are concerned about the *praxis* of information organization, processing, and provision. Second, we stress the *user-driven approach* as a major input to systems design, complementing the content-driven and the technology-driven models which dominate present design practice.

We have used the term ''model'' in various contexts, and it should be explicated. In the context of this book a model is not predictive, though the value-added model has potential in that direction. At this time and in this place, a model is a means for organizing observations, a device for describing, defining, analyzing, and synthesizing data about the operation and effects of information systems. Eventually, we would hope that the models presented here will become useful devices for comparing, measuring, experimenting with, and generating hypotheses about information transfer.

The Praxis of Information

We start from operating information systems, from the ''ordinary contexts of practical action.'' This is our reality: ''practice-driven and not, as is mistakenly assumed by those who squat in the shade of the natural sciences, a product of 'basic' research'' (Dunn, 1982; p. 293). This is not meant to deny the validity of scientific inference or empirically derived knowledge. Rather we are saying that, at this time, we in the information fields must be practice-driven. We have systems that work. That is to say, these fortuitous mixtures of professional know-how and technology called systems gather, operate on, and provide information to an amazing array of people in every kind of imaginable situation. Not that it is always done well. In fact, in many cases it is done poorly. But it is, historically considered, a remarkable set of practices that has evolved to organize, store, manipulate, retrieve, analyze, evaluate, and provide information in a variety of chunks to a wide range of people. We need now, more than anything else, an overall model of these practices, together with rigorous definition of identifiable system activities, values that are added, client types that are served, and the resultant problems that can be illuminated if not resolved by empirical research.

The field is basically at a prescientific stage, if indeed it will at any time be amenable to scientific analysis as we know it now. It is a mistake to demand rigorous quantitative measures or to expect useful and cumulative knowledge to emerge at this time. The field is at the naming, taxonomic, descriptive, and defining stage. To repeat, we have information systems that work. We need to be able to describe in rigorous terms what it is those systems do and how they do it. Then we can begin to apply experimental and quantitative techniques. This is descriptive, not prescriptive.

An analogy can be made to the invention of the steam engine in the seventeenth and eighteenth centuries, and especially with its improvement by James Watt in the 1780s. The engine worked and performed many useful functions; pumping water out of mines, powering the newly invented steamboat, driving manufacturing machinery, and providing the power for early rail transportation. It was not, however, until some sixty to eighty years later in the mid-nineteenth century that Carnot, Joule, Clausius, and others could state the thermodynamic principles of heat and energy that explained how and why the steam engine worked. When this happened the steam engine would undergo extensive alteration and improvement, and in fact new generations of power sources could be foreseen and supported. The analogy between the steam engine and information systems should not be pressed too far. The formal processes of information are much more complex, and, as we have implied, as a practice-driven discipline, it may not be amenable to the quantitative rigors of the natural sciences in the same way that gases, condensers, and governors are. As T.W. Hutchison points out:

> Because of constancies in their basic materials, predictive capacity, once attained, regarding many physical or chemical phenomena, can be preserved, added to and accumulated to an extent significantly beyond what is possible in the social sciences. In economics and the social sciences it might well be that painfully and fleetingly achieved predictions and predictive capacity may not only lose practical relevance but may break down and even become more difficult to replace, because the basic material might be becoming more difficult, or impossible to predict. (Hutchinson, 1979; pp. 32–33)

The User-Driven Model

The user-driven model is one of the foundations of the approach to information systems presented in this book. It is discussed in Chapter Three. The model supports the argument that major input to the design of information systems must come from an analysis of the information use environment. That environment essentially (a) establishes the conditions of information flows into, within, and out of any particular entity; and (b) determines the criteria by which the value of information messages will be judged. The user-driven model is perceived here as complementary to the content-driven and technology-driven models which are presently the major inputs to systems thinking and design. The content-driven model stems from the traditional divisions of knowledge, a concern with the classification of knowledge and information that has been the focus of scholarly and scientific attention for over 2500 years. The technologies of the technology-driven model have essentially prescribed the size, shape, function, dynamics, and even the content of information systems. Most people think of these technologies only in terms of the computer and associated technologies. Historically, the book and, before it, the papyrus roll, the clay tablet, and other forms of knowledge storage were also technologies which affected what our knowledge systems would store and how that stored knowledge could be accessed. It is not that these content-driven and technology-driven models are poor. It is rather that they are no longer enough in our information-rich world. They need to be tempered and informed by a frame of reference that begins to get at the uses and utility of information and ultimately to fundamental concerns of the value of information.

THE VALUE OF INFORMATION

The "value of information" is obviously a major thread in this book. Not that the term is defined unambiguously—that would be a foolish venture at best. In Chapter Two we discuss the problems of value in information contexts and the potential utility of the value-added approach to the analysis of information systems. There is no doubt but that the question of value is central to the study of information transfer. As a profession and possibly a science, we will need to come to some mutual agreement as to how we will talk about and use the term "value." We will need to be able to present, criticize, and even test mutually acceptable methods of quantifying value. In our impatience for certainty, however, we must be very careful not to freeze and enshrine top-of-the-head measures or to derive and present to our public figures on information value without appropriate qualification.

The concern with value of information is not new. The desire for measures of value, however, increases in parallel with our awareness of the pervasiveness of information in Western society. In 1970, Slamecka, in discussing the design of information networks, wrote:

> An incidental result of the requirements analysis research could very well be a partial insight into a most difficult property of information measure—its value. The development of a pragmatic measure of information utility must rank as the most important task of information science research in the next decade. An adequate functional description of the major information-using processes of man may, however, shift the responsibility for applying this measure on the information users, and away from the service designer and vendor. (Slamecka, 1970; p. 567)

The Rouses in 1984 reiterated this concern with value as the "central theoretical issue" of the field (Rouse & Rouse, 1984; p. 135). Keen and Morton in their work on decision support systems state that "this book would be far stronger if we had an operational set of concepts and techniques for discussing the value of information" (Keen and Morton, 1978; p. 44). It is significant and relevant to the argument of this book that the value of information is user based. In other words, value is not something intrinsic to, that is, contained within, an information message. An information message is given value by someone who "uses" it. (The reason for the quotation marks around "uses" will become apparent later in the chapter.) A message has potential for value. And therein, of course, lies the trouble. We cannot determine a priori the value of an individual message. We must work at the system level, not at the level of the individual message. What we can do, and this harks back to the brief discussion on use environments, is to analyze the population who will be the users, i.e., the beneficiaries, of the information in the system: their need for and mode of use of information. This is, of course, why the user-driven model is of such importance: It is the key to the value-added approach. In this way we can make estimates as to the probable utility of certain kinds of information, the preferred modes of access, and the kinds of enhancements or signals the system can provide so that use can be facilitated in that particular context.

When we make these estimates and have transformed them into a formal series of activities, we have in essence designed an information system, responsive to a particular information use environment. The merit of the system is based on how well it reflects and reponds to the needs of that environment. An information system, then, is a series of *value-adding processes*, the results of which help the users or clients to make choices or which assist them in clarifying problems. A system invests time, staff, equipment, and know-how into these processes. These are the costs of information provision. *Provision* is also an interesting, but ambiguous, word. Does it mean giving someone a pile of paper which might contain information relevant to the person's needs? Does it mean providing the means whereby clients can better and more easily find what they are looking for; or the means whereby they can manipulate the data so that they can estimate possible futures in order to make a decision today? Does it mean the provision of analyzed, evaluated, and interpreted information for use in a particular situation? Provision indeed means all of these. It depends on the interpretation of context as to what a system actually provides and delivers.

If we take a systemic view of the information process from the point of generation of new data to the point of actual use of that data, then there is a total cost (time, energy, money, know-how, equipment, etc.) attached to that information. That total cost is shared by the system, by a whole series of mediating activities, *and* by the user of that information. From the vantage point of the user, everything that happens to the information up to the time it is made use of, can be seen as cost external to the user's costs. From that point of view those costs are system costs. Given this total cost of a chunk of useful information, each system then must decide where its costs (and therefore its function) end and where the user begins to assume the costs. That total cost may not vary, though this may be a much more complex question than we can deal with at this time. That cost will be shared by system and user. How that cost is apportioned between system and user is in part the subject of this book. In general, then, we can say that as system costs go down, user costs will rise. Unfortunately, such a convenient statement is simplistic because of the dynamic nature of systems, user environments, and information. Nevertheless, the basic principle remains of a cost apportioning—a ratio between system and user.

THE VALUE-ADDED SPECTRUM

Figure 1-1 is a rough generalized chart of the value-added spectrum from initial data gathering and processing through various transforming processes to final use. It illustrates the four general processes which group examples of the activities supporting that particular process. These activities, e.g., classifying, comparing, and presenting options, are value-adding activities. In Chapter Four these are translated into 23 values—the basis for the value-added model. In Chapters Five and Six, document-based systems (libraries, abstracting and indexing services) are discussed and described as value-adding entities operating principally at the organizing level. In Chapter Seven, we look at the analyzing and judgmental processes as reflected in information and data analysis centers, in information evaluation centers such as the Congressional Research Service, and in corporate knowledge centers such as strategic planning offices. Organizational decision environments are examined in Chapter Eight in order to provide preliminary ways of (a) understanding information use in these contexts, and (b) defining the value-added activities necessary in those information systems which support decision formulation and decision making.

Information systems, then, are a series of formal processes by which the potential usefulness of specific input messages being processed is enhanced. These are the steps by which value is added to the items going through the system, however those items are defined. This point needs to be stressed, for this is the primary, if not the only, reason for the existence of formal information systems. These processes add value, whether or not we have an appropriate definition of value. These systems indeed work at some level. The value that is added may be either external or internal to the message, or both. They may be tangible signals, such as a descriptor; or an intangible value, such as validity of data. This is discussed further in Chapter Four.

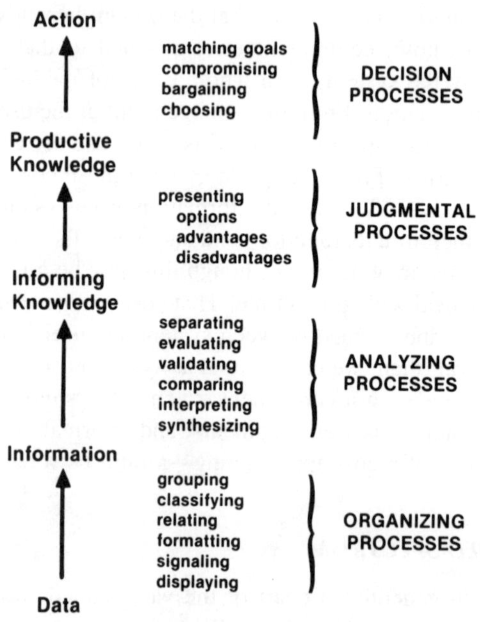

Figure 1-1. Value-Added Spectrum

The use in Figure 1-1 of the words "data," "information," and "knowledge" is tentative and approximate, let alone fraught with danger. Each of these terms carries all sorts of semantic baggage.

Data are basically symbols "that designate the states (conditions) that characterize an entity at some point in time" (Dunn, 1974; p. 78). "Data" here means:

1. numerical data: for example, the residential and commercial consumption of energy in the U.S. in 1980 expressed by BTU's;
2. tables of numerical data: for example, U.S. consumption of energy by end-use sector and year;
3. non-numerical fact: for example, the name of the Office in the State of Illinois responsible for collecting data on energy use.

These data are labeled in various ways appropriate to the context and intent of the system. This labeling process is not a simple one, as most people may assume. The proliferation of data and data bases fostered by the needs of a complex society and the exploding size of hospitable computer memories has made data access much more difficult than it was, say 30 years ago. These problems are explored in Chapters Seven and Ten. Without further processing, that is, adding value, data alone are useless. Each system must define what its data are.

To take an example from the abstracting and indexing operation (A&I), we can say that the original paper (document) is one of the forms of data input to the system. This is not to imply that a scientific paper per se is useless, but that in the context of the A&I system such papers are input data. The paper becomes the input definer for factual data: a unique bibliographic citation and a brief summary called an abstract. An example of the value-added activities might be seen in the following gross illustration. In one case, all papers coming into the system are dumped into a large room like coal in a coal bin. No index terms are added, no citation record is made, nor is there any abstract. Each time someone wants something, each paper must be handled and scanned. In this sense the data sources (i.e., the papers) are "useless" because of the amount of effort (the cost) necessary to isolate a single useful item. At the other extreme, each paper would have all possible enhancements and surrogates to allow any potential user with minimum effort to decide whether or not the item was of value. Indeed to take this a few steps further, the "system" might select, compare, analyze, and evaluate the output and make a new synthesis before presenting the information to the client. Obviously, in the context of A&I systems these are absurd extremes, but they do represent the range of the value-added spectrum. The A&I process normally organizes, labels, summarizes, and displays. These activities "involve a tradeoff of costs and benefits. In general the more finely the sorting is done, the greater the benefits [to the user]—and the costs [to the system]. Beyond some point, making the sorting categories finer would not be worth the additional cost for the particular decision-making purpose" (Sowell, 1980; p. 83; brackets added.)

Data become *information* when we establish relationships among data. That is, information is not just more labels. It is the structure and relations among data, and, most important, the rules and conditions used to establish those relations. Unfortunately, the word "information" is pervasive and ubiquitous throughout our society. Indeed the variety of professions and disciplines in the information field are built around its many faceted meanings. We do not intend to discuss or to analyze these meanings here. "Information" is used as a portmanteau word, covering data, information, and knowledge; and it will be used in that sense in this book. There is, however, one fundamental and critical caution to be made. On a practical level there is a basic definitional problem which exists throughout the field of information (science, studies, management, systems, transfer). There is a need to distinguish between two things: the *information content* of a message, and the *services* or *resources* that provide or contain the messages (Braunstein, 1979; p. 79; Machlup, 1979; pp. 62–63). These are frequently mixed in discussion and block good communication. In commonsense terms, information is the content of message, the "meaning," that which informs or that which influences a decision. *Information resources*, on the other hand, are the services, the packages, and the support technologies and systems used to generate, store, organize, move, and display these packages. We manage information resources so that we can raise the probability that the content of formal messages, that is, the information, will be useful to a client or group of clients sitting in a particular environment with particular kinds of problems.

To become useful or productive, information must go through several more steps before it can become knowledge. This is not an attempt to redefine knowledge. Because of the poverty of the vocabulary in this field, it is necessary to use what seem to be appropriate terms from everyday language, fully cognizant that these terms may carry meanings beyond the intent of the author. There is no other choice except to coin new words, a process for which this field is not yet ready. With this disclaimer and in this context, knowledge then is seen to have two properties or functions. The first is to inform, and knowledge with this property is called *informing knowledge*. The second is action or decision oriented, and knowledge of this type is called *productive knowledge*. Through the processes of selection, analysis, and judgment, what were once data, then information, have become something that can educate, inform, and contribute to personal, professional, and cultural growth. This, for example, is what education is. This is informing knowledge, which can add to or change one's picture of the world and therefore affect a person's actions and decisions. It is contextual, it is nutritional, but it is not immediately useful or productive knowledge. By no means does all knowledge become productive in the practical sense used here. In fact, most knowledge remains part of the educating, informing, and enjoying context, from which we extract portions to help us make data productive. The process of moving from informing to productive knowledge is a judgmental process, where options are presented and advantages or disadvantages weighed.

This last step, the judgmental, is usually done by the final user, the one who says: "If I do this, then X will probably result: if I do that, then Y will happen." We will see in Chapter Seven, however, that in the past thirty years, new knowledge centers have grown in organizations which monitor the outside environment for new information, and which formulate decisions, present options, and even perform many analyzing and filtering functions right up to the point of decision. The decision process is and must remain a personal one. Utilization of formal knowledge in these contexts will depend not only on its validity, quality, and ease of access, but also on the degree of "fit" between the knowledge available and the information environment within which users operate and wherein they must make decisions. It is this fit that determines the value of that knowledge. This fit is discussed in Chapters Four, Seven, and Eight, under the criterion of system adaptability and especially as the value "closeness to problem."

This fit is related to a *distinction* made *between question and problem* which travels, as it were, under the skin of the book, surfacing occasionally as a signal of subterranean differences. In general our systems (narrowly conceived as specified formal processes) have evolved to answer questions, rather than to address problems. Questions are compromises. They are only part of the larger problem situation. Questions require answers. That is to say, questions are satisfied by the most precise chunks of information we can provide. Users, however, are not interested in just receiving answers to questions, but rather in addressing problems. Problems require clarification, resolution, and perhaps even solution. This distance (one could call it a vacuum) between the output of formal systems and the actual needs of clients has been filled by a range of analysts, knowledge experts, and consultants, who massage, combine, manipulate, and interpret information to fit the problem needs of the end-users of information. These interpreters are part of the total information transfer chain between system and user. The user-driven model is one way of deriving problem-related information as input to the design of systems and their operation.

A FEW TROUBLESOME TERMS

There are a few specific terms used in this book which require some early explanation so that the reader will be alert to certain problems, realizing that there might not always be consistency of use throughout the text. In addition, as mentioned before, the author has not tried to invent new terms, but rather has used standard words in full recognition that these terms carry a load of semantic trappings. The reader might wish to run up a red flag when these terms appear.

We have already remarked on the term "information," which will generally be used as a portmanteau word to cover data, information, and knowledge. The phrase "chunk of information" is used in a rather informal sense: from Webster's Third Unabridged Dictionary: "a short thick piece often crudely or roughly formed." During the past 25 years, however, the term "chunk" has been used in cognitive psychology as a means for talking about a mental grouping of data in which complexity, recall, understanding, and familiarity are significant factors. A chess master can "see" much more on a chess board than can a novice, because the master groups potential moves into a strategy—into understandable chunks. Expert computer programmers seem to use chunks to understand a program rather than individual instructions (Davis, 1984). This is a most interesting area of concern for the information field, and will eventually have impact on how formal messages may be put together for different audiences. This is related to the discussion of problem dimensions and information traits in Chapter Three.

As interesting as this future may be, we have used "chunk" as a generalized unit of information, "a short thick piece often crudely or roughly formed." The field of practical information service and systems has no well-defined unit. We can talk about a single datum or fact, about the images in an instructional film, about an abstract or a reference, about an idea expressed in a paper surrounded perhaps by other ideas, about part or all of a structured report on production, or sales, or enrollment, or any other attribute to which we care to point. Other resources have well-defined and mutually acceptable units: a ton of anthracite coal; the dollar, mark, or yen; 500 cubic feet of space; an automobile. The "bit" and "byte" of information are really not useful as units in our context. Hence we have used the term "chunk" as a purposely ambiguous means of identifying any generalized unit of information, from single fact to complete report. The context in which the term is used will generally determine more precisely how it is used. This is, by the way, an area of fundamental concern to the profession: a taxonomy and consequent rationalization of outputs from information systems.

The word "technology" or "technologies" is used throughout the book. Though we are usually referring to current information technologies such as the computer, we need to remind ourselves that various information technologies have been used for many millenia. The process of writing, the formation of the alphabet, and the invention of printing, are all information technologies which have had profound effects on our culture. The computer and associated technologies will have an equally fundamental effect on society, perhaps as great as the development of writing. Our use of the word "technology" spans the range from a device such as the microcomputer or copying machine to what we have labelled *intellectual technologies*, for example, indexing, classification, systems analysis. The process of alphabetization, for example, is an old, familiar, and powerful intellectual technology, frequently overlooked because of its pervasiveness. In the last chapter, in discussing education in this field, technology is differentiated from science and engineering, as dealing with the processes of production and delivery of goods and services. The reader should be aware of this range of use of the term "technology."

The term "system" is used in a very broad sense to encompass any formal set of value-adding processes which have been designed or which have accumulated historically to provide chunks of information to some set of potential users. A system may be entirely machine based or entirely human based. Most likely a system will be a mix of the two. In Chapter Seven we discuss the formal and very human processes of information analysis as a system. As mentioned earlier in this chapter, from the end-user's point of view, the system may be perceived to include everything up to the point of actual use. It is important to keep this range of meaning in mind.

The concept of "use" of information is quite ambiguous. Depending on context, it may mean the act of choosing a reference to a document from an abstracting and indexing service. In another case, it may mean receiving an answer to a question or clarifying a problem situation. "Use" can mean the actual insertion of a chunk of information into a report or the direct input to a decision. In a more general sense, use can mean the messages that are part of the educating process, where new information and knowledge form part of the base affecting future decisions and actions. In our context, however, it is a formal process, the result of either a search for and/or a conscious reception of information. The field needs a classification of information *use* and *uses* (they are different) which would allow both practitioners and researchers to evaluate and investigate information environments in mutually understandable terms.

In the value-added context, information systems are designed and built on estimates of future use. This concept of "probable usefulness" poses another set of concerns. The phrase tends to imply only short term use. We should not lose sight of the fact that the value a user may perceive in any particular chunk may be related to either (or both) (a) short-term needs, that is, immediate consumption, or (b) long-term interests which are essentially contextual or nutritional. In the latter case, by far the larger, the information may not be consumed at all in any conventional sense, for example, as a trigger for action. Rather (c) it provides context affecting future information consumption needs and patterns, or (d) it becomes input to a smaller, highly individualized information system in which case the information may be recycled through a similar process sometime in the future. The case of (d) is especially true of the formal document-producing processes such as scientific and technical A&I systems, because scholars and scientists tend to maintain their own personal collections of information chunks, collections which in turn become candidates for new value-added processes.

The terms "user," "client," "customer," "consumer," though there are some slight differences in meaning, are assumed to have the same general sense as an active agent who seeks or receives information from an information system. They are used interchangeably principally for stylistic reasons. The important point is that it is this agent and the situation surrounding him or her which establish the criteria by which the value of information is judged.

These assumptions and meanings are threaded throughout the book and, indeed, have colored the way the author has approached problems. The value-added model is an early attempt to focus on a different set of problems than has hitherto been the case. It does not pretend to new knowledge, unless one can say that a change of focus generates new knowledge. The book is rather a reexamination of some of the things we know and do. This has been done in the expectation that such a reexamination will develop more fruitful and more powerful ways than we have at present for describing information processes and information contexts. To some extent, the book poses more problems than it provides answers. This is done in the belief that for now our principal concern should be the identification of problems and practices of providing useful information to users, and the rigorous description and definition of those practices.

Chapter Two

THE VALUE OF INFORMATION

Like narrow escapes in that marvelous children's story *The Phantom Tollbooth,* value "comes in all different widths." There are esteem value, apparent value, use value, positive value, dollar value, exchange value, negative value—to cite but a few of these "widths." This variety—these qualifiers—is an indication of the utility of the word, as well as the immensity and many-sidedness of the concepts it is intended to cover. The problem of value definition is compounded when we attempt to apply it to information. Information has attributes which make it quite different from other resources. These are discussed later in this chapter.

EXCHANGE VALUE AND USE VALUE

Our concern with value revolves around two principal qualifiers of value: exchange value and use value. Exchange value basically says that for a particular entity one would exchange something for something else. This exchange is usually stated in concrete monetary terms: I will give you $80,000 for that house; $20 for that book; 40DM for filling two teeth. If the buyer and seller agree to that figure (the price is usually set before the negotiation) then there is an equivalence relation (King Research, Inc., 1982), and an exchange takes place: a formal amount of money in exchange for the particular entity. As a result of this transaction, the entity has received a monetary value, because that is what someone is willing to pay for it (Fallon, 1971; pp. 48–52). The exchange could also be on a barter basis: I will provide you with dental service if you will repair my furnace. This is a process that drives economists and taxing authorities up the wall, because it exists outside the tidy universe they have constructed. Information, in many instances as we will see, also exists outside that universe.

Exchange value is not the same as use value. However, use value, in the sense used here, is basic to exchange value, because use value establishes the conditions for the exchange of one thing for something else. Our concern is principally with the "establishment of the conditions" noted in the last sentence. That is to say, we are concerned with the description, however primitive at this stage, (a) of the potential or actual audience for the information output of formal systems, and (b) the environment in which they sit which causes members of that audience to need information and to make choices among the information chunks presented, thereby giving value to that information.

This concern with use, and concomitantly with value, attempts to isolate and describe two important aspects. The first are those environmental variables which form the basis for a client to say "this chunk of information may be of use," that is, have value, and "that chunk will not be of use." Hence that client is willing to exchange something for one chunk of information but not for the other. This aspect, that is, the setting from which the need for information arises, is fundamental to the value-added approach argued in this book. The second aspect has to do with information systems, which are seen as a series of processes that enhance or add value to the messages coming into and going out of the system.

These rather bald statements need to be discussed, qualified, and placed in perspective. That is the purpose of the chapters that follow. Their basic statement at this point, however, has been necessary for the discussion and understanding of value.

The phrase "exchange value" needs to be qualified, because we include not only a formal dollar price a client is willing to exchange, but also the time and effort a client is willing to invest in order to receive what is perceived as benefits from the information process. This has been called "the apparent value of information" (King Research, Inc., 1982, p. 15). We should also point out that clients may not incur any formal dollar costs that they are aware of, for example, "free" library service. They may be vaguely aware that some small portion of their local taxes will go to support the local public library. However, they still must make the decision to expend time and energy, and to forego other activities or opportunities, in order to utilize the system. "Apparent value" is obviously an extension of exchange value, and something rather difficult to pin down.

At this stage, it is important, indeed necessary, to recall one of the cautions mentioned in Chapter One. We must distinguish between two things:

- the value of the information content of messages, that is, the "meaning," that which informs or that which influences a decision;
- the value of the information resources (i.e., the services, technologies, and systems) that store, process, analyze, package, and deliver messages.

We must keep this dichotomy in mind, even though, as technology becomes more interactive, the division may become blurred. In discussing value-added processes we are talking about the second category above—information resources, and how these information services, technologies, and systems increase the probability that clients in a given environment will find useful messages in the systems output.

In the context of this approach, the value of information, then, has meaning only in the context of its usefulness to users. There is no way of analyzing exchange value of information except by reference to the environment of those who are the intended or actual clientele of the information system. Except for certain aspects of esteem value, use value is "the pivotal concept which gives rise to the other aspects of economic value" (Fallon, 1971, p. 42).

An example of this from the realm of aesthetics may illustrate more clearly the dependence of value on circumstances.

> Is a lady's elegant-looking hat elegant? Evidently so, by definition. Its owner displays it proudly and excites the admiration of all who are present. What happens if we introduce some change in the clothes of the lady who wears it? If we take her shoes off, for example, or if we replace the dress which matches her hat with a bathing suit? It is obvious that the elegance of the hat is diminished, since it cannot be isolated from the rest of the garments which go with it. Nor can it be separated from the milieu, the style, the social prestige of the person who wears it, the accepted customs, the age, and other personal and social factors. Hence, the woman's elegant hat looks ridiculous on her husband's head, or if she wears it while washing dishes.
>
> More complex examples in the aesthetic or ethical realm can reveal better the dependence of value on a host of factors, transitory and permanent, individual and social, which intervene in the valuation of an object.
>
> If the name "situation" is applied to the complex of individual, social, cultural and historical elements and circumstances, then we maintain that values have existence and meaning only within a specific situation. (Frondizi, 1971, p. 158)

From the foregoing discussion, it is quite obvious that we will disappoint those who expect some quantification of the value of information. We agree with Kent Hall: "We are left where we started—there is no simple, reliable, generally accepted means of measuring the value of information, particularly *ex ante*. *Ex post* estimates of the value of particular scientific and technological breakthroughs have been made using cost-benefit analysis" (Hall, K., 1981, p. 162). The question of value assessment is a large and very complex set of problems. There are no accepted or standardized ways of assessing value (Black & Marchand, 1980). In fact, as we have seen, consensus on a basic definition of value does not exist. In the field of information science this difficulty is compounded by the nature and attributes of information when considered as a resource. We believe, however, that a beginning and solid base can be constructed by identifying (a) a set of criteria by which users seem to make information choices, and (b) the system activities that make those choices easier to make. The purpose of this book is to explore, discuss, and structure, in tentative fashion at least, notions about value and value-added processes that will be useful in the design, operation, and evaluation of information systems and services.

VALUE IN THE USE CONTEXT

With the foregoing as background we can say something about the value of information in the context of the systems and services that provide it, and of the people who use it. We need again to recall the basic dichotomy between (a) the information content or "meaning" of messages, and (b) the packages, transfer mechanisms, and the systems that store, provide, and display information. As will be seen in the statements and discussion that follow, there is a basic question in value theory which has to be faced and which runs something like this: "Do we desire things because they are good or are they good because we desire them?" (Frondizi, 1971; p. vii). Within the frame of reference of this book, and without prejudice to wider concerns, we have chosen to affirm the second part of that question: Things "are good because we desire them.'' This is obviously a subjective approach, and it carries problems with it.

Value is not inherent in nor is it carried by a message. We might draw the parallel with coal. Once mined, coal must be sorted, graded, transported, marketed, delivered. At this point, coal only has potential for use, that is, to be of value. Not until it is burned and the energy released in the form of heat have we made use of it, that is, given it value, to heat a house, to melt iron ore, to produce methane gas, which in turn will provide better ways of releasing the stored energy. Human ingenuity and effort has, through a variety of processes, turned a black stone that is buried in the ground and of no apparent value into something of great potential value. This analogy should not be pushed too far because there are some significant and fundamental differences to be remarked on later between information as a resource and other resources. The basic point here is that the book on the shelf, the weekly production report, the paper in a journal, or thermal conductivity data stored on disk have no value until someone ''uses'' it and thereby gives it value because that person has expended time, energy, perhaps dollars on that particular item. It should be noted that the word ''uses'' is in quotation marks because there are problems with the concept of use to be discussed below.

A message has value only in context. Clients or sets of clients live and work in particular environments. It is from this environment that tasks and problems are generated. The structure of the environment, in many complex ways, determines what information is acceptable (i.e., has value) for clarification, solution, or alteration of a problem, or for the accomplishment of a task. A message then is given value by a ''user'' who sees its potential ''usefulness'' because he or she is in a particular environment and can relate the message to the problems and tasks of that environment. This is called the information use environment. It is discussed in Chapter Three.

Messages therefore carry potential for value. We assume that the generators of messages, in communication terms the senders, initiate the process because they believe they have something to communicate, that is, something that has potential value. That this assumption may not always be correct is indicative of some of the causes of information glut, of information pollution. People may produce messages for ego support, for status purposes, because it has always been done this way, or for many other ''non-valuable'' reasons. One of the functions of information systems is (or should be) the filtering or selection of input. Somewhere in the input process, someone has made choices of data types or information packages, based on knowledge, however limited, of the probable needs of the clientele or customers of the system. This is a value-added process because it reduces noise for the systems clientele. This points up the fact that information systems are future-oriented systems. That is to say, choices of input today are based on anticipation of usefulness tomorrow, next year, or even next century in the case of research libraries and archives. This assumption—messages carry a potential for value—is important because it demands that we see system and user in a larger systemic sense.

''Usefulness'' means that a person or groups of persons have chosen a particular

message for one of several reasons. "Chosen" implies that messages have been extracted from a larger set of messages because the content bears some meaningful relation to their activities, problems, tasks. "Meaningful relation," at the moment, is not a significant concept except to acknowledge that choices are made because people perceive that relationship. We are not concerned with the process of choice at this point but rather with the context of choice, that is, what are the conditions that shape the act of choosing? It is the knowledge of these conditions by the system designer that facilitate those choices. That knowledge leads to the design of processes that add value, because they save costs, however defined, for the user.

The set of messages, for example, may be incoming correspondence, some of which is thrown out or redirected to someone else (in both cases, forgotten of no value to the recipient); some may require response and "permanent" storage for the record; some may be stored for potential future reference; and some items (we suspect a very few) may alter the recipient's current image of a problem and hence have decisional impact.

In speaking of information, Machlup advised, quite correctly we feel, that "it seems more reasonable to keep use and effect of use separate" (Machlup, 1979; p. 64). We must separate the fact that something is chosen from the store, from how it is used. We are not yet able to deal very well with the effect of information on performance *and* with evaluating that performance. We discuss this in later chapters and especially in connection with decision making and productivity in Chapters Eight and Nine. For document-based systems, however, we define "use" as the process of making choices. That is to say, the determination of usefulness rests entirely on the decision as to what to do *with* a letter, not what is done as a result of a letter. It is this decision that determines the usefulness *at that moment* of the letter: Throw it away; file it (frequently a cop-out because one is not sure of potential use and the Law of Unused File Space operates); file it because one feels that it will be useful sometime; or act on it. Note that each of these decisions implies something about the usefulness (i.e., value) of a message to a receiver who is in a particular environment at a certain time.

We have discussed this in the context of a mail system in which, in a sense, the receiver (the user, the client) is passive. Where the user is an active searcher for information, he or she makes the same range of decisions as to the value of the information messages scanned or received, even though the context for decision may be much more specific, even dynamic. Note particularly that information value is not a yes/no choice, but much more frequently the decision is made along a continuum of value as judged by a client. Person, environment, and time—each of these is an important determinannt in this process. If we wish to derive a scale of value, we could say that (a) if discarded or redirected, the message has no value; (b) if stored for whatever reason, a tentative judgment hs been made that the content of the message may have potential for value (this implies an additional filtering process sometime in the future); (c) if action is taken because of the message, then the message has high value.

Since messages carry potential for value, *value-added processes are defined as those activities of information systems which provide mechanisms that (a) can signal this potential, and/or (b) can relate the potential to a specific problem in a specific environment.* The mechanisms mentioned above are myriad and depend on the function, shape, and style of particular system types. Systems are perceived in much broader terms than is conventional, and may in fact be completely human activities formally organized to process and provide information to others. These are discussed in various settings in the latter chapters of this book.

The merit of an information system is determined by its success (a) in signaling these potentials, (b) in constructing forms which facilitate choice, and (c) in the long run, in providing the basis for better results in the organization, however defined, for example, decisions, solutions, and clarification. This essentially means that information systems should be perceived as a series of processes that enhance, that is, add value, to the information items going through the system. Indeed, if a subprocess does not add value in the sense used here, there may be good reason to consider dropping it. One of the arguments in this book is to suggest that there may be new ways of evaluating systems, more fruitful than exist at present, based on the added-value concept. In addition, there is a need to focus on the output of systems, be they products or services, because such a vantage point will allow us to look backward at the processes which produced the output, and forward to the customer or client or environment serviced. Looking backward provides an approach for the analysis of system efficiencies. In the latter case, looking forward to the use of information provides a base for the determination, quantitative or qualitative, of the usefulness of outputs, that is, what effect that particular output has on the performance of a recipient or on an organization.

These are very important considerations, for the approach provides a means of moving beyond system efficiencies to system effectiveness. If it is agreed that the customer or user is the appropriate focus of the system (and this attitude is by no means universal), then the value-added approach does indeed provide a new focus for managerial control, one better attuned to customers who in the future will become more benefit- and cost-oriented (i.e., more information literate).

INTERPRETATIONS OF "VALUE-ADDED"

The concepts "value" and "value-added" become mixed in many complex ways. It is appropriate here to summarize and comment on some of these interpretations and usages, because an understanding of them and some agreement between author and reader are a necessary base for the rest of this book. Within the context of value-added processes there are four possible ways we might interpret and use the term "value" in this book.

The first interpretation is the use of "value-added" or "added value" as used in the discipline of economics. (The two phrases, by the way, are used interchangeably.) Basically, added value is the creation of wealth. The concept is not new. The idea was probably first enunciated by Tench Coxe (Wood, 1978; p. ix), an American political economist, who was Assistant Secretary of the Treasury and

Commissioner of the Revenue in the Washington and Adams administrations, and from 1803 to 1812 Purveyor of Public Supplies under Thomas Jefferson. Economists have been using the idea for over 100 years in national accounting.

> Added value is the kind of wealth generated by the efforts and ingenuity of mankind. . . . A manufacturing business buys raw materials, components, fuel, and various services. It converts these into products which can be sold for more than the cost of the raw materials and other purchases. In doing so the business ''adds value'' to the materials by the processes of production. (Wood, 1978; p. 1)

In book publishing, for example, the publisher purchases a manuscript (or promises payment in the form of royalties and other benefits), edits it, prints it, binds it, and markets the resulting book. In economic terms, the difference between the initial cost and the final price is added value, the creation of new wealth. There are some complexities here, especially in the publishing business, for example, between author, agent, publisher, bookseller, and with the notion of ownership, that is, copyright. In addition the situation is further confounded by the fact that we are dealing with an intellectual product—with information and knowledge—and such products are different in some ways from other products.

In considering the economic approach to added value, we need to ask how nonmarket activities, such as government services, education, and medical service, are treated in the value added context. Unfortunately, they tend to get short shrift, because they do not produce a ''profit'' and, therefore, are not measurable in conventional economic terms. As Wood has said: ''There is general agreement about the concept of added value, i.e., it measures the wealth created by business and industry'' (Wood, 1978; p. 3). This statement is preceded by the following paragraph in which Wood dismisses the idea of added value in services, and by implication in the information field.

> Does a hospital or school generate wealth? When a doctor enhances the health of a patient, both the individual and the society benefit from the service. When a teacher inculcates knowledge and develops skills in the pupil, both the individual and society benefit from the service. In this sense, medical and educational services can be said to generate wealth. Of course, it is not wealth in the sense of a manufactured product or a material possession. Nevertheless, these services help to raise the standard of living. But when these services are financed by taxation, it is not easy to measure the ''added value.'' If there is no ''profit'' or ''loss'' it is difficult to know whether the added value created is greater or less than the sum total of the costs involved. It is easier to discuss added value in terms of the more strightforward examples of industry and commerce. (Wood, 1978; pp. 2–3)

The attitude portrayed here, of course, begs the important questions. That omission has special import for the information processes, for a great deal of information transfer activities, maybe even most, take place in a nonmarket context. Such contexts include government activities for the public, such as publishing, and information analysis centers, and the ''quasi firms'' that process information for internal use within private, as well as public, organizations, such as computing departments, legal departments, and research and development divisions. These are basically overlooked in the traditional value-added process.

The economists' interpretation of "value-added" becomes a highly practical and political matter when it is translated into a taxing mechanism, called the Value Added Tax or VAT. Since 1967, 24 countries in Europe have adopted VAT as one of their basic taxing mechanisms. In a 1980 Report on the Value Added Tax to the Congress, the Comptroller General stated:

> The value added tax . . . is a tax on the value added to a product or service at each stage of the production/distribution process. . . . The difference between it and the sales tax, is that the latter is collected only at the retail stage, while VAT is collected incrementally throughout the production/distribution process. (U.S. Comptroller General, 1980; p. 1)

The second interpretation of the concept is one more central to the concern of this book: value-adding processes. Basically, we ask the question: What characteristics or attributes are added to the data and information items being processed that make them more useful (i.e., valuable, beneficial) to users, clients, customers, than they were at the start of the process? This interpretation of value goes beyond that of the economist, for in a sense we are asking precisely what values are indeed being added during the period of processing or producing, activities into which the producer invests capital, labor, and materials. We ask this question because we wish to ascertain, at some level, whether those values are worth the expenditures invested. This is, of course, a "dirty question" in several ways. It is not at all clear how such worth can be ascertained in a formal and quantitative way. But we can, indeed we must, evaluate these information systems on subjective and qualitative grounds—and that base can be rigorous. As a matter of fact, such systems are being "evaluated" now, principally by inaction (no decision is decision) or by incomplete sets of criteria, and sometimes in the marketplace. Our purpose here is to formalize and structure this process within a broader user-focused context. Such considerations also may point up the weaknesses of some of the cherished technological assumptions we hold concerning information systems. This is discussed more thoroughly in the next chapter on user-driven systems.

The third possible interpretation of value has to do with the relationship of the customer or client to the information. What, for example, would a person in a given situation pay in dollars for the information? This we have called "exchange value" already discussed above. An extension of this is "apparent value": what a customer is willing to invest in terms of energy, time, lost opportunity, *and* dollars for the information. We are not particularly concerned with exchange value, but we are interested in apparent value. The latter seems to come closer to the real costs of information *for the user,* because the user makes choices, and in our model this is an important concomitant to value.

> In an information-rich world, most of the cost of information is the cost incurred by

> the recipient. It is not enough to know how much it costs to produce and transmit information; we must also know how much it costs, in terms of scarce attention, to receive it. (Simon, 1971; p. 41)

Apparent value is also pertinent to our interests because within organizations, information is often perceived as "free" in dollar terms, that is, the organization pays for it in many hidden and nonaccountable ways, such as overhead. The individual, however, must spend time and energy to search for, to select, and to use information. That is to say, the individual, by expending effort, has given value to that chunk of information. Now economists recognize and can deal with the first kind of value noted—exchange value. But, apparent value is of more concern to us, because it provides a clue as to how a client values information of a particular type in a specific context.

A fourth interpretation of value also has to do with the client or user and with the context within which information is used. Despite the strictures stated earlier in this chapter, we cannot avoid discussing the question of the effect of information use on client perception of their world and hence on their behavior. Nor can we avoid discussion of the effect of information on organizational performance, and on decisionmaking and problem clarification. Value, in this context, has to do with the benefit a user or an organization accrues as a result of information use (or even, dare we say, of nonuse). This is obviously much more difficult to deal with, principally because of our cultural bias for objective—measurable and quantifiable—knowledge. Rigor in description, in definition, and in the derived structure of relationships, albeit subjective, can be, and indeed must be, just as necessary and substantive as are so-called objective measures. These questions of benefit and cost from the user standpoint are treated throughout the book, but are discussed principally in Chapter Nine.

CHARACTERISTICS OF INFORMATION

Earlier in this chapter we made passing comment on the fact that information has attributes which make it quite different from other resources. Such differences tend to heighten the difficulties of placing a value on information. We need again to recall the basic dichotomy between (a) the information content of messages, and (b) the systems that provide these messages. We do not wish to get into extended discussion of information per se; nevertheless, any consideration of value in this field must point to some intrinsic characteristics of information that separate it from other types of resources. These obviously have some effect on the way information as content is valued in given situations.

One of the major characteristics of information in our context is that a person cannot know before seeing (hearing) the information, whether or not it is of use. Such a statement, however, implies a "yes" or "no" answer, that is, it is or is not of use. It also implies something immediate: a decision in which the information will be used. This sense of immediacy we believe has utility in only a very small number of incidences. It is not an "on" and "off" decision, but rather a whole spectrum of choices, compromises, filters, and temporary storage that heighten, but delay, actual choice.

This characteristic, however, should be tempered by the degree of knowledge one has *about* a chunk of information. The level of this knowing in some ways decreases the need for that chunk because one may already possess a part of the information. Braunstein discusses this characteristic as the "alienation or transfer of property."

> Ordinary goods have the quality of being easily "alienated" or transferred in exchange for value, either in kind or in money. A seller can describe the goods to a prospective buyer in considerable detail without having parted with the object of primary value. Information poses a logical conundrum, however, because to the extent that one has information *about* the product, one already *has* the product itself. Hence an information seller is often guarded about what he reveals, and a buyer may not be sure of what he is getting. (Braunstein, 1982; p. 4)

Such guardedness is most noticeable in such things as a letter one receives which attempts to sell a financial/stock market newsletter. The sender of the letter is very careful not to give away any information of use, but rather, by adroit wording and tempting questions, to lead the receiver of the letter to buy the newsletter in anticipation of future information of value.

"Information is not depleted as it is consumed" (Hall, K., 1981); p. 150). In the earlier example of coal and its use, coal turns to ash as it is used and no longer has value as a source of energy: Its function and nature have changed completely. The nature of a chunk of information may change as it is used; it may become obsolete, but it is never used up. The nature and speed of that change, however, is quite different: In fact, its value may appreciate as it is combined with other chunks of information, or its basic nature may be altered entirely. In one particular situation it may have far more value than in another situation. We are dealing with uniqueness here of course, and with the ability of human beings to combine these unique qualities of information into new patterns. Scientific and technical information, for example, may be superceded, may be absorbed in a larger context, or may just depreciate over time. Only through a better understanding of the nature of information use, both in pure form of information and as an information good, will we begin to provide some clarity here.

In contrast to other goods, a chunk of information can be owned by or, known to, many people at the same time. Other goods or resources can usually have only one owner at a time, and the use of that good deprives others of its use. As Braunstein points out, however, "by the marketing procedure of controlling information and its price . . . information can be made to appear in very short supply" (Braunstein, 1982; p. 4). Generally, however, many people can know the same facts, or own the same chunk of information without depriving others.

We tend to overproduce and to overconsume information. As Feldman and March point out:

> Organizations provide incentives for gathering more information than is optimal from a strict decision perspective. . . . Since the information-gathering functions are typically separated from the information-using functions of organizations, incentives are modest for gatherers to avoid overloading users . . . [and] it is better from the decision-maker's point of view to have information that is not needed than not to have information that might be needed. (Feldman & March, 1981; pp. 175–176)

We have very little understanding of what might be called "informational safety factors." This is the reason we have so many filters in the information process. Such filters, of course, raise the costs (both system costs and user costs) relative to the benefits of information. They are there because we do not understand well the effect of information on decision and other information-rich processes. Only by a better understanding of situational factors of information use can we begin to control this process.

Chapter Three

THE USER-DRIVEN MODEL AND INFORMATION USE ENVIRONMENTS

Historically, our extrasomatic knowledge and information systems have been technology driven and content driven. The technology was represented in the early bullae and seals which probably were used for scheduling supplies of food and other resources (Pfeiffer, 1977; pp. 185–187), but which in themselves, in their physical shape as hollow clay balls, dictated the form and structure of the storing, recording, and accessing mechanisms. Clay tablet, papyrus, and paper, all forms of technology, have had an important influence on the storage and dissemination of knowledge over space and time. According to its characteristics, as Innis points out, a medium of communication "may be better suited to the dissemination of knowledge over time than over space, particularly if the medium is heavy and durable and not suited to transportation, or to the dissemination of knowledge over space than over time, particularly if the medium is light and easily transportable" (Innis, 1951; p. 33). For the past 500 years, the book and its associated technologies of printing, graphics, and binding have had a profound effect on present day information and knowledge systems, and their associated dissemination channels. Today, the computer and its associated technologies are gradually altering that landscape again. We do not understand it well, because we are early on the course. As the late John McHale has stated:

> We are faced . . . with the emergence of a new and powerful fusion of technological capabilities which not only potentially amplifies our capabilities to deal with our social and physical environment transactions but which by its function as screen, channel and multiplexer of information actually reshapes the information content and perception of society—in ways that our conventional wisdom and traditional institutional means may not be able to foresee, comprehend or effectively control. (McHale, 1976; pp. 16–17)

These are indeed technology-driven systems, and they affect the ways we store, access, and disseminate information and knowledge. These technologies have essentially prescribed the size, shape, dynamics, and even the content of information systems. What is stored in a book or similar artifact, or what is stored and is manipulable in a computer is perceived and accepted as knowledge or information.

The constraints of the book, up to now, or the computer, in the future, are the determiners of the technology-driven models.

On the other hand, content-driven models are derived from the traditional classifications of knowledge, together with the elaborate schemata that have grown around them over the past 25 centuries. These models have provided a variety of powerful ways of dividing, organizing, and hence thinking about knowledge and perceiving the world around us. These have provided us with a means of organizing packages, such as books on shelves, or papers in a file, or references in an index. They have established disciplined ways of perceiving knowledge and its applications, for example, the formation of academic departments, the taxonomy of living phenomena, the periodic table of chemical elements, and indeed the identification and structure of researchable problems. In terms of information systems, it is what is in the package, the subject matter, and its storage relative to other similar subject matters and their retrieval, that has established the boundaries and objectives of content-driven systems.

It is not that these models are poor; it is rather that they are no longer enough. As our society becomes more information based, the systems that store, organize, and provide information and knowledge will become increasingly critical. We may hazard a guess that one of the major characteristics of the early period of an information society is information glut, or information overload. The explosive growth of potentially relevant information in research, managerial, educational, social, and policy contexts is altering the information environment in rather basic ways. This does not mean that we have too much information; it means rather that the sytems that filter, transmit, and distribute information do not operate well. The inadequateness is due in part to a failure to understand the contexts from which the need for information arises and to the perceptions we hold concerning the information systems themselves (Mick, Lindsey, & Callahan, 1980). The major—perhaps *only* as this book argues—reason for the existence of an information system is to store and to provide information and knowledge in usable chunks to those who presently or in the future will live and work in certain environments, and who, as a result, have or will have certain problems which information may help in clarifying or even in solving.

THE USER-DRIVEN MODEL

With this as background, a third model is proposed: the user-driven model. This model is not a substitute for the technology- and content-driven models. It is rather a complementary approach, providing a perspective for more fruitful use of the insights of the other models. As might be anticipated by the name, a major input to system design and operation is derived from an analysis of information use environments. These are defined as the set of those elements (a) that affect the flow and use of information messages into, within, and out of any definable entity or group of clients; and (b) that determine the criteria by which the value of information messages will be judged in those contexts.

Figure 3-1 is an overall graphic illustration of the model. The diagram may be thought of in three parts: (a) the information use environment (No. 1 in the figure) which provides input to the design process, and which generates the problems which the system may or may not respond to; (b) the design process (steps 2–7); (c) the operational context (steps 8–13) with particular emphsis on the value-added implementation (No. 8) and the negotiating space (No. 13). We will briefly discuss each element in the total model, and then return to a more extensive description of information use environments.

Design Processes

Analysis of the information use environment implies the description of organizations, people, and problems in ways that are useful to the design of information systems and to the understanding of the interface between system and human user, called "negotiating space" (No. 13) in Figure 3-1. This is not limited to organizations but may also include any definable cultural/social/intellectual group. Such an analysis is especially concerned with those patterns intrinsic to any particular group, patterns that can be identified and that affect information behavior. In common-sense ways, we do know a fair amount about the information behavior of different groups, for example, managers, engineers, lawyers, and students. We have not, however, developed suitable methods of organizing those data; nor have we ways of translating those characteristics into systems design. This process is inhibited in part by our

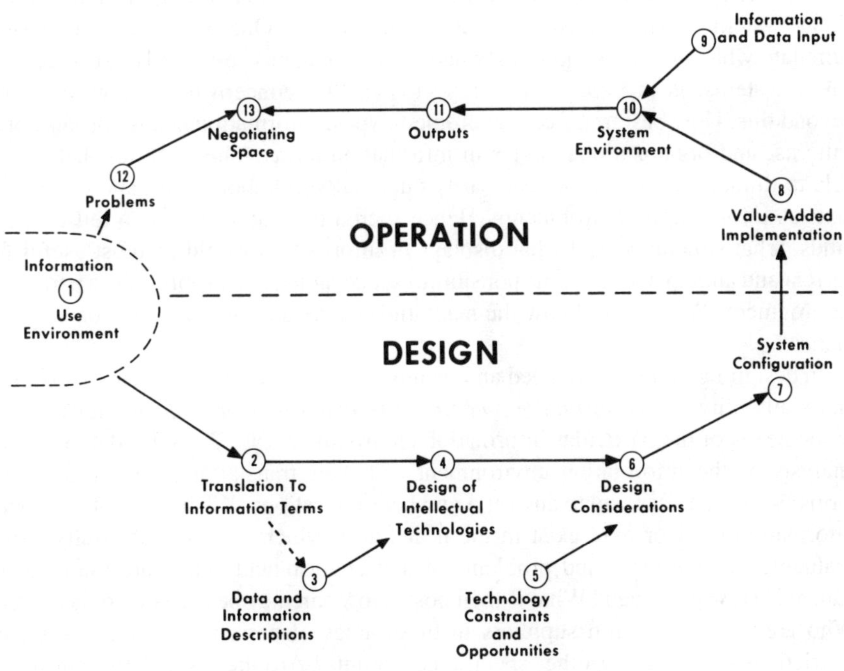

Figure 3-1. The User-Driven Model

dependence upon technology as a solution to all problems, and to our traditions of content, or subject, analysis as the sole means of access for all clients or users.

This step is essential for any initial consideration of the design of an information system because it refers to the user and to the user environment which creates the information need. For what other reason do we have an information system? The other parts of the model should be designed and implemented as a response to this analysis.

There is an assumption which forms the basis of the value-added model and which precedes this first step of analysis of information environments. That assumption is that people, organizations, and problems can be described, at least in preliminary fashion, in information terms, and that those data can be organized in aggregate groups or along generalized dimensions. These components can then become inputs to the design and structure of any particular information system and/or service in terms of important information dimensions which reflect the user and the user's world and values. There is consequently a real need to identify the dimensions of the information environment and information systems and in forming predictive relationships between them. This is discussed in the latter part of this chapter.

The analysis of the use environment needs to be *translated* into information terms (No. 2). Such translation must contribute to the design of information systems. This means that the descriptive criteria and typologies should have some predictive quality. They should have a positive effect on systems output and on the client–system interface (positive = useful to clients). One of the few attempts to cumulate what we know about information environments, especially for document based systems, is in Fabisoff and Ely (1974). Our concern here, however, goes beyond this: How best to reflect the problem types, information needs, professional patterns, and organizational styles in information terms. This requires that we be able to think rigorously (not necessarily quantitatively) about work and other contexts as information environments. Hence such a translation needs to tell us what kinds, what structures, and what displays of information would be most useful for current and anticipated tasks, responsibilities, decisions, and problems in a particular environment. We need to know the magnitude of the data and information requirements.

In designing systems, we need an inventory of the type, subject, scope, quantity, and availability of *existing and/or potentially derivable data and information* relevant to the needs of the particular information environment (No. 3). With data from the analysis of the information environment and their translationn into information terms, we need to ask and to answer a number of questions. What types of organized information exist or may exist in the near future which will be potentially useful (valuable) for the tasks and problems of that environment? How are the data organized? How packaged? What is their cost? How can they be acquired or accessed? Who are the information suppliers in these areas of concern? What, if any, are restrictions on use? Any other specific constraints? Are there specialty consulting firms that provide a knowledge base in the field? How can they be used and built into the total information resource? What "make or buy" decisions are feasible and possible?

The *information specifications* are generated at this stage (No. 4). These are the intellectual technologies best suited to meet the information needs of the environment within the constraints of the relevant data and information available. As Brinberg has pointed out, *intellectual technology* is "the intangible capital of information production." It is "the area somewhere between information as an intellectual work product and information technology as machine technology, where the application of the human-intellect–driven systems and procedures makes possible the management of information resources. Included within intellectual technology, for example, are such concepts as indexing methodologies, vocabulary control, searching logic, and systems design" (Brinberg, 1980; p. 9).

These technologies may range from the design of simple forms to artificial intelligence techniques for scanning and fixating in retrieval systems (Paisley & Butler, 1977), from indexing a report to the design of the software which allows personalized analysis in a decision support system. The specific intellectual technologies used in a particular system should reflect the needs and contexts of the clientele, the market, and the users. These technologies dictate the size and shape of the output products and services and, to a large extent, their effectiveness. That is to say, their primary function is to provide the intellectual frame of reference for adding value to the messages in or produced by the system. Any audit of products and services should attempt to describe these technologies at several levels: the kinds of structures in information products and their relationship to use patterns; ease of access and use in varying contexts; difficulty of duplicating the intent of a particular intellectual technology through computer software.

At this point, the translation of the information environment and the description of existing data merge and the information specialist can generate specific information requirements for the system. It is certainly possible, for example, that step 2 (translation of the information need), could produce a need that was beyond the ability of available information and data to provide. In this case, the intellectual technology may become more than just matching. It could become a stage that indicates need for research and development to see if a new structure or package is feasible in response to the analysis of the use environment. Therefore, this step may identify an information/data vacuum, where it is necessary to develop additional information or, possibly, better input mechanisms.

It is appropriate here to pause a bit in order to summarize and illustrate by example these elements of information use analysis and translation. For example, if we were developing an information resource to support the legal staff of a large corporation in the petroleum industry, there are rather specific peculiarities of lawyer behavior and of legal information, its provision and use, that will dictate design. The law is based on precedent, and therefore its information resources are historical in the strict sense. Not only is it historically based, but its coverage of specific topics must be exhaustive, because detail, specific interpretation of a law or regulation, may be of critical importance in presenting a case or considering a course of action. The kinds of problems and questions generated in a legal context tend to reflect these biases. What precedent exists for this or that interpretation? What regulations exist that are relevant to a particular process or incident, and how are they interpreted and enforced?

Legal and regulatory information resources tend to reflect these contexts and forms of use. They are mainly printbased, with the usual types of indexes, computer or print, especially citation forms that have become associated with the law. It is interesting to note that corporate legal staffs tend, on an individual basis, to become experts in certain fields of legal knowledge reflecting the interests of the corporation. For highly specialized or large-scale legal work, the corporation will usually call on outside expertise and counsel. As a result of these information behaviors in the legal profession, the information resources can be highly concentrated in fairly formal collections, which may be computer accessed, and in the specialized expertise which exists in a small group of experts called the legal staff. It must be emphasized that these are all components of the legal information system we are "designing": print systems such as a case law collection and reference books; computer accessing systems such as LEXIS; corporate legal staff with special knowledge, competencies, and connections to outside information sources; and external legal expertise.

This contrasts with the information behavior and needs of top corporate management in the same petroleum industry. Managers are concerned with two principal types of information. The first is control information, which tells them how things are at present. However, the higher managers are in the corporate structure, the less use they make of the financial accounting systems and the conventional management information systems (Rockart, 1979). More importantly, managers must also be able to forecast future change, be knowledgeable about market share, and be able to act on less than complete information. Managers generally favor the verbal media, namely telephone calls and meetings (Mintzberg, 1975; p. 52), and they will use systems through assistants (Keen & Morton, 1978; p. 77).

To accomplish these ends, as Huber points out, a manager needs to have two kinds of general information systems.

> . . . every manager has and uses a management information system, a combination of information sources and channels, and procedures for drawing on these sources and channels. Such systems typically consist of the trade magazines, file cabinets, sales reps, recollection, telephones, organization charts, and other resources and programs that the manager uses when seeking to answer a "What is. . . .?"-question. . . .
> . . . every manager also has and uses a decision support system, a combination of his or her information system, and a set of decision aids for examining the desirability of possible choices. Such a system might include decision rules, policy manuals, recollections, and staff analysts among the programs and resources that the manager uses when seeking to answer a "What if. . . .?"-question. (Huber, 1981; pp. 1–2)

These descriptions of management information system (MIS) and decision support system (DSS) obviously do not agree with the accepted definitions of computer-based MI and DS systems. The point is that, if we truly are concerned about clarifying or solving a problem (i.e., *what is* the situation? or *what if* this happens?, then we will utilize any and all available information and data whether or not they happen to be labeled MIS or DSS by the data processing people.

Now both of these groups—the lawyers and the managers—work and face problems in the same environment and their concern is with the same petroleum industry. Their questions may to some extent be the same, but the kind, quantity, and even quality of information deemed relevant to their specific problems will be quite different. They will require different kinds of information support. It is these differences that the analysis of the information use environment is intended to uncover. The differences will determine the kind of criteria each type of client uses in determining the usefulness (value) of information. And it is around these clues of value in specific situations that the value-added system is developed.

The fifth step (No. 5 in the diagram) is a review and analysis of the *available machine technology,* both hardware and software, that would be appropriate and feasible for the system design as defined in the previous steps on information specifications and intellectual technologies. What is the range of options? What are the price tags? What are the specifications and constraints of off-the-shelf equipment and software? This is an area of importance and breadth, and is covered, in a technological sense, in many texts. It is not, however, of primary concern here. The primary question to be answered here is the degree to which this hardware and software will contribute to the value-added processes as developed from the analysis of the environment, and reflected in the system processes.

At the next stage (No. 6) the *design specifications* are established, which merge input from the intellectual technologies necessary to respond to the information environment and input from the analysis of available hardware and software. Stage 6 is much like stage 4, in that research and/or development, this time into technology, may be indicated because some specification cannot be fulfilled with available components. Different or more sophisticated software, for instance, may need to be developed to accommodate the requirements of the designated intellectual technology.

At step No. 7 in the design process, the *configuration of the system* is made final, reflecting the specifications derived in the preceding step. This is the process of choice, translating what is desirable into what is feasible within the constraints of cost, equipment, availability of expertise, and time limits. One important (but seldom examined) concern here is the consideration of the extent and role of human beings in the total process of delivering truly useful information to those who can use it. This is an important part of the user-driven approach. It assumes a total systemic perspective, in which *all* the steps between the system and the user or client are important. Despite the variety of historical reasons and mandates for information systems, the ultimate objective of information system design must be the construction of a system that will enhance the delivery of useful information in some usable chunk at the right time to the right place. The only way we can achieve this goal is to recognize that human beings play a major role in the process. We tend to think of systems only in technological terms—hardware, software, and relevant labor. The value-added model demands that we think of the total process from data input to use, including whatever or whoever is necessary. The output of this process will be a final design with sufficient flexibility to accommodate implementation of value-added processes and output variety.

Operation Processes

We now move to what is labelled in Figure 3-1 the operations side of the user-driven model. The division between design and operation is in part arbitrary. It has been made in order to emphasize the interface side of the information process, between system and environment. The first step (No. 8) is the formal *implementation* at the elementary level of *value-added activities*. This step is based on the assumption that, if a subprocess of an information system does not add value (in terms of potential users), then there is reason to question the existence of that subprocess or activity. The remaining chapters in this book are a description of and commentary on the implementation of value-added processes in various settings. Consequently, we will not comment further on this step at this time.

At this stage the full *data input* is introduced into the system environment (No. 9). Though attention had been given to the anticipated types of input previously in the design process (No. 3), actual input requires testing, feedback, evaluation, system change, and iteration before becoming truly operational.

Systems

The *systems environment* basically brings all the pieces together in an operational sense and establishes accounting, interfacing, and evaluation procedures (No. 10). It is appropriate here to summarize what we mean by "system".

The phrase *information systems* is used as a shorthand for activities with the following characteristics:

- They are formally designed processes that select, acquire, organize, store, retrieve, display, analyze, and/or interpret messages.
- These are processes where messages are enhanced in a variety of ways, either by signals or by fundamental alteration of content.
- Messages are formal communications that people consciously design and issue in some form, for example, publish, record, present, or put in memo form.
- Messages are also generated through various computing devices and processes, and may be massaged, formatted, or organized by programmed instructions.
- These messages are sought by or automatically routed to other people who may or may not choose to make use of them.

This definition covers those systems normally called office, library, data processing, management information, information analysis, decision support, and information retrieval systems. In our interpretation, *systems may also include those human beings who extend the system to the true point of information use*. By this is meant not just systems labor, but intermediaries of various kinds, including analysts (see Chapter Seven) who fit information output to user problems. This may be an unorthodox view, but from the standpoint of the final users, everything before them in the information chain is part of the system. This approach is important in the user-driven model, though the combination may not always be made, nor is it always apparent. Comments on systems which follow should be seen in this light.

Systems are constructed from three basic components: intellectual technology, software, hardware. The ordering of these three components is purposive and reflects the user-driven approach of this project—the necessity, as much as possible, to see the client or user as a prime design factor. We have already commented on intellectual technologies in the notes on step 4 above.

The level and sophistication of *software* development, within some cost framework, will determine the degree of success of the translation of an intellectual technology into machine terms, which in turn reflects an image of a client population. Meadow, in his paper on languages in information retrieval, suggests some evaluative measures in the context of retrieval. His comments are especially pertinent here, because they take the user of the retrieval system into account.

> In what way should a language "match" a user? Strangely, given the amount of discussion on the subject of languages, we have no generally accepted definition. The following are at least candidates for measures of goodness of fit, or match:
>
> (1) *Accomplishment:* what can be done with the language in the sense of retrieving desired information and not retrieving undesired information, as well as processing that which is retrieved.
>
> (2) *Performance:* how one achieves the accomplishment—means rather than end, process rather than product. It is the kind of measure receiving much attention in the programming world and might be termed "elegance of the process or means by which an end product is achieved."
>
> (3) *Cost:* an obvious consideration, but one with several interpretations:
> (i) Cost of learning—a pre-use cost which includes the cost of learning what one must know in order to use a language, such as database structure.
> (ii) Cost of acquiring rights to use, another pre-use cost.
> (iii) Cost of human use in composing programs or searches, a during-use cost.
> (iv) Cost of executing, a pre- or during-use cost which includes compiling, interpreting and executing of programs and communication to and from the computer.
> (v) Cost of iteration, the repeating or revising of programs or queries because they did not produce the desired results—a most difficult cost to determine.
>
> (4) *Attitude:* Ultimately, people make a decision on what language to use and, for all the objective measures that might have been considered, a major factor is how well users or potential users *like* working with the language, or how well others think they will. (Meadow, 1981; p. 315)

Meadow points out that "matching users and languages is not a simple matter of choosing a 'best' language, on a scale of values. . . . The trend seems to be toward use of the computer to help bridge the gap between the user's state of knowledge and the retrieval/processing system that can perform the required tasks" (Meadow, 1981; pp. 316–317).

The constraints of the *hardware,* including costs, will establish boundaries within which the translation from intellectual technology to computer language takes place. In many ways the technology will dictate the shape of the interface. The application of information technology alters the shape of the interface in many ways, with major effect on costs and benefits. The cost on the system side, however, may be high, especially for appropriate software. These changes will affect the design of input information and hence the varieties and forms of information available to clients. The client's "working space" will be augmented by various techniques of artificial intelligence: scanning, fixating, feature extracting, comparing (Paisley & Butler, 1977). These, however, may be offset by an increase of "noise" in the system, because the increasing size of computer memories will make it easy *not* to select at input, but rather to pass those choices on to clients, hence raising their costs. At present, information technologies tend to raise the number of options open to a client, on the assumption that a wider range of choices is more beneficial. It may possibly be more beneficial, but the cost to the client in making these choices will also be higher.

At this level systems are usually described by flow charts and diagrams, showing linear and/or parallel progression of activities that take place between input and output, or just "start" and "stop". Such diagrams are principally concerned with showing relationships between activities or with the flow of material and/or, in a few cases, with the flow of information.

In describing information systems, there are four general categories of data necessary: goals and purposes; input data and data organization; processes; outputs. A formal understanding of the goals and purposes of any system is in one very real sense the objective of this book. One cannot describe value-adding processes without a clear recognition of what a system is intended to do, for whom, with what, and presumably with some implicit assumptions as to what effect the system will have on those who use it.

The term "data" is used to encompass any kind of information input or throughput: raw unorganized numeric data; references to or text of scientific papers; references to books and reports; organized routine data as in production or sales; soft data, if formalized, as in business intelligence. There are no good ways of comparing data across types of systems, nor of structuring the relationship of data to the "reality" they are supposed to represent, so that data bases can be designed and constructed in more rational fashion than is now possible. Dolby and his colleagues are doing fundamental work in this area (Dolby & Clark, 1982). In any particular system, how data are defined and how they are collected and organized become binding on the structure of the output, with consequent effect on the patterns and habits of use. We wish only to call attention to this problem, and to point out that data description is necessary not only for the description of systems, but also for the output of products and services. It will not be pursued further.

An information process is a series of steps by which inputs are altered, grouped, tagged, enhanced, stored, and/or displayed in some form (output) for the use of someone outside the system. In our terminology, this should be a value-added process, a series of activities that enhance input. These processes may be either machine or human based. As we will argue, from the user or customer viewpoint, those that are human based will tend to produce outputs that are more valuable.

The *outputs* (No. 11 in the diagram) are the products and services produced by the system. Outputs of systems may range from a simple form which triggers an order for materials to a periodic activity report required by management, from an online search in support of research and development to an ongoing filtering and evaluation of data for decisionmaking. The important point in the model is that this is the face the system presents to its clients. These outputs are the chunks (be they product or service) which the system provides in response to some question or problem. There are complexities in defining outputs of information systems. These are discussed in Chapter Nine on Productivity and Information.

Negotiating Space

The other side of the negotiating space (No. 13) reflects the specific concerns that arise out of the information use environment, which we have called *problems* (No. 12). Traditionally, the profession has taken a piecemeal view of the information process, separating information use and use environments from the actual system and the provision of information. The system is several times removed from the problem which generated the need and the criteria for evaluating the information received. This distance is the result of perceiving systems only as formal linear strings of operations built around a particular technology. Today, the technology is usually the computer. The system ends where the technology ends; there is a sort of no-man's land between the system and a human being who could benefit from the output of the system. This we have called the "negotiating space." This separation must be of concern in future system design.

In discussion the negotiating space, it is necessary to look first at the broader problem of information transfer. In his ARIST essay, "An Economist's View of Information," A. Michael Spence points out that "economic agents engage in rationally limited search; that is to say, people stop searching before their information is complete. The reason for this is that *at some point*, the benefit from acquiring additional information does not cover the additional cost" (Spence, 1974; p. 61; emphasis added). The threshold implied in the phrase "at some point" suggests that there is an interface between the agent (user, client, customer, etc.) and that which is searched (an information service, however designated and activated). Now most people in the field acknowledge the existence of such an interface; but, aside from certain evaluative procedures and feedback, the dynamics of that interface have not been explored, nor has the knowledge derived been made useful in system design.

The dynamics of the negotiating space in a very real sense define the time, effort, initiative, and even dollars a customer must invest (cost) in order to extract information of use from the system (benefit). It is here that the match between system and customer takes place, where the system must be evaluated. The understanding of and options within the negotiating space will reflect the success of any analysis of the information use environment. The negotiating space has three elements: the problems as generated by people sitting and working in a specific environment; an array of outputs supplied by the system; and a variety of mechanisms (e.g., a human intermediary or a computer display) to best match these two.

It may be important to view the service–interface–client interaction as a single total entity, emphasizing "wholes rather than parts" (Levitan, 1980; p. 249). This is illustrated in Figure 3-2. The line *AA′* is the point of input to some formal information entity, for example, a management information system, an information analysis center, or an abstracting and indexing service. The line *DD′* is the end of the process, if indeed there can be an end, where satisfaction (or unsatisfaction) or closure has been reached. The space *BB′CC′* reflects the belief that the threshold is not a single point, but rather a negotiating space, the dimensions of which will vary under different circumstances and in different contexts. The dynamics of this threshold define the environment within which (a) information need is defined and generated, (b) where a repertoire of messages and signals are displayed, and (c) where a few of those messages may be chosen (or not chosen). The elements of this negotiating space essentially define the user/system tradeoff in benefits and costs.

INFORMATION USE ENVIRONMENTS

An information use environment was defined earlier as the set of those elements (a) that affect the flow of information messages into, within, and out of any definable entity or group of clients; and (b) that determine the criteria by which the value of

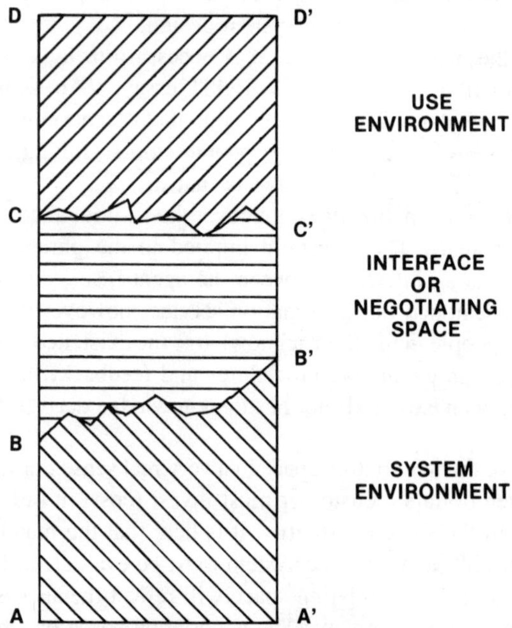

Figure 3-2. The Negotiating Space

information messages will be judged in those contexts. Within the framework of this book, the second part of this definition is important. What follows is an early exploration of those contextual determinants of information value. There are three general types of information use environments.

Geographical: defined by some physical limit, for example, a neighborhood, a city, a region, or a nation. The neighborhood as a definable entity is probably the only one that is meaningful at this time in the value-added context. The local public library and local social agencies (basically information processes) have a concept of information need and use that fits well in the value-added approach. Larger geographical entities, such as a city or country, may be useful for inventorying information resources, but they have little meaning in our context until we can analyze at the local level and then perhaps aggregate.

Organizational: An organization is a complex social unit deliberately designed to achieve a specific purpose or set of purposes (Knight & McDaniel, 1979; p. 5). In this context, an organization may be part of a larger organization, such as a research and development division of a corporation, or the financial and accounting section of a public agency. It may be a real estate office, a hospital, a police department, or a consulting firm. In each case it meets the criteria of the initial definition.

Social/Intellectual/Cultural: a group of people, very possibly unknown to each other, whose professional or personal interests provide a basis for various kinds of information services and products. At the social level, examples are: all Masons, all Catholics, all stamp collectors; at the intellectual level: all chemists, all modern historians, or all bankers: at the cultural level: all Chicanos, all chamber music players, and so forth.

In our context, we are principally concerned (a) with certain classes of people, grouped by their information behavior, who work (b) in specific organizational information environments. We recognize that the geographic neighborhood, providing it can be bounded and described in information terms, may represent an important user population. Our concern, in this book, is primarily with organizational contexts. In our information culture today, it is for the most part the organization that provides the context and establishes the tasks and responsibilities from which problems, and hence information needs, are generated. For example, abstracting and indexing services, whether print or online, are produced and disseminated for specific intellectual groups, such as chemists, lawyers, or medical researchers. These services are usually filtered through a library or information center in an organizational context before being used by an end user. The organization essentially establishes the boundaries, direction, and rules, but it is the engineer or biologist or manager who defines the problems. Consequently our description of information use environments focuses on three defining factors:

- the structure, purpose, and direction of the organization as they affect information behavior:

- the variety of people who work in the organization and who, because of their training and responsibilities, display different kinds of information needs;
- the dimensions of problems which are generated by these people and which reflect the specific context in which they work.

People and problems, and their reflection in information requirements, will of course exist in any type of environment, not only in organizations. To some extent the broader context is considered in Chapter Five on libraries.

Organizations

In many ways the organization establishes goals, style, rewards and penalties, and access channels for information use and validation. The organization may be small or large; it may be the whole or part of something larger; it may have formal relations to other organizations that affect its information processes. Whatever the size, structure, or relationships, the organization sets the context for the use of information. Organizations today are quite different from those of 50 years ago. In good part, it is the utility, effect, and perception of knowledge/information in those entities that signal and describe this change. As Paisley has pointed out:

> Social systems have six primary functions with respect to work: they *mandate, justify, enable, guide, evaluate,* and *reward* work. Each social system is responsible for most of these functions, but each social system carries out the functions in its own way. For example, an organization enables work by providing space, equipment, and material; a work team enables work by providing know-how and direct assistance. An organization rewards work with pay and advancement; a work team rewards work with esteem and an exchange of services. (Paisley, 1980; p. 136)

The way each of these primary functions is viewed and implemented by the organization has an effect on information transfer and utility. For purposes of structure, and in very simple terms, it is suggested that there are four general factors useful in describing an organization informationally: (a) goals, demographic data, and clientele; (b) style; (c) formal flows of information; (d) work structures.

The *goals, demographics,* and *clientele* or *publics* of any organized entity set direction and boundaries. It is not only necessary to be able to describe what an organization does (manufacture integrated circuits, sell beer, or educate adolescents), but also what its knowledge base is. That is to say, from where does its strength, growth, and innovation come, and how are its objectives established or changed? It is, of course, necessary to consider the vital statistics of the organization: size, structure, share of market, legislative mandate, types of workers, and so forth. The clientele of public agencies vis-à-vis private for-profit corporations have widely differing perceptions of what they expect from those organizations. The organizations themselves have differing objectives, and therefore varying criteria for evaluating success or nonsuccess. Because of this, these clientele or publics impose differing constraints for ascertaining the value of information within the organization. So we need to be able to describe the clientele, market, or publics of this particular entity. Even an organization within a larger entity has its clientele. For example, the research and development division of a large corporation has top management as clients, and the information that division produces must be relevant to the style and concern of management. The technical information center has the scientists and engineers of that research and development division as clients, and its information services must fit their interests and problems.

Each organization provides a setting for a *style of operation and function*. Van de Ven and Ferry point out that "the structure and functioning of organizations are the result of strategic choices made either implicitly or explicitly by management or by people who are the key decision makers in an organization" (Van de Ven & Ferry, 1980; p. 15). Structure establishes differentiation in function, reporting and responsibility channels, and the distribution of power and authority. The functional design establishes specializations, personnel requirements and composition, performance norms and standards, and interunit relationships. This is the formal style of the organization and, though we are well aware of the informal styles that may develop, these are defined and enhanced or constrained by formal structures. The formal style of the organization establishes the channels for formal messages and the procedures and assumptions for the validation of messages. To a large extent the structure determines what information is worthwhile, who in the organization should get it, why they get it, and what they are expected to do with it (Zand, 1981; p. 9). Because these questions are asked here does not mean that an organization answers them in any formal sense. In fact such questions have often been ignored; but such a situation itself is an important index in the understanding of the information environment.

Concern with the *formal flow* of information into and within an organization is provisionally organized in four areas. *Activities at the boundaries* of the organization monitor and scan the external environment, and select and filter information from that environment deemed appropriate to the organization. The capability of those activities to know and to match organizational information needs is a key process in both having an informed organization and exercising some control over information overload. Organizations recognize this monitoring need and the varieties of expertise necessary to accomplish those ends, by staffing different kinds of people to watch for different kinds of problems and information from the external environment. Financial managers monitor the economy; engineers the technical advances; and lawyers the legal and regulatory environment. Each of these specialized staffs may be supported by agencies such as libraries or information centers which also scan the external environment, and formally collect, organize, and provide access to both external and internal information.

Internal information collection is critical in providing a continuous flow of information to answer the questions "What are we doing?" and "How are we doing?" A critical point here is who decides (a) what is to be collected and (b) how it is to be structured. In other words, who owns the information? In the past, responsibility for data bases in organizations has been widely scattered, with the result that users such as top management are poorly served because they have not originated, do not control, and hence do not own the data. Top management therefore frequently gets only the by-products (Berry & Cook, 1976). This is discussed at more length in Chapter Eight.

The *direction and size of information flow* is an important consideration in the process of informing. The copying machine, computer printout, and the assumption that the more information the better have made it easy to avoid decision controlling this flow. Consequently, overload and high costs frequently mark the information process. We do not yet know very much about informational safety factors. How much is enough information? How much is too much? We do not have answers. Hence to be on the safe side, we tend to overload. A sensitivity to the processes by which information moves within any organization is an important step in understanding the information environment.

Information systems are a series of formal processes by which the *potential usefulness of specific input messages are enhanced*. Though this value-added process is the subject of later chapters, it is necessary to call attention to it in the context of the information environment. It is also a reminder that while messages may be enhanced (made more useful) the flow of messages may be impeded by inefficiencies at the systems level.

The importance of how an organization structures itself for work has been noted above. It is of concern here that we look at departments, work teams, offices, etc. as information processors. Each of these has varying criteria, need for, and disposition toward information. Within any given unit the managerial structure has established or fostered, inadvertently or otherwise, an attitude toward information and its usefulness. In research and development laboratories, for example, what executives emphasize and reward (useful products/processes or publishing a paper which adds significantly to the technical literature) has a great deal to say about the importance of different kinds of information (Pelz & Andrews, 1966; pp. 297–299). At the research end of the spectrum (publishing a paper), literature support, online searching, and similar activities become important. At the development end (useful products/processes), specifications, properties data, materials information, patents, and computer-aided design systems become important. As information literacy grows in organizations, the information support services will need to discriminate among these varying types of need.

People

The kinds of people who make up the clientele or customers of an information system are an important element in describing the environment, and hence a determinant of system design. That is to say, different classes of professionals need and use information in quite different ways and indeed have differing innterpretations of information, its delivery, structure, and utility. This is not just a matter of subject content, but rather, that the kinds of problems and kinds of concerns that one professional group has is quite different from those of other groups. For example, we would not (or, at least, should not) design the same kind of information system(s) for lawyers, design engineers, corporate strategic planners, undergraduate students, physicists and chemists, legislative staffs, medieval scholars, or manufacturing production managers. Generally, most people would agree with the last statement. However, we know very little about why we would design different systems or about the structure of problems in these different professions and their reflection in information requirements and information services and systems.

Gerstenberger and Allen, in their study of engineers and choice of information channel, note:

> Engineers, in selecting among information channels, act in a manner which is intended not to maximize gain, but rather, to minimize loss. The loss to be minimized is the cost in terms of effort, either physical or psychological, which must be expended in order to gain access to an information channel. (Gerstenberger & Allen, 1968; p. 277)

It may be, and this is offered as a tenative hypothesis, that this behavior is due less to the type of person or profession, but rather to the types and structure of problems that engineers deal with, or at least to problems at different stages of a process (see also Allen, 1977, pp. 35–98). This is discussed further in the next section on problem dimensions. There are general classes of problems called engineering-type problems, or scientific-type problems, or legal problems, or managerial-type problems. They affect the way information is needed and the way it is used. Our concern here is with these large aspects of differences among classes of information users. We will later discuss the dimensions of problems and their relation to the traits of information as it is stored in formal systems.

As illustration, we look at three classes of professionals and their general patterns of information use: scientists, engineers, and executives (Brinberg, 1980, pp. 5–6). Worth noting is that these three classes are portmanteau words for classes of problems and information needs. That is to say, scientists do not always behave like managers or engineers. With this caution, we can say that *scientists* can be characterized as follows:

- They produce documents and thereby constitute and draw upon the information store. Paper is their product. They are paper centered, papyrocentric, in the words of Derek Price (Price, 1965).
- Their work progresses over long time periods; it is cumulative.
- They are interested in theory and source data.
- They are interested in comprehensive coverage; they find bibliographies helpful.

Generally traditional information services such as libraries and abstracting and indexing services have grown to serve these needs.

On the other hand, *engineers,* when behaving as information seekers, can be characterized as follows:

- They have a focused direction of inquiry; an exception to this is at the beginning of the design stage when they browse literature and talk to many people for stimulation and idea formulation.
- Their primary goal, in contrast to scientists, is to produce products or to design operating systems; these, rather than formal papers as in the sciences, are the carriers of their information.

- In their choice of information channels, they tend to minimize loss rather than maximize gain (see Gerstenberger and Allen quote above); they satisfice, i.e., "look for a course of action that is satisfactory or 'good enough' " (Simon, 1976, p. xxviii).
- They prefer informal sources of information for the first steps in problem solving, regardless of engineering job activity or industry (Shuchman, 1981; p. 21).
- They generally seek reliable answers, not guides to source literature.
- They work within time constraints.

Executives or *managers,* especially those who are policy makers, have information requirements that can be characterized as follows:

- They rely heavily on evaluated, aggregated data.
- They make a variety of short- medium- and long-term decisions, each frequently requiring different configurations and quality of information.
- They must operate on a good deal less than total information; 70 percent is considered high availability for business people (Brinberg, 1980; p. 6).
- They suffer from an abundance of irrelevant information (Ackoff, 1967; p. 147).
- They seek options and alternatives, rather than answers.
- Subjective (human) judgment plays an important role in executive decision making.
- They strongly favor the verbal media, namely, telephone calls and meetings (Mintzberg, 1975; p. 52).
- No manager can depend solely on information generated internally in the organization; external information, often unpredictable in occurrence or impact, is critical.
- They tend to use formal information systems through assistants and secretaries who act as preliminary filters.

These are only summaries and are not intended to be complete characterizations. They illustrate the need to distinguish between different types of professional settings, and their translation in information terms. They imply that there are characteristics inherent in both setting and response that are *not* subject determined. They are intended to illustrate above all that there are important characteristics of different user populations that need to be built into the design of information systems.

Problems

One of the major constraints of most current information retrieval systems is that they are designed to serve preclassified sets of people defined by disciplinary interests: all chemists, all historians, all economists. Because of this disciplinary bias and its effect on system structure and organizations, large classes of problems are not served, or served only poorly, by present systems. Among these types of problems are policy making, decision making, managing, planning, engineering design, legislating, and the vast array of coping problems in the everyday world. The object here is to suggest the development of a practical framework of problem dimensions, useful as a way of looking at systems and their design (see Newell & Simon, 1972, pp. 787-868). In this context, Neelameghan points out:

> information needs of planners and decisionmakers are not structured according to ''subjects'' in the usual sense of the term, but are essentially function or task oriented. That is, the ''information package'' would be used in performing better situation analysis, extrapolation and forecasting future trends, contingent decisionmaking and problemsolving, anticipating consequences of action, etc. (Neelameghan, 1980; p. 206)

Such ''packages'' imply value-added processes that go beyond conventional subject oriented systems.

At the other end of the use spectrum—everyday coping—Brenda Dervin points out, in discussing the relationship between the information needs of the general public and the ''functional units'' of our information systems:

> if we look at the individual and his informing processes we can see that his functional unit is more likely to be responses, instructions, reinforcements, solutions, answers, ideas, assistance, wherever and however they may be found. We find, for example, that as citizens begin to use information systems designed ''for them,'' they collide with those systems. The citizens, on the one hand, are asking for a functional unit that is meaningful to them. The system, on the other, is protecting whatever functional unit in which it has a vested interest. (Dervin, 1975; pp. 12–13)

In order to respond at these levels, it is necessary to provide more filters and, more importantly, to design systems adapted to a different set of concerns than is now the case. As a result of present approaches, our systems and those who design and interpret them, tend to respond only to such concerns as ''What do you want to know?'' And they do this rather well. That is to say, we do quite well with systems organized by subject matter and the imposed hierarchies and relationships we have developed over the past few centuries. In the context of the problems cited above, however, there are other equally important concerns that need to be responded to: ''How do you need to know it?'' ''Why do you need to know?'' ''In what form do you need to know it?'' ''What do you know already?'' ''What do you anticipate finding?'' ''How will this help you?'' ''What does your problem look like?''

The consideration of problems in this context then moves beyond subject matter as the only arbiter of response to other concerns related to the concerns noted above. Problems do not require just answers, as do questions, but rather they require solutions, resolutions, clarification, options, and compromises (Taylor, 1962). Problems represent the use environment and contain enough that is important about it to indicate that the exercise of defining problem dimensions may allow the information professional to infer needs for information in a more structured and systematic way than is now available. Good reference librarians and information specialists have been doing this for some time (Taylor, 1968). Despite the euphoria for expert systems and artificial intelligence approaches, the human interface will continue to be an important part of the negotiation and response process for some time to come. It may indeed become even more important.

Problem Dimensions[1]

Problem dimensions are those characteristics that, beyond specific subject matter, establish the criteria for judging the relevance of information to a problem or to a class of problems. Saracevic, in a 1971 paper on relevance, hinted at this in noting that "the human factor, i.e., variations introduced by human decisionmaking, seems to be a major factor affecting the performance of every and all components of an information retrieval system" (Saracevic, 1971; p. 138). Those variations may be interpreted as reflections of the problem dimensions discussed briefly here, which exist in the nonsubject part of the question response by the system. They are presented below as dichotomies, though they probably exist as continua.

1. *Design/discovery:* Discovery is the description of the natural world, the things and processes which are apart from human activities. Natural sciences, such as astonomy and physics, are disciplines which involve the process of discovery, i.e., describing what is "already there." In contrast, design concerns things and processes made by humans. Economics, cognitive psychology, education, and information studies are examples of disciplines which concentrate on problems of design. Man does not create what is "described," but does create what is "designed."

Very simply, design and discovery are analogous to the processes of inventing and finding. Information for design would include an option range, while information for discovery would concentrate on a single piece of data. Information systems generally have been designed only as discovery mechanisms.

2. *Well-structured/ill-structured:* Well-structured problems (WSP) are those which can be solved by application of logical or algorithmic processes. Ill-structured problems (ISP) are those which cannot be resolved through strictly analytical means. Reasons for the existence of ISP can be that the problem is nonroutine or too complex to be properly analyzed. Variables within the problem are not well understood (e.g., human motivation), and therefore may vary over time and space. Random factors exist in the problem, such as weather prediction. WSP lend themselves to the use of hard, quantitative data. However, the assumptions behind the quantitative data and the method of collection may introduce hidden subjectiveness into the information. ISP require decisions based on probabalistic information on how to proceed, for example, development of a policy for the management of information resources by federal agencies.

3. *Complex/simple:* Complexity of a problem refers to the number and interactions of problem variables. A simple problem is one where a path from initial statement to solution is easily defined. Complex problems need to be reduced to manageable

[1] The sections on problem dimensions and information traits have been derived from MacMullin and Taylor (1984), and may be seen in fuller form in that publication.

blocks. Complexity and structure (well- or ill-structured problems) may influence the choices as to which problems to pay attention.

4. *Specific/amorphous goals:* This problem dimension introduces the use of proxy goals which are substituted when goals are too ambiguous to be operationalized. For example, "office productivity" must be made measurable in order (a) to make specific plans for reaching a set goal, (b) to recognize plans for reaching that goal, and (c) to recognize when the goal has been reached. Proxy goals are then used, such as, reducing the time needed to compile a report or to write a program. Efficiency measures are based on specific goals. Amorphous goals are an indication of the direction one wishes to go and not of the result that one wants.

5. *Initial state understood/not understood:* Initial states, that is, the specific problem state, are confusing because at least some of the interrelationships among the contributing factors are not well understood. In science, there is no progression unless each step is explained. In many ways, the task of science is to understand a state by observation and description. Social science research, on the other hand, is the means by which we attempt to define and understand aggregate behavior. In many cases we may produce too many conflicting and unsupported results to describe easily most initial states in these areas. This means that, in information terms, soft and qualitative data may be of more use in helping to define the initial state.

6. *Assumptions agreed upon/not agreed upon:* Problems in the management and policy sciences do not have one accepted knowledge base such as those which exist in the natural sciences. Natural laws are largely consistent; axioms which include inferences about human behavior, on the other hand, may not be mutually acceptable. Approaches to economics, for instance, center on contradictory assumptions. Problem definition is made difficult by these disparate assumptions. Perceptions about the world lead to different basic assumptions which are further diversified by various ways of coding information and the motivation to use it and to make sense of it.

7. *Assumptions explicit/not explicit:* Whether assumptions are agreed upon or not, they often get buried and become normative imperatives which are not taken into account in higher levels of debate. Often argument is at cross purposes because such assumptions are not made explicit, and positions are worlds apart from the beginning. This is intensified by packaging and form. Information may seem more objective when it appears in certain forms, for example, statistical tables, data sets, and computer printouts. Numbers and machines carry an authority in themselves at times, with no reference to the possible vagaries of data collection.

This is an opportunity for information systems to be valuable in a substantive way. Analysis and explication of assumptions that were made at the time of data collection and reflected in the information provided would be of high use in clarifying complex issues. Because there is so much information in so many forms, synthesis and critical comparison of salient studies and opinion is necessary. Critical/informative summaries, for example, are one way of relieving the burden of the first level of analysis and synthesis from decision makers and their staffs. These processes are discussed at more length in Chapter Seven on information analysis.

8. *Familiar/new pattern:* Many problems are essentially procedural. Professions such as engineering, medicine, and teaching rely on well-established method. Engineers calculate safety factors and material strengths when designing structures. Specifications provide guidelines to assure quality of the work. If the problem pattern is familiar, then the information needs are largely procedural and historical. If the problem pattern is new, however, the information needed will tend to be more substantive and future oriented. Experienced professionals have built up a repertoire of analogies which they can use to assess problems. Novices need more information because they are not used to seeing similar problems and do not have the experience to draw upon.

For both familiar and new patterns, option ranges are important. In managerial fields, clinical (one case) information may be useful. For instance, if the problem of office productivity is addressed, useful information could take the form of the experiences of similar offices in raising their productivity. Information which addresses itself to the analogy and comparability between problem situations would tend to reduce duplication of effort.

9. *Magnitude of risk great/not great:* This problem dimension is based on the consequence(s) of failure to resolve a problem. High-risk, high-reward problems would justify expenditure of resources in securing the best available information. Some professions tend to be perceived as high-risk situations. The industries which deal with nuclear objects, medicine, engineering, pharmaceuticals, biogenetics are in large part high-risk industries. Therefore, it would be expected that the information which was gathered would be as accurate (precise) and comprehensive as possible. Low-risk industries would be able to tolerate a potentially higher rate of failure and still be able to succeed in the marketplace, and hence could use less precise information. The questions of uncertainty and risk are discussed in Chapter Eight.

10. *Susceptible/not susceptible to empirical analysis:* Some problems are judgment calls in that no amount of research can evaluate the alternatives fairly. They are not susceptible to empirical analysis. Resolution of such problems is helped by subjective information, advice of experts, weighing of values and options, and forecasting. Those problems subject to empirical analysis rely on data which is objective and aggregated. Most problems are not purely one or the other. There is often a mix of empirical analysis and judgment in the resolution process.

11. *Internal/external imposition:* Problems either are sought out or they are imposed. Problems which are sought out tend to be goal directed. Useful information, then, needs to be relevant to and supportive of the chosen goal. External problems come from the environment, for example, competitors and government regulations. Information needs at this point generally are those which describe the environment as it affects the organization. The environment supplies the stimulus, such as new regulations; and the organization must define how it will respond to the new problem situation (e.g., cost compliance, resource availability, penalties for noncompliance, alternatives). Organizations generally do not like purely reactive situations. They have less time, less control, and fewer alternatives than does a

planned activity to an anticipated event. To this end, companies employ people who monitor government regulations, competitors, and economy, legal matters, etc. in order to reduce the surprise factor.

Information Traits

The problem dimensions represent one side of the negotiating space; see Figure 3-2. They reflect the needs of the environment. The other side of this equation is, of course, the information available through the system, however that system may be defined. The information and data contained in these outputs reflect a range of attributes relevant to the problem dimensions just discussed. These are called *information traits*. They are the special attributes that can be used to define the ways that information can be identified and presented. More importantly, these traits can be related directly to the dimensions of a problem. Some traits appear to exist on a continuum, while some seem to be dichotomous and mutually exclusive. Following are brief descriptions of information traits important to the *need* for information.

1. *Quantitative continuum:* Quantitative information is derived from phenomena that can be measured, and is represented numerically. Otherwise, qualitative and descriptive information is presented. The latter may provide reasons, assumptions, nuance, and details.

2. *Data continuum:* Data which can be empirically derived can be called *hard data*. Hard data are a result of observation and should be able to be replicated. *Soft data* exist when the data cannot be observed but must be inferred, or where assumptions must be made in order to collect the data. See discussion in Chapter Seven on data types.

3. *Temporal continuum*—historical (precedence) forecasting (future modeling): This continuum concerns information on what has been (historical), what will be (probabilities), and what should be (prescriptive). Litigation support systems, for example, consist of historical legal information. Financial business information is a mix of information about past performance and potential performance.

4. *Solution continuum* (single solution/option range): The criteria, which define a situation, yield a distribution of possible good and bad solutions (Meindell, 1982). There may be one desired best solution or, in some cases, any number of solutions will do. Satisficing, or finding the first solution that meets minimum criteria, is the standard operating procedure, for example, of the engineer. Information is collected until a reasonably good solution is discovered. There is no need to go beyond this point if cost and functional factors are met. There is more to this continuum, however, than satisficing and optimizing. Generating solution options is also a way of understanding or clarifying a problem.

In some cases a problem may be solved, or, better said, resolved, by redefining it in accord with the information a person has (Johnston & Gibbons, 1975; p. 28). Frischmuth and Allen comment that:

> When a study is initiated, an engineer is normally provided with a set of dimensions on which to evaluate any solution he may propose. In the course of the project, the

> engineer often discovers that [n]one of his proposed solution alternatives is acceptable according to a given set of dimensions. The normal reaction in such a case is to modify the solution or to generate a new one. . . . These two alternatives are not the engineer's only course of action. It is also possible to alter the set of dimensions, thus changing the problem. The concept of a variable problem is of great importance to problem solvers, yet many of them do not recognize it. This is partly the result of the way we educate engineers, training them almost exclusively on closed-form problems in which there is only one correct solution, and the nature of the problem is immutable. (Frischmuth & Allen, 1969; p. 63)

5. *Focus continuum* (precision/diffusion): The focus continuum is based on the extent to which facts are identified and associated for a situation. Precise information is useful for a situation which is well-defined, whereas diffuse information may be more useful in an ill-defined situation. Precision requires exactness of information. Diffusion is an asset if a problem is not well understood or is in a definitional stage. Brainstorming and idea generation produce scattered diffuse information which can be used to orient or to gain a pespective on the situation in question.

6. *Specificity of use continuum* (applied/theoretical): This continuum is concerned with levels of concreteness or specificity of use. Applied information is immediately useful in an operational sense. It tells how to do something, explains process, or establishes procedures. Theoretical information gives possible reasons or clues as to why/how something works or behaves. The theoretical principles and logic of an event are sought in order to explain and predict.

7. *Substantive continuum* (applied/descriptive): This continuum is defined through form and content. Applied information is defined here just as it was above in the specificity of use continuum. It is instrumental or operational information which describes the protocol or how to do something. Substantive information, however, seems to be different than theoretical information in that it describes the content and meaning of a phenomenon without necessarily predicting the process or behavior. A theory links the item in question to the environment. Substantive information focuses on the object and describes it.

8. *Aggregation continuum* (clinical/census): Information can be presented quantiatively, from a sample of one to a large population. Situations which are highly complex and contain variables which are not quantitative can be researched by case studies. This kind of research yields information which has depth and detail, but that cannot be easily generalized or aggregated. On the other end of this continuum are studies done on entire populationns, and there is, of course, no need to generalize. Aggregated information, taken from population samples, gives us information on the most central measurement of the population (i.e., mean, mode).

9. *Causal/diagnostic continuum:* Causal information (why something happens) is an implicit need in all problem solving. Diagnostic information (what is happening) is the information which must be gathered by defining a situation carefully. This is the first step toward causal information (Kahneman & Tversky, 1979; p. 263).

These information traits are as characteristic of stored information as are subject descriptions. Just as we now have subject classification and subject-naming systems, we need to have schema for locating and classifying these information traits. When we learn how to do this, these traits can be identified and used in decisions about information selection, organization, retrieval, and display. They become legitimate and useful signals affecting user choice in the complex process of selecting relevant information for problems which have certain dimensions. They can enhance the information being stored and transferred. They can add value. At present many of these information traits are interpreted by human beings who filter and give form to information output so that others can make use of it.

Chapter Four

THE VALUE-ADDED MODEL

The previous chapters on the value of information, on the user-driven model, and on information use and information systems environments were necessary preludes to the model of value-added processes presented in this chapter. The user-driven approach is a basic assumption. An analysis of information use environments is a necessary base to the understanding of the kinds of judgments users may (or may not) make in choosing one particular set of messages over another, that is, giving value to the former, but not to the latter.

In order to better understand and discuss the value-added model, it is presented early in this chapter in diagrams with definitions of the criteria and values that users seem to apply in making choices of messages from formal information systems. The remainder of the chapter then discusses the model's frame of reference, its derivation, and a commentary on the values as they are defined, their strengths and weaknesses. The question of what purpose an information system serves will in large part determine the kinds of values that will be added by any particular system. That is to say, different information systems add different sets of values. The question here is whether or not the 23 values which have been defined are sufficient to cover information system variety. We think they are. But this cannot be said with any certainty until different kinds of systems have been analyzed and evaluated in the value-added context.

Most studies on *evaluation* of information systems have concentrated either on system efficiencies or in the area of recall and precision (relevance). As Swanson has stated in her seminal review of evaluation in this field:

> The information science literature on evaluation has been dominated by studies of retrieval measures. The retrieval powers of indexing languages have been compared in laboratory and operational settings and retrieval effectiveness has been assessed in terms of relevance judgments by various categories of people. Studies of other elements of information systems, for example the coverage of data bases, document delivery capabilities of systems, and use of information products by customers, are far less numerous. (R.W. Swanson, 1975; p. 140)

The paucity of other criteria was also noted by Saracevic in 1970: "It seems no other effectiveness criterion than relevance was or is being seriously contemplated, or at least none exists that has caught some general attention" (Saracevic, 1970; p. 118).

The frame of reference presented here has grown out of this dissatisfaction. The question of information value is a fundamental one for the field of information. It is argued that the value-added approach may open a useful and fruitful base for those disciplines and professions that study or design systems for the provision of information. The point is that we are making judgments of value continuously—both on the system side and on the user/client side of the interface. All long-term information systems—those that acquire, process, store, and disseminate messages—are essentially a gamble that in the next minute, next day, next year these messages will be useful (have value). The concept of value-added in this process is and must be a future-oriented risk. One of the purposes in formalizing this model is to better understand the nature of that risk. On the client side, the user is continually monitoring a variety of information systems, and extracting what seems to be of value, based on his or her current situation and, if the user is prudent, on his or her perception of the problems that may be faced in the near future. These processes of storage and display on one side and choice and use on the other are based throughout on conscious and unconscious assumptions about the value of information.

The diagrams in Figures 4-1 and 4-2 are the basic value-added models. They illustrate the three parts of the information process: the *user* or client; the *interface* between system and client which in the user-driven approach is labelled "negotiating space"; and the *system* which is defined as a coherent series of value-added processes producing varying outputs. Figure 4-1 is a general and highly simplistic model of the total interaction. Figure 4-2 is more specific, listing from left to right: (a) the user criteria of choice; (b) the specific values added by the system; and (c) a small sample of formal information processes that add those values.

The *user* (client, customers, etc.) is defined as an agent who actively seeks (or receives) information from a formal information system in order to achieve some objective, either personal or related to the organization in which he or she works. The user's primary criterion in judging the usefulness of the system is cost savings—savings in time, dollars, energy, and so forth. Such a statement does not mean that we subscribe wholeheartedly to the economist's picture of the decision maker (usually writ large). The economist's model of the decision maker (DM) requires that

> he or she has *full knowledge* concerning the different alternatives and their outcomes . . . that the objective of the DM is *to maximize* his or her utility . . . and that the DM is *rational*. This rationality is defined in terms of the utilization the person makes of his or her limited resources (money, time, effort, etc.) to achieve his objective or maximization of utility. (Farid, 1982; pp. 54–55)

User	**Interface**	**System**
Problems which establish the criteria of choice	Display of values added by system to assist user in making choices	Specific processes that add specific values

Figure 4-1. Value Added Model

Such a position seems unrealistic, as Farid points out, and not very useful in trying to model the information process. A number of behavioral scientists and organizational theorists criticize the rigidity and unreality of this concept of objective rationality, and would substitute the notion of subjective or bounded rationality. As Simon has pointed out, the latter is "a rationaliity less grandiose than that proclaimed by economists" (Simon, 1970; p. 21). Indeed bounded rationality may be really a sort of sophisticated and experienced common sense, "simply natural rationality" (Loasby, 1976). The assumptions and discussions in this book perceive the user in this light.

It is worth noting that, with document-based systems in particular, a client's objective may include building a small, but personal, collection of information resources on a specific topic of ongoing or potential interest. In this sense the user has established a new information system—personally controlled—which in miniature may have the same structure, values added, and other attributes of larger systems. Such a system is closer to the user's problems, hence more relevant, and presumably more accessible and, therefore, easier to use.

USER CRITERIA OF CHOICE	INTERFACE (Values Added)	SYSTEM (Value-added Processes: Examples
Ease of Use	Browsing Formatting Interfacing I (Mediation) Interfacing II (Orientation) Ordering Physical Accessibility	Alphabetizing Highlighting important terms
Noise Reduction	Access I (Item identification) Access II (Subject description) Access III (Subject summary) Linkage Precision Selectivity	Indexing Vocabulary control Filtering
Quality	Accuracy Comprehensiveness Currency Reliability Validity	Quality control Editing Updating Analyzing and comparing data
Adaptability	Closeness to problem Flexibility Simplicity Stimulatory	Provision of data manipulation capabilities Ranking output for relevance
Time-Saving	Response Speed	Reduction of processing time
Cost-Saving	Cost-saving	Lower connect-time price

Figure 4-2. User Criteria and Values Added

For convenience the user criteria have been broken into six categories. These are the criteria the user consciously or, perhaps, even unknowingly makes use of in choosing among the variety of information presented. These are not graven in stone. They seem, however, to be a useful way of organizing the values that are added to the system.

In Figure 4-2, the center column labeled "Interface" lists these values in each of the six user criteria. This *interface* is the negotiating space between system and user. These are the values added by the system which aid customers in matching their needs. These added values are discussed individually below.

The *system processes,* right-hand column in Figure 4-2, are a sample of activities that enhance (i.e., add value to) the items going through the system. In many systems, such as abstracting and indexing operations, the values added are mostly external. That is to say, the item coming into the system is the same as the item going out of the system. What has happened in the process is that, through a series of subprocesses, a whole range of tangible signals has been attached to the item, without altering its content. These activities and processes for document-based systems are discussed at length in Chapters Five and Six.

In other types of information processes, such as information analysis, the information going through the system is massaged, altered, evaluated, combined, and interpreted in a variety of ways. The important point in such processes is that the output is not the same as the input. The information chunks being processed are altered by various activities which make them of more value to the client than they would have been without the performance of those activities. Information analysis is discussed in Chapter Seven.

DERIVING USER CRITERIA AND VALUES

One of the problems in deriving user criteria and values added in information systems is that there are not many studies specifically directed toward this concern of user benefits and costs. To be sure, as a well-read professional is aware, there are hidden bits and pieces concerning these interests tucked away in many studies of information systems. Many are the common sense perceptions of capable professionals, carrying the authority of education, experience, and close knowledge of operating systems and information markets. We tend too frequently to overlook, even belittle, this valuable know-how and experience, perhaps the only real knowledge we have of the operation of information systems. There are a few studies concerned directly with the statement of values, user benefits, and user criteria of channel choice. Consequently, the criteria and the values to be discussed in this chapter have many formal and informal sources, including the author's need to provide structure for system activities that to some extent may not yet be perceived in terms of user benefits and costs.

In one study on the criteria used in the selection of an information channel by R & D engineers, Gerstenberger and Allen (1968) discuss four such criteria: accessibility, ease of use, technical quality, and degree of experience. With the exception of the last criterion, degree of experience, these are values in the terminology presented in this book. Even, as we will see, degree of experience may shed light on the interfacing and orienting values that systems frequently support and encourage. As the authors say, "each criterion provides subjective estimates of 'channel costs' and 'channel payoff' or value" (Gerstenberger & Allen, 1968; p. 274). *Accessibility* implies physical access, especially proximity. *Ease of use* is related to physical accessibility but also says something about the perceived comfortableness of use. *Technical quality* has to do with the anticipatory perception of reliability or integrity of the information contained in a message. It is worth noting that *degree of experience* is something the system may wish to strengthen, for user experience with a system tends to enhance the user's perception of its utility. This is commented on below under Interfacing.

In a study of the perceived benefits of information analysis centers, Mason (1979) identified nine characteristics of information services, described by four independent dimensions. These characteristics are "values" in our terminology.

1. data/information *quality*
   precision and accuracy
   source credibility
   (Gerstenberger's and Allen's technical quality)
2. *scope*
   recency
   completeness of information
   (This may also be included in Gerstenberger's and Allen's technical quality, though "scope" may also mean breadth and coverage of a specific subject.)
3. The *difficulty,* or hassle, associated with using the service
   time lag in receiving information
   ease of access
   ease of use
   degree to which in-house personnel are required
   (Gerstenberger's and Allen's accessibility and ease of use)
4. The *cost* of the service, i.e., the dollars exchanged for the service
   (Note: the more appropriate term is "price" instead of "cost." (Mason, 1979; p. 36.)

In an earlier study, Mason cited the following "characteristics of information and channels of technical information judged to be important" to potential and actual users of information analysis centers:

> cost, accuracy, currency, response time, ease of access, ease of use, technical quality, coverage of topic, understandability, format, media, recall, and relevance. (Mason, 1977; p. 57)

Mason went on to recommend further research to "define the relationships among these characteristics and to deduce the relative value of each characteristic to the IAC users." This is just what the 1979 study did with the results as noted.

In a review of cost-benefit analysis of computing systems development and operation, King and Schrems (1978) define a benefit as "the consequence of an action that protects, aids, improves, or promotes the well-being of an individual or organization. Benefits take the form of cost savings, cost avoidance, improved operational performance, and 'intangibles' " (King & Schrems, 1978; p. 21). To fit the frame of reference of this book, we would say *value is an assessment of the anticipated consequences of an action*. In this case "action" equals "making a choice" of an information channel or of a specific chunk of information by a user.

The authors further state: "Accuracy, response time, security, reliability, and flexibility can significantly affect costs and benefits of an information system relative to a task" (King & Schrems, 1978; p. 31). The last phrase "relative to a task" implies some direction and purpose, and hence a utility or benefit to a user down the line. Though the authors write in the context of computer systems, these attributes are types of criteria by which clients or customers place value on a system's output.

Paisley and Butler (1977) in their work on computer assistance in information work, discussed three categories of functions by which the computer aids a user: acceleration, augmentation, delegation. These are operations which support the values perceived by a user in using a system. In the computer they are represented by such value-added processes as scanning, fixating, feature extracting, decoding, comparing, deciding, inducing, retrieving, selecting, transforming, and producing.

Acceleration is basically doing something (e.g., comparing) faster in the computer than it can be done by a human being. Now this of course is what computers do very well, and today we accept this as commonplace. Forty years ago, however, this speed of response was not possible. Until recently such speed, together with better physical access to larger stores, have been the major values added by the raw power of computers in operational information systems.

Augmenting is assisting the user in the substance of his or her task, not just in the pace of its execution. Paisley and Butler point out:

> There are two related senses in which information tasks are augmented and not just accelerated:
>
> 1. If the information system is more than two or three orders of magnitude faster than the user in performing a task, then acceleration yields to augmentation in the sense that the user can perform the task in a reasonable amount of time with assistance but would forego the task without assistance.
>
> 2. If limitations in human perception/cognition other than time requirements make a task almost unperformable, and if assistance from an information system makes the task readily performable, then the task has been augmented and not just accelerated. (Paisley & Butler, 1977; p. 45)

When the processes of augmentation become common and truly operational they can and will have a positive effect on certain specific values. Browsing, for example, can certainly be enhanced by processes such as scanning and fixating. Almost any process of augmentation can give a value such as flexibility more utility for the client. Formatting can certainly be aided by the possible presentation of varied outputs—graphs, charts, or lists—and by feature extraction.

Delegation, in the framework of Paisley and Butler, means that decisions are made by the system itself.

> These decisions are made normatively via one of three procedures: according to rules that the system itself stipulates; according to decisions that a majority of the system's users have made in similar contingencies in the past; according to decisions that the individual user has made in similar contingencies in the past. The second and third procedures require the system to learn from its users. In human systems these procedures call for intelligence; in computer systems they call for artificial intelligence. (Paisley & Butler, 1977; p. 46)

The Paisley and Butler approach has been included here because, as the technology becomes more interactive in information systems, the more the technology will contribute to the value-added process, with major effect on user benefits and costs. In the value-added context this interface has the following characteristics. From the system side, the system *qua* computer system

- displays its contents, either in menu/instruction form or in text as direct response to a query;
- transmits signals concerning the potential value of portions of its content;
- provides a variety of means to aid the user in making choices.

On the other side, the user

- matches the signals or displayed contents against perceived information needs;
- makes (or does not make) choices from the system.

The foregoing description assumes an active search for information. We need continually to remind ourselves that a great deal of formal and valuable information is transferred and passively accepted by a recipient (user?) for a variety of reasons that has nothing to do with active search. These reasons may include such things as the fear of not being informed, the maintenance of status in an organization, or a genuine necessity to be informed without precise need.

VALUES ADDED

The definitions and interpretation of the 23 values listed in Figure 4-2 (center column) are of some concern. As discussed above, the values were generated after extensive literature review, by examining one particular information process—the abstracting and indexing process—and by putting together bits and pieces from the observations and experiences of skilled professionals and persons who have a high level of information literacy. It is not a very elegant process, nor can it be at this point in time. What we are trying to do is to construct an early model of a complex human activity, a model that would be useful in the description of information-providing systems of any type, and eventually in their design.

Some of these added values are tangible, that is one can "see" their manifestation, for example in index terms, in feedback displays, in classification systems, in formats, in file systems, or in speed of delivery. Others are intangible values, such as accuracy, reliability, or currency. In abstracting and indexing systems, for example, the user trusts (or does not trust) a system to be correct in its citations and reasonably valid in its indexing. The system invests money in editing and verification and in staff training to assure accuracy of output. In a report stemming from extensive information analysis, the recipient places trust, in varying degrees, in the human analysts who evaluate and recombine raw information to prepare the report. In this case the analysts are part of the system. The system invests money in these highly skilled and knowledgeable people who can turn raw data into coherent bodies of information and knowledge relevant to and useful in such managerial processes as strategic planning. These are values that one cannot point at. They are intangible.

Essentially what is being asked is (a) what do users want from information systems that would enable them to perform better, however "better performance" is defined in their context; and (b) upon what basis do users make choices when presented with large amounts of potentially relevant information? We contend that it is the enhancements added by the system, including all its human parts, that assist a client in making informed choices. An understanding of these enhancements (values) would help us as information professionals understand the total information process somewhat better. The 23 values discussed individually below should be perceived in this light. For purposes of discussion, they are grouped by the six user criteria shown in Figure 4-2. One-sentence definitions are given for summary reference in Table 4-1 at the end of this chapter.

Ease of Use

Ease of use has to do with system elements which, in physical, human, or software terms, tend to reduce difficulty in using the system. These elements can be divided into four categories: (a) browsability; (b) the level and skill of the human interface, if any, between system and user; (c) gross ordering of display (e.g., alphabetizing and subject division) and formatting for ease of scanning; and (d) physical accessibility (e.g., proximity) (Rosenberg, 1966).

Browsing is the capability of a system to allow a client to scan an information neighborhood, with the probability that the client will serendipitously find information of value. The value of browsing, of course, is only useful in certain types of situations where the client, as an active information searcher, is not clear as to the boundaries of the problem, nor of the relationships among the available data and information. It must be an active searcher, however defined, for, as Neville's First Law of Serendipity states: In order to find anything one must be looking for something.[1]

To be informed in an area of concern requires that a person be able to scan a good deal of relevant information without being able to define precisely what is wanted: not knowing what is looked for until it is found. Highly specific newsletters, such as *Plat's Oilgram,* allow a person to be informed by regular browsing in such

[1] Harvey A. Neville, 1898–1983, chemist, scholar, and President of Lehigh University from 1961 to 1964.

information sources. Classification systems in libraries allows one to scan shelves for items of interest in a particular subject.

Formatting is the physical presentation and arrangement of data/information in ways that allow more efficient scanning and hence extraction of items of interest from the store. As a very basic beginning, formatting includes such mundane things as standardized formats in print display or terminal display so that the same type of information will always appear in the same place on a page or screen. This is done not only for system efficiencies but, in our frame of reference, so that a repeat user of the information product can scan faster and can focus more quickly on those things with the highest potential of displaying information of interest. Formatting may include emphasis by highlighting significant words or phrases. It includes presentation by means other than text: graphics (is a picture indeed worth a thousand words?), charts, graphs, or maps. In relation to tables and charts, there are questions of some importance, which Nancy Clark has discussed.

> There seems to be little real agreement about whether tables and graphs should communicate at all—that is whether they should be viewed as a medium of communication or as storage containers for data. Tables, for example, are a tremendously efficient means of storing data. They are also a primary means of communicating in statistics. . . . Whether the function is storage or communication, the reader needs access to the data. But in the case of data storage such access is the end, and in the case of communication it is the *means* to an end. (Clark, 1983; p. 1)

Clark, of course, has called attention to a basic dichotomy of approach to any information system—whether it be a table of data, a large corporate data base, or an archival research library. Is it storage container or communication process? It should be obvious by now that this book is concerned about the communication processes that make the contents of storage containers more accessible and useful to users. In this book, those "communication processes" are called "value-added activities."

Interfacing is the capability of the system to interpret itself to users. This may be accomplished either by the system through a variety of displays or programmed instruction, or by human intervention. The purpose of interfacing is to help users get good answers from the system or to help users understand and gain experience with the system, on the assumption that, in this case, familiarity does not breed contempt but, on the contrary, raises customer expectation of accessibility. There are two ways that interfacing can be achieved: mediation and orientation.

Interfacing then is not only mediation between system and user or the presentation of instruction. More important is how these are done, and whether they provide good answers or effectively interpret the system in helpful ways. For purposes of the value-added model two forms of interfacing are used.

Interfacing 1 (mediation) is the means used to assist users in getting answers from the system. It may range from such mundane things as "see" and "see also" references in indexes and library catalogs to one-on-one human assistance in finding an answer. The search intermediary for online bibliographic retrieval systems or conventional reference services are examples of human intervention. The whole process of information analysis may be viewed as a mediating activity between the incoherent and often low-quality mass of information and the user.

Interfacing II (orienting) includes the means used to help users understand and gain experience with the system and its complexities. In contrast to mediation which may take the form of on-the-spot and immediate assistance without instructional payoff, the intent of orienting is to help clients develop the ability to use the system themselves. The recent interest in the information center environment of computer systems is a relevant attempt to improve the system–user interface. It is aimed not only toward helping users solve their problems, but toward educating and encouraging more sophistication among users so that they can make better use of the system (Hammond, 1982).

There is an important distinction to be made between the value added by interfacing and that added by *adaptability* (described below). Interfacing is concerned with system interpretation, or how the system interprets itself for users. Adaptability is concerned with how well the system fits the context and the problems arising from the environment of the users. Interfacing is systems oriented; adaptability is context oriented.

Ordering covers the basic methods of initially dividing or organizing a body of subject matter by some form of gross structuring: large groupings, alphabetization, etc. We tend to forget the power of alphabetization as a form of ordering. Our dictionaries, encyclopedias, indexes, and other forms of compact information storage are completely dependent on alphabetization for ordering the knowledge stored. The idea of ordering is placed under the rubric of "Ease of Use" because that is precisely its intent—to make a body of information easier to use.

Physical accessibility is just what its name implies: ease of access to information in a physical sense. The invention of printing 500 years ago made information and knowledge more accessible to more people than before. There is nothing strange about this: The book could be mass produced; it was portable; it could be distributed easily; and, because of its low cost, it no longer had to be restricted by chaining or locked rooms. The book itself was cheap (much cheaper than the parchment codex), portable, *and* randomly accessible. These are physical attributes that opened up the wealth of knowledge to anyone with the ability to read a language. Printing provided the necessary technological base for the rise of science, for the industrial revolution, democratic governments, and for universal public education. It made recorded knowledge more accessible (Eisenstein, 1979). Today's computer networks and office terminals, though still very complicated because of lack of standardization, make vast stores of data available to those who have the money, patience, and time to use them. These newer technologies are, however, based on older information processes. As a consequence they will not only carry all the problems of the earlier processes, but will magnify those problems, such as overload or poor data quality.

Noise Reduction

Noise reduction basically includes three processes. The first is the process of *ex-*

cluding, or withholding information, that is reducing noise. The second is the process of *inclusion,* of supplying information within some (possibly rather large) boundaries. The third process is *precision,* which has to do with focus, with specific data or fact. Though these are interrelated in ways that are not quite clear at present, it would appear that both the processes to accomplish these ends, and their intent, are quite different.

The intent of exclusion is to restrict or to contain the amount of information presented, without denying access. Its processes are built around differentiation, the capability to discriminate among data and information that under other circumstances might be considered similar. The intent of inclusion is to assure that nothing of conceivable value is omitted. Its processes tend to be all encompassing. They emphasize similarity, connection, and linkage. Discrimination is not important in inclusion processes.

The idea of precision is to assure that, if something can be defined, then the information concerning that entity, and only that information, will be presented. If information cannot be precisely defined, then the system will resort to some of the elements noted under the criterion of adaptability below (flexibility, feedback, and manipulability) in the expectation that these will induce clarification and restatement.

This criterion has been labeled *noise reduction* in the belief that this particular concern, exclusion, will be of major concern in the future as information overload becomes a principal problem of information systems. The computer with its emphasis on storage and speed will not help this process without a basic change in attitude as to the function of information, and some primary development to provide better filtering at the point of input. Present intellectual technologies such as indexing systems and data base file management systems are not capable of handling these problems. Simon has put this most succinctly.

> It is conventional to begin designing an Information Processing System by considering the information it will *supply*. In an information-rich world, however, this is doing things backwards. The crucial question is how much information it will allow to be *withheld* from the attention of other parts of the system. (Simon, 1971; p. 43)

Our present systems tend to be supplying systems (inclusive) rather than withholding systems (exclusive). A major viewpoint of this book is that such inclusive systems are no longer viable as principal information providers. The principal summary point to make is that the major problems in future information systems will revolve around the processes of reducing the amount of and raising the quality of information brought to the attention of the user.

The word "access" has been used here. In this sense *access* differs from the phrase "physical accessibility" used above under "Ease of Use." Access here means intellectual access, the intellectual technologies that provide the systematic means of narrowing the information universe to a set of data and information which has some probability of containing material that is wanted or needed. The signals provided are tangible—visible to the user. Different kinds of intellectual access provide different cuts of the information universe in approximate accord with the desires of the user.

Access I is the value achieved by the identification of any information chunk or discrete piece of data by systematic physical description providing a user with location information and a "name tag." In business data bases, this form of access might identify a datum such as, for example, employee name and social security number with links to home address, salary, work grade, and/or corporate location. Under the best of circumstances each of these records could provide a means of access. For a variety of reasons discussed under "Access II" below, this is frequently not the case. In traditional bibliographic systems, the citation becomes the basic form of Access I. Computer-based reference retrieval systems can now access separate parts of the record—author, title, journal, date, institution—each of which can provide additional means of exclusion or inclusion, that is, ways of slicing that particular information universe. The business data and the bibliographic data processes are, however, somewhat different. In the former, the data items are kept separately and combined as need requires. At least, this is the intent of data base management today. Past files, however, at their inception were not well thought through. Hence, there is today a very large problem of rehabilitating those structures so that they can become organizationally more useful. In the latter, the basic record *is* the complete bibliographic citation, and that becomes the pointer to full information. The individual data item (title, author, etc.) can be broken out and searched on if required.

Access II is a second cut of the subject information universe: the provision of a subject description through the addition of new access points, such as index terms, descriptors, and names of data items. In bibliographic systems this is a highly sophisticated capability with a long and rich historical background.

In business and commercial information systems, a data base is defined as "a collection of data from which multiple end-user views are derived" (Martin, 1981; p. 50). The phrase "end-user views are derived" seems to imply that the data have an effect on the client or the user of the system, and, therefore, have value. This value is enhanced by the capability of the system to identify, name, and locate the data items. Unfortunately, in business data systems, the problem of naming is exacerbated by the haphazard ways the data bases were originally put together, and the speed the magnitude of their growth.

> A data base contains hundreds (and sometimes thousands) of types of data items. Five thousand or more types of data items may be used in running a big corporation. . . . In order to computerize the activities of a corporation, the data items it uses must be defined, cataloged, and organized. This is often difficult and time consuming because data have been treated rather sloppily in the past. What is essentially the same data item has been defined differently in different places, represented differently in computers, and given different names. Data items which were casually thought to be the same are found to be not quite the same. In one insurance company the term POLICY NUMBER was widely used, but as the data bases were being defined it was found that it was used with a dozen different meanings in different places. If a simple term

like POLICY NUMBER causes this problem, think of the problem with some of the more subtle terms. (Martin, 1981; p. 38)

Access II then is basically a bundle of value-adding activities which provide other cuts of the data/information universe, specifically naming items by discrete and unique terms understandable to the customers, and useful to them in the process of identifying information chunks of potential benefit to them.

Access III is a third cut of the information universe in the process of isolating information of use. Its purpose is to provide a summary and/or brief explanation of the content of an item. The function of such processes is to benefit the users by reducing a large amount of information into a compact item without losing too much information in the process. This assists the uses in making choices or in keeping them informed. These processes have, in some cases, developed into highly sophisticated forms. They may take the form of an abstract, an executive summary, a news brief, or a table of contents (sometimes called a menu). Charles Bernier's suggestion of "terse conclusions" in scientific and technical literature, which he equates with the aphorism, is an interesting proosal in this context. As Bernier points out:

> Interesting properties are expected of terse conclusions. Keeping up on knowledge in fields 10 to 100 times broader than can now be read is the most important. Conservation of reading time is the next most important. Such terse conclusions provide better guidance than do indexes, abstracts, or extracts because the terse conclusions carry advocacy (direct or implied) and the wisdom of one or more specialists. (Bernier, 1970; p. 318)

There are many additional forms that are information compressing: a chemical structure diagram; a map; a graph or chart; a mathematical formula. These examples require that the client have a special knowledge of particular sets of symbols. For that group, however, the compression of information is very large and extraordinarily valuable. One can get a sense of this by trying to describe in verbal terms the geography of New York State: relationships, distances, rivers and their direction of flow, large bodies of water, mountains, roads and their condition, cities and their size. Then compare that description (if one ever gets that far) with a road map. These are common but remarkable forms of data compression, which we tend to overlook because of their commonness. In every case, however, they require a knowledge of and facility with the symbols used. All of these forms, from abstracts to mathematical formulas, are a very real form of value added, for they allow a user to make choices or to be informed in less time and with less effort.

Linkage is the value added by providing pointers and links to items, sources, and systems external to the system in use, thus expanding the client's information options. It would be as if the library catalog also included under its subject headings the names, addresses, and phone numbers of specific people who are experts on that particular subject. In a sense the library catalog does this by listing directories, handbooks, and other formalized reference tools. But it does this in such gross form, and the tools are frequently out of date, that it is usually necessary to work through another filter, the reference librarian. For the most part, links today are provided by people: the invisible colleges of the scientist and scholar; the "good old boy" networks; the professional societies; peers and colleagues in the organization. Thus far, the technologies from the postal service, to the telephone, to computer links only provide the means of support for these links. When, for example, a management information system dynamically provides links to financial, production, and marketing data external to the organization, then we will begin to add this value in significant fashion.

Precision is the capability of a system intended to aid a user in finding exactly what is wanted, in terms of subject matter. Precision refers specifically to those processes a system performs to assure that a user has a high probability of retrieving information of value to a specific question. This, of course, assumes that the user can define and describe what is wanted in fairly exact subject terms. There is a paradox here in that the better one can define the information required, the more one knows about it, and therefore the less it may be needed. In the extreme case, precision holds, for example, where a precise datum or fact is required, somewhat like searching for the last piece of a jigsaw puzzle in a large bag of woodchips. Precision is subject oriented. In this sense, it can be contrasted with those values of adaptability discussed below which tend to be problem oriented. To some extent precision works in parallel with the process of selectivity, except that precision comes at the system output end, whereas selectivity occurs at the system input side. This important point is explored below under the discussion of selectivity. This distinction is a small but critical point, for it says something about where an information system or service will invest its money and effort—at the input side or at the output side.

Selectivity is the value added when choices are made at the input point of the system, choices based on the assumption of the appropriateness and merit of certain information chunks or data to the client population served. There are three major points to emphasize and discuss. Selectivity takes place at the *input side* of the system processes. Secondly, it is consciously *based on the user-driven model*. Thirdly, it is not a one-shot process, but requires *continuous filtering* of data and information already in the system.

The activities that add the value of selectivity are at the input side of the system. Their function is to filter information chunks and to reduce noise before the information is allowed into the system. These are in contrast to those activities associated with and supporting the other values added under this criterion (access I,II,III, and precision) which filter at the output end. Selectivity reduces the amount of information coming into the system.

The value added in the processes that provide selectivity is a conscious application of the user-driven model. A system is only able to establish criteria for these choices called "selectivity" if it is knowledgeable about its clients, their problems, and hence their probable information needs. In contrast, a system based on comprehensiveness (another value added, see discussion below under "Quality") needs to collect and cover completely the literature and data of the field to be covered.

Coverage becomes important. Systems which emphasize selectivity tend to ask "How small should my information store be?" rather than "How large. . . .?" Selective systems are especially important in managerial environments and in applied situations where satisficing and minimizing loss are of particular concern. Information analysis plays a critical role here. It is worth noting that the establishment of undergraduate libraries, such as Lamont at Harvard University and Uris at Cornell University, were, in a way, attempts at selectivity. They were conscious attempts to select and limit, in contrast to the comprehensive collections thought to be required for scholarship and other research.

Selectivity, in addition, implies continuous review of information already in the store, asking whether data and information added yesterday will be of use tomorrow. This purging process unfortunately seldom happens, because of inertia and indecision. That is to say what is in the store tends to stay in because it is easier and less painful for the system *not* to throw something out. This is especially true today as computer memory capacity expands. The failure to weed or purge means, however, that gradually the costs of information choice will be shifted to the client or that investment in output filters, such as information analysts, must rise dramatically. This may be inevitable under any circumstances.

Quality

Quality is a user criterion which has to do with excellence or in some cases truthfulness in labeling. Several categories of values are included under this rubric: (a) the reliability of the data/information or, in grosser terms, of the service (reliability, accuracy, precision); (b) the assumptions made in original selection or generation of data (comprehensiveness, currency, validity).

It is worth noting that quality values are for the most part intangible values. That is to say, we tend to be suspicious of a system or a package which needs to advertise its reliability or its accuracy by words only. These are characteristics earned over time and by reputation. It is somewhat like a restaurant with a sign in front, "Fine Food" (sometimes spelled "Fyne") which by itself is no guarantee, as we often learn to our dismay, of the quality of its food.

There is a second aspect of quality which goes beyond the value (reliability or accuracy) itself. Contrary to comments in the last paragraph, this does require labeling. It has to do with the degree of that particular value: level of accuracy or level of reliability of a source of data. Such qualifications as to level and degree are necessary because different user activities will have differing quality requirements. The discussion in Chapter Three of magnitude of risk as a problem dimension is pertinent here. The level of a particular quality value necessary, such as currency, in a given situation is dependent on the information use environment from which the need for that information arose.

Accuracy is the value added by system processes that assure error-free transfer of data and information as it flows through the system and is eventually displayed to a client. In a sense, accuracy guarantees a true copy. It should be emphasized that accuracy does not necessarily say anything about the validity, the truth or falsity, of the data or information in the system.

This is an intangible value, the result of which, if the user believes that accuracy is high in the output from the system, allows that user to trust the system. The system itself invests labor and money in editing, proofreading, verification, and staff training to assure accuracy. The typographic error, the incomplete and inaccurate citation, the transposed figure are all examples of low accuracy, which force the client to expend unnecessary effort, or worse, to make critical but poor decisions because the data was inaccurately transmitted. Perhaps, unfortunately, we do not have the subtlety and play-sense of the Chinese printers who purposely made typographical errors in a text so that their readers could feel superior when they found them.

Comprehensiveness is the value added by the completeness of coverage of a particular subject or discipline (e.g., chemistry) or of a particular form of information (e.g., patents). As we discussed above, comprehensiveness is the converse of selectivity. Comprehensiveness has high value for a historian, a scholar, a lawyer, and in certain situations for the scientist. Consequently, we can say that the level of value here is dependent on the user problem environment. See the discussion above on selectivity.

Currency is the value added (a) by the recency of the data acquired by the system; and (b) by the capability of the system to reflect current modes of thinking in its access vocabularies. In the first instance, the system invests time and money in obtaining the most recent data available. The users can feel assured that the system indeed contains the most recent information and that they can obtain it. There are, of course, varying degrees of currency necessary, dependent on the users' environment and problem. The air controller at the airport needs absolutely current, that is real-time, as well as accurate information about the location of planes within the boundaries of his or her responsibility. Here currency implies real-time or instantaneous information about the location of planes. The strategic planner may require current information, but it certainly does not have to be real-time information. In bibliographic systems, *Current Contents,* published by the Institute for Scientific Information, is a response to the need of scientists for currency, providing them with a means of scanning the tables of contents of journals in their fields as they are published.

In the second instance cited in the definition above, the system attempts to maintain, for example, a current vocabulary in its descriptors. This has been especially true of bibliographic systems where vocabulary in the sciences, and perhaps even more so in the applied fields, is changing constantly. This is no longer, however, just a problem for bibliographic and text systems. As Dolby points out, in relation to larger-scale scientific, technical, and social data bases we can no longer "keep in mind the meaning of each and every datum." Dolby then continues:

> The obvious next move is to use the machine to help manage the meaning problem. The question is: How? Intuitively it seems clear that meaning is not carried by the

> numbers, but by the descriptors that are used to identify the numbers. The weakness in current statistical packages is that they use user-supplied descriptors as labels for output but for little else. Data base management systems use descriptors primarily as access pointers for the numbers, and little else. Connecting a statistical package to a DBMS provides a great convenience in a number of ways, but does nothing to assist in the management of meaning, if neither piece has any concern for meaning. (Dolby, 1983; pp. 1–2)

The point of this is that numerical data systems will soon require all the intellectual paraphernalia for naming that text systems have been struggling with for centuries. Questions of descriptor appropriateness as well as currency of terms will be especially critical.

In a very real sense, the value *reliability* may be the summation, from the client's standpoint, of many of the other values. But it is something more: It has to do with consistency and hence possibly with familiarity. Reliability then can be defined as the trust a user has in the consistency of quality performance of the system and its outputs over time. That is to say, the system and the apparent processes of system change will, in the user's view, be the same tomorrow as it is today. The system will be consistent in maintaining its accepted level of accuracy, of currency, of comprehensiveness (or selectivity as the case may be), and it can be relied upon to do so in the future. Hence its output will be perceived as reliable and worthy of trust. The perceived value of consistency results from use of the system over time, from familiarity with the system's idiosyncracies and benefits, which inspires a sort of comfortableness with the system. Reliability, consistency based on familiarity, is an important but intangible value for the client and in support of which the system invests labor and effort.

Validity is enhanced when the system provides signals about the degree to which data or information presented to users can be judged as sound. These signals could consist of indicators of bias (assumptions behind the data) or of analytic notes on the comparability of the data presented. These can take the form of a critique of the research methodology or of the experimental design; violations of statistical assumptions in the data; or disclosure of partiality of viewpoint. These are signals which allow clients to make decisions as to what level of validity they require or level of bias they can tolerate in the problem that has to be attacked. Though the following quotation was written in the context of fundamental physical constants, the approach and cautions are part of the concern here for validity of information presented.

> Measurement of some property of a thing in practice always takes the form of a sequence of steps or operations that yield as an end result a number that serves to represent the amount or quantity of some particular property of a thing—a number that indicates how much of this property the thing has, for someone to use for a specific purpose. . . . In general, the purpose for which the answer is needed determines the precision of accuracy [equals validity in our terminology] required and ordinarily also the method of measurement employed. . . . The *bias* or *systematic error,* of a measurement process is the magnitude and direction of its tendency to

> measure something other than what was intended; its *precision* refers to the typical closeness together of successive independent measurements of a single magnitude generated by repeated applications of the process under specified conditions; and its *accuracy* [i.e., *validity*] is determined by the closeness to the true value characteristics of such measurements. (Eisenhart, 1968; p. 120)

Though far more determinant than is possible in concerns other than the physical sciences, the direction is important for business, economic, and social concerns. Many present political and economic decisions are based on measurement that are largely meaningless. Data are compared that are really not comparable, because there is no explanation of their origin or method of calculation, and hence of their validity. A recent report of the National Aacademy of Sciences on productivity states this most succinctly.

> Reliable comparison of national income and product levels in different countries are a prerequisite for international comparisons of productivity levels. The widely published comparisons of output (expressed in yen, marks, dollars, etc.) by use of exchange rates are virtually meaningless. . . . (National Research Council, 1979; p. 17)

It becomes quite obvious that some sort of tangible signals are needed to alert clients as to the degree they can trust the data to be good approximations of reality. We know very little about information safety factors, partly due to our inability to signal the validity of a particular message. Hence we tend to overload. As we have discussed before, validity signals in information systems will be one of the major concerns in future information and data systems. Otherwise we are truly condemned to the neverending cycle of "garbage in, garbage out," which all too frequently becomes "garbage in, gospel out," with dire results on ensuing decisions.

Adaptability

The criterion *adaptability* is made up essentially of those measures provided by and investments made by the system which will strengthen the responsiveness of the system to problems that users have in their working/living environments. The basic assumption here is that there are many reasons, besides subject matter, why a message will be accepted or rejected. These have been discussed at some length in Chapter Three under problem dimensions and information traits. That is to say, once we have ascertained with a fair degree of confidence the subject matter of a particular problem, the appropriateness or relevance of the information displayed will depend on other attributes of the problem situation. It is these other atttributes around which the concept of adaptability revolves. The kinds of values grouped here respond to the concern with *how* something is needed, and *why,* and how well the system, including the human actors, can respond to the environment in which the user operates. It attempts to match type of response with problem context. This approach may seem somewhat strange, because our training and our categorizations tend to cluster around subject matter, or, what something is "about." The idea of adaptability asks instead what the dimensions of the problem are in nonsubject terms. Adaptability, which is problem specific (user oriented), contrasts therefore with the criterion of noise reduction which is subject specific (content oriented). It also contrasts with the value of interfacing which is systems specific (technology oriented). At the present time, much, if not most, of the value included under adaptability is added by human intermediaries because they are the only agents who can understand the problem setting and can interpret its dimensions and needs in nonsubject terms. It needs to be noted here that there may be a gray area between the value of interfacing and those values grouped under the rubric "Adaptability." A search intermediary who filters the output of a search by indicating that some chunks are more important than others is beginning to adapt the output to the needs of the user.

This book makes the assumption that the best information systems are those that will tend to address problems rather than only answer questions. The difference between questions and problems was discussed in Chapter Three and in MacMullin and Taylor (1984). Consequently, how useful the output of a system, be it product or service, is for the processes of clarifying or even solving a user's problem is a significant value. That value can only result from some level of problem understanding and empathy, which at present can only be provided by human beings. *Closeness to the problem* then, is the value added by those activities of a system which meet the specific needs of a person in a particular situation with a particular problem. This usually means a human interface, for it implies knowledge of the person's style, bias, idiosyncracies, and sophistication, as well as the politics and other constraints of the context.

During the past 30 years we have seen the rise of the knowledge worker in organizations. They usually appear in such activities as legal counsel, research and development, marketing, tax accounting, data processing, and associated consultants in many very specific interests. These staff activities have flourished, not only to monitor the external environment, but to adapt their special types of information to the well-being of the organization. They are closer to the problems than are conventional information systems (computer based or otherwise). These knowledge workers, and their ability to work fruitfully with those who have problems are very important parts of the total information systems of the organization. This is discussed in more detail in the specific setting of information analysis in Chapter Seven.

Flexibility is the capability of the system to provide a variety of approaches for working dynamically with the data/information in a file. Flexibility is in a way a continuum of methods, ranging from the associations provided in indexing systems, both manual and automated, to the potential of highly dynamic access systems built around data bases that can be "played with" in a wide variety of ways useful to the client. In decision support systems, for example, it is critical that the system users be able to play with the data, asking "What if. . . .?" questions, and getting a variety of output forms illustrating possible scenarios in response to their questions (graphs, tables, charts, and maps), adapted to their particular visual set and the needs of the information itself.

In the context of reviewing human factors in interactive computer dialog, Ramsey and Grimes note several senses in which the word "flexibility" is used.

> Systems are flexible because they: 1) are applicable to a broad range of tasks; 2) allow multiple approaches to a given task; 3) allow multiple ways of invoking the desired next computer operation; 4) adapt well to different user classes, particularly different levels of user experience; and 5) allow personalization of system behavior based on user preferences. (Ramsey & Grimes, 1983; p. 35)

The authors add "this is too great a burden for one word to carry . . . yet these various kinds of flexibility are going to become increasingly important as we develop more appropriately integrated information systems."

One of the major obstacles to flexibility of information systems in the modern organization, as James Martin has pointed out, is that data are frequently not independent of the application for which they were collected in the first place.

> Most *ad hoc* queries from a user employing a generalized query language cannot be answered. Although the data exist, information cannot be provided relating to those data. The data cannot be processed in new ways without restructuring.
> One sometimes hears the protest from management: "We paid millions for that computer and we cannot obtain the information we want from it." (Martin, 1981; pp. 9–10)

In further remarks, Martin states: "One of the most difficult tricks that we have to learn is how to introduce automation without introducing rigidity. The computer industry is now only beginning to glimpse how that can be done" (Martin, 1981; p. 61).

In literature-based systems, flexibility has been limited principally to the browsing mechanisms discussed above. However, as electronic publishing, computer-stored text, and expert systems become more common, the potential for flexibility in asking questions of text will become enormous. Flexibility in operational computer-based systems will depend a great deal on the ability to develop for everyday use the augmentation and delegation routines which Paisley and Butler discussed and which were cited above. This, however, is for some time in the future. Present online encyclopedias and handbooks, while useful for maintaining currency, are a long way from the flexibility that is necessary. For the most part, flexibility today is based on the skill and adaptability of the human intermediary.

Basic to any attempt at interfacing are simplicity, clarity, and the absence of ambiguity or overrefinement in the way information is presented or displayed. This does not mean that the ideas expressed need to be simple. They may, in fact, be quite complex. It is the clarity of expression and organization which is important. *Simplicity* may be a combination of several values, but its basic intent is to make the content or meaning of an information chunk easier to understand, hence easier to use. Those who have had the misfortune to be presented with a set of instructions that read as though they had been written by a semiliterate chimpanzee have an inkling of the other side of the coin. One of the banes of computer information systems is that instructions and examples are written by specialists who communicate only to other specialists who speak the same language. These specialists lack empathy, and in fact may be illiterate in natural language. They use excessive jargon. The instructions do not scan easily. They are not written for those outside the magic circle. They are not simple.

Legalistic prose tends also to undermine simplicity. As Jane Fonda said in *Cat Ballou:* "Why, they did terrible things to my father—they put manure in his well and they made him talk to lawyers."[2] The Allstate Insurance Company, in its new easy-to-read Auto Policy, states: "We've simplified the language making your policy easier to read *and* understand." They made the information in the policy easier to use, by simplifying. They added value to this small information product.

No discussion of simplicity would be complete without mention of Occam's razor, sometimes called the Principle of Parsimony. William of Ockham (Occam) 1300?–?1349, was a Fransiscan scholar and scholastic philosopher, who taught at Merton College, Oxford University in the early fourteenth century. He defended evangelical poverty against Pope John XXII (c. 1330), was imprisoned, escaped, and probably spent the rest of his days in Munich. In his *Dialogues* (1343) he stated the principle, that has come to be known as Occam's razor, that "entities must not be unnecessarily multiplied." In more idiomatic language it commands: Among equally plausible hypotheses, prefer the most simple.[3] Make it simple!

To some, the value called *stimulatory* may seem out of place, because the activities in support of it appear to be at some distance from what are perceived to be the normal concerns of an information system. Examples of these activities are provision of space for community meetings, planning and hosting seminars for the parent organization, editing speeches, papers, and newsletters, and advising on equipment and software purchases by other departments. Most of these activities are not central to the concerns of the information system. They provide, however, a means for gaining visibility for the system, of making the strange familiar, and of performing useful services for the larger organization or community. This is a form of good will, of adapting behavior. It is probably not measurable though it plays a role, for example, in the sale of a business, where a difference is recognized between good and ill will. Buyers (customers) will attach positive value to the former, and negative value to the latter. It results from certain effort and resources allocated on the part of the information system in the commitment of staff time and possibly space. We have called it "stimulatory." It should not be overlooked.

Time Savings

Although all values could conceivably be included under the rubric "Time Savings," because they presumably reduce the time and effort a client needs to make choices, we include only those that are specifically time related. During the past 30 years, there have been two major impacts of the computer. The first has been to accelerate processes which were already in existence: bookkeeping/accounting

[2] Quoted by W. Leslie Peat in *Library Journal, 106*(19), p. 2086 (November 1, 1981).

[3] This idiomatic expression is from a speech by Lee Loevinger, former Associate Justice of the Minnesota Supreme Court, given at the American Bar Association meeting in San Francisco, August 5, 1962. His talk was appropriately and succinctly titled *Occam's Electric Razor*.

systems; inventory systems; personnel records; library circulation and processing; production records; and similar kinds of standard transaction processes needed to operate and manage basic activities. The second has been to provide the means for performing calculations not possible before because of the immensity and intricateness of the calculations required, such as large-scale number crunching and Boolean search operations in online retrieval systems. Placing a man on the moon would not have been possible without computer processes. Though scientists knew what calculationss had to be performed, the task was far too large for human manipulation of the data. In this sense, human capabilities were augmented by the computer, and the act of moon flight made possible. These have been time-saving processes. The threshold from large-scale number crunching to true augmentation of human cognitive processes, however, has not yet been crossed except in very elementary ways.

Basically, as far as users or customers are concerned, the value by which they judge the time-saving merits of the system is the response time of that system: How fast can a reference be retrieved? How fast can a document be delivered? How long need a customer wait at the terminal for a response? How long does it take to generate a special report?

Cost Savings

Cost savings is the value achieved by conscious system design and operating decisions that save dollars for the client. Like the time savings criterion, many if not most of the values added may reflect in the user's total cost. However, this criterion is concerned only with real dollars saved. Usually this criterion and its attendant values added can only operate in a situation where dollars actually change hands, for example, where there is a price in the marketplace for the information product or service, or where there is a chargeback system in an organization. The question of cost saving becomes less clear when we consider such activities as "free" public library service. We talk as though this were free, but we know quite well that there is a cost in tax dollars. It is best if this point is not pressed too much. In the context here, cost saving is limited to actual dollars exchanged either in the marketplace or in a chargeback situation.

Table 4-1. Definitions of Values Added

Following are brief definitions of the added values discussed in this chapter. They are alphabetized. The expression in parentheses following the value name indicates the section in the chapter where more extended discussion may be found.

Access (Noise Reduction): the values added by the intellectual technologies that provide the systematic meanings, based on subject matter, of narrowing the information universe to a set of data and information which have some probability of containing material that is wanted or needed. Different kinds of intellectual access provide different sets of the subject universe.

Access I (Noise Reduction): the value achieved by the identification of any information chunk or discrete piece of data by systematic physical description and location information.

Access II (Noise Reduction): the provision of a subject description through access points such as index terms, descriptors, and names.

Access III (Noise Reduction): the result of proceses which reduce or compress large amounts of information into compact items, such as executive summaries, abstracts, terse conclusions, chemical structure diagrams, mathematical formulae, graphs, or charts.

Accuracy (Quality): the value added by system processes that assures error-free transfer of data and information as it flows through the system and is eventually displayed to a client.

Browsing (Ease of Use): the capability of a system to allow a client to scan an information neighborhood, with the probability that the client will serendipitously find information of value.

Closeness to Problem (Adaptability): the value added by the activities of the system, usually through human intervention, to meet the specific needs of a person in a particular environment with a particular problem; this implies knowledge of that person's style, bias, idiosyncracies, and sophistication, as well as the politics and constraints of the context.

Comprehensiveness (Quality): value added by the completeness of coverage of a particular subject or of a particular form of information.

Cost savings: the value achieved by conscious system design and operating decisions that save dollars for the client.

Currency (Quality): the value added (a) by the recency of the data acquired by the system; and (b) by the capability of the system to reflect current modes of thinking in its structure, organization, and access vocabularies.

Flexibility (Adaptability): the capability of a system to provide a variety of ways and approaches of working dynamically with the data/information in a file.

Formating (Ease of Use): the physical presentation and arrangement of data/information in ways that allow more efficient scanning and hence extraction of items of interest from the store.

Interfacing (Ease of Use): the capability of the system to interpret itself to users.

Interfacing (Mediation) (Ease of Use): the means used to assist users in getting answers from the system.

Interfacing (Orienting) (Ease of Use): the means used to help users understand and to gain experience with the system and its complexities.

Linkage (Noise Reduction): the value added by providing pointers and links to items, sources, and systems external to the system in use, thus expanding the client's information options.

Ordering (Ease of Use): the value added by initially dividing or organizing a body of subject matter by some form of gross ordering, such as alphabetization, or large groupings.

Physical Accessibility (Ease of Use): the processes of making access to information stores easier in a physical sense.

Precision (Noise Reduction): the capability of a system to aid users in finding exactly what they want, by providing signals on such attributes as language, data aggregation, sophistication level, or by ranking output.

Reliability (Quality): the value added by the trust a system inspires in its clients by its consistency of quality performance over time.

Selectivity (Noise Reduction): the value added when choices are made at the input point of the system, choices based on the appropriateness and merit of information chunks to the client population served.

Simplicity (Adaptability): the value achieved by presenting the most clear and lucid (explanation, data, hypothesis, or method) among several within quality and validity limits; not to be confused with simplistic.

Stimulatory (Adaptability): those activities of an information system that may not be directly supportive of its primary mission, but which assume importance in establishing a presence in the community or organization served and which encourage use of the system and/or its staff expertise.

Time savings: the perceived value of a system based on the speed of its response time.

Validity (Quality): the value added when the system provides signals about the degree to which data or information presented to users can be judged as sound.

Chapter Five

VALUE-ADDED PROCESSES IN LIBRARIES

DOCUMENT-BASED SYSTEMS

Document-based systems are those formalized activities that we have traditionally associated with the graphic record, with print, with documents and books, and with their predecessors in clay, papyrus, quipu, and parchment. For millenia, the archives and libraries that grew around the need to preserve and to organize the records of historical civilizations (civilizations with a written record) have served as a memory for society. The records had become too complex and dynamic for the older oral traditions. This was especially true as commercial transactions across the Iranian Plateau increased spectacularly in the third and fouth millennia B.C. There appears to be good evidence that goods were passing through more and more hands, requiring identification, receipts, and records of orders made and filled (Pfeiffer, 1977; pp. 183–187). These required organization, storage, and access. One might call them libraries, they were certainly data bases of a sort.

It is worth noting, in passing, that the oral tradition had its own formalisms for memory in ritual, poetic rhythm, and in the internal structure of tales and oral sagas. The songs of people in the Carolines and other Pacific Islands included detailed sailing directions, a primary means of preserving crucial information for survival, what Eric Havelock has called "the tribal encyclopedia" (Pfeiffer, 1977; p. 473). There is a West African saying that "when an old man dies, a library is burned."[1] The high art of medieval Japanese sword making has been called the supreme metallurgical art. This complicated process was preserved in a highly stylized ritual passed from generation to generation by a small elite (Smith, 1981; pp. 292–299). These forms were the means of preserving knowledge in nonliterate societies or, in the case of Japan, in order to maintain control by an elite over the process of swordmaking, because the sword was a symbol of power and purity. The point here is that this knowledge was not recorded in ways we would consider conventional.

This transition from an oral culture to a written culture based on an alphabet was not a simple one, and echoes of that ferment can be heard today as we may

[1] From Professor Marta Dosa, School of Information Studies, Syracuse University.

be moving gradually away from a print-based society. The following quotation from Plato's *Phaedrus* illustrates not only those difficulties, but in a way foreshadows some of the arguments we hear today about the loss of reasoning ability due to the computer.

> I heard, then, that . . . in Egypt, was one of the ancient gods of that country, the one whose sacred bird is called the ibis, and the name of the god himself was Theuth. He it was who invented numbers and arithmetic and geometry and astronomy, also draughts and dice, and, most important of all, letters. Now the king of all Egypt at that time was the god Thamus. . . . To him came Theuth to show his inventions, saying that they ought to be imparted to the other Egyptians. But Thamus asked what use there was in each, and as Theuth enumerated their uses, expressed praise or blame, according as he approved or disapproved. The story goes that Thamus said many things to Theuth in praise or blame of the various arts, which it would take too long to repeat; but when they came to the letters, "This invention, O king," said Theuth, "will make the Egyptians wiser and will improve their memories; for it is an elixir of memory and wisdom that I have discovered." But Thamus replied, "Most ingenious Theuth, one man has the ability to beget arts, but the ability to judge of their usefulness or harmfulness to their users belongs to another; and now you, who are the father of letters, have been led by your affection to ascribe to them a power the opposite of that which they really possess. For this invention will produce forgetfulness in the minds of those who learn to use it, because they will not practise their memory. Their trust in writing, produced by external characters which are no part of themselves, will discourage the use of their own memory within them. You have invented an elixir not of memory, but of reminding; and you offer your pupils the appearance of wisdom, not true wisdom, for they will read many things without instruction and will therefore seem to know many things, when they are for the most part ignorant and hard to get along with, since they are not wise, but only appear wise."[2]

This brief digression into the oral tradition has served principally to point up the primacy of the role of memory in document-based systems. That many other functions and processes have accumulated around this primary function is an indication of the complexity of the human record and the varietyof uses to which it is put.

With the advent of the computer and its associated technologies, the whole mechanism of extrasomatic memory (for example, libraries, museums, and computer memories) is at the beginning of profound change, in which some time in the future even the role of human memory itself may well change. The technology may indeed be available for massive change, but three factors will tend to restrict its application. The first is the natural inertia inherent in the way information is organized at present. This is also reflected in managerial, academic, and bureaucratic structures which in themselves are ways of organizing and ordering information and knowledge, and from which decisions will be made determining how computer power will be used or not used. These attitudes will take a long time to change.

---

[2] *Plato,* with an English Translation by Henry North Fowler, Volume 1, pp. 561,563. London: Heineman, 1923 (The Loeb Classical Library, Plato, V. 1).

The second factor is that, despite our theoretic models of decisionmaking, we really have little inkling of how the human mind works in decision situations, nor of the role of information in those processes. Efforts to mimic the human mind, or even just to augment it in ways beyond the most elemental, are obfuscated by a need for a reductionism that must omit most of the variety requisite in human mental activity.

The third factor inhibiting the full use of computing power is that, in truth, we really do not know what to do with that power except to automate early twentieth-century processes. We are like the little boy with a hammer—everything becomes a nail, something to be hammered. Up to now and for the next few decades, the impact will be felt principally in the automation of traditional information processes.

The lack of an historical perspective together with its concomitant belief in instant progress, may force document-based systems to change faster than would be appropriate had we more control over the circumstances. Present forms, such as the book and present institutions, such as the library, will be with us for some time to come, for, despite the rhetoric of computer technologists, they offer a variety of advantages that the computer is not able to match. The book, for example, is portable, randomly accessible, and requires no technology, except perhaps spectacles, for its use. The computer per se can match none of these capabilities. It can of course produce booklike packages, which then assume the properties of the book. New systems which are computer based, will begin to parallel and to occupy some of the territory of document-based systems. The computer will allow the latter to perform faster, though there may be some sacrifice in quality. These are basically the standard routinized processes inherited from and perfected over the past century and a half. When the computer begins to move into the provision of reference information presently available in handbooks and similar standard sources, as is beginning to happen now, there will certainly be an improvement in the currency of the information and perhaps even in its accessibility. The process, however, will tend to freeze or even to intensify inefficiencies or, worse, mistakes in the basic data and their definitions. These problems unfortunately, will, probably not detract from the perceived utility of such systems, and hence their continued growth and application.

> The suspension of critical judgment, not recognizing underlying data quality problems, not recognizing the incomprehensibility of much of their own software, leads inexorably to acceptance of the system reality as the only reality. (Laudon, 1980; p. 134)

We will be living with two systems for some time to come, the older of which has the advantage of being in place, built on several centuries of comfortable use and growth. The newer systems have the glamor of novelty, endowed with a halo of progress and improvement. It is very possible that improvement will be substantial. The process of changeover, however, will be expensive. We tend to automate a process, then wonder what to do with it or ask what its implications are for other related activities.

LIBRARIES

Libraries, throughout the centuries, have provided the means for storing and physically accessing the accumulated knowledge of the human race. This is of course a simplistic assertion, but it does represent the historical function of libraries. During the last half century there have been changes especially in public and special libraries supporting the development of user and people-oriented activities. These are directly relevant to the user-driven approach for value-added processes, and are discussed at greater length later in this chapter.

Roles of the Library

In a societal sense, a library generally assumes one or more of several roles: archival, educational, informational, volitional reading,[3] and there may indeed be one more function—community service—somewhat more difficult to define as we will see.

In general terms, these primary functions and their adoption by any particular library is a response to a perceived user environment, though the statement of that response may be put in more library-centered terms:

> . . . the essence of library service is providing books to be read. . . . (Buckland, 1983; p. 6)

> . . . the company technical library has to dispense a more tangible product—answers to problems of interest to the company on a day to day basis. (Max Mueller as quoted by Aspnes, 1980; p. 5)

In the chosen context each library tends to develop its own processes of adding value, in response to the perceived needs of the environment in which that particular library sits and the way those needs are interpreted by the professional staff or by the governing board.

Most librarians would say, with justification, that their type of library performs more than one of these functions. Within their defined spheres, each size or type of library serves to some degree an archival function. In a societal sense, however, it is the large research library that principally serves this function. Indeed a large university library may have two separate facilities, not including branches or specialized collections: one a research library built around the archival function, and one an undergraduate library built around the educational process. The public library tends to be more diffuse in its purposes and hence, some will argue, less effective. It certainly serves as a source for recreational reading. By its services to children and young adults, it serves a conscious educational purpose. As its base has been affected by new channels—the paperback, the book club, and television—and by changes especially in urban neighborhoods served, the public library has sought new foci of concern. Its business section or its art and music section have become specialized information activities directed toward meeting the needs of special interests of its publics. Incipient probes at providing information services for those

[3] The term is used by Lowell Martin (1974).

not normally reached by conventional public library services are attempts to capture an audience which, despite the rhetoric, has been beyond the usual library's realm. Special libraries, particularly those in corporate, industrial, and commercial settings, serve first an informational role and, when reincarnated as technical information centers, an archival referral role, and maybe even an analytic role. The technical information center, either as metamorphosis of the special library or as a new format for providing service, moves beyond the traditional role of the library into the processes of information analysis. As Kertesz has pointed out: "The most important feature that differentiates the information center from a special library or document collection is that the output of the center is not the same as the input" (Kertesz, 1980; p. 719). The process that makes this difference is called information analysis, and is discussed in Chapter Seven as a number of critical processes that add value, that is, the making of sense from disparate pieces of data and information. The present chapter is limited to the conventional patterns of libraries and their services. This is done in full awareness that libraries and librarians may indeed be moving onto new grounds. This process is discussed in this chapter as well as in various sections throughout the book, especially in Chapters Seven, Nine, and Ten.

Value-Added Processes

In looking at libraries of any type there are two questions to be considered in the value-added model. First, where, among these values, does the library allocate the available energy, time, materials, labor, and money? This question can be (and should be) asked of any size or type of library. The second question asks what kinds of activities does the library perform in support of these values. It should be kept in mind that the basic consideration behind these questions is what the library does to facilitate choice by its users. For emphasis we repeat that choice does not necessarily mean information for solution to an immediate problem, but, more likely, information that may be useful in the future or that helps to make sense of a particular situation. The interplay and degree of emphasis between problem-solving information and contextual or sense-making information will tend to separate different types of libraries.

When seen in terms of value added, all types of libraries perform similar basic enhancing activities. (The reader should refer to Figure 4-2 for a structured list of values added, and to Table 4-1 for definition of those values). Probably the most important value added by libraries of all types is *physical access* to an organized collection of materials. It is of interest here, however, to note that there has been a gradual change in the meaning of physical access. Sixty years ago, it meant access to a collection of books in a single location called a library. On occasion and by prior agreement an item might be lent by one institution to another for use by a patron of the latter institution. With the gradual realization that no single library, academic or otherwise, could afford to acquire and store all the materials needed by its publics, local union catalogs, the *National Union Catalog*, and the *Union List of Serials* were developed. These were means of providing a central record of the holdings of a group of cooperating libraries. In the beginning, access among the institutions in these networks was entirely by mail. Telephone, teletype, and now the computer and associated telecommunications technologies provide quick, even instantaneous access to materials, bibliographic information, and quantitative data anywhere in the country, or the world. Thus the activities of providing physical access have in the past 30 years changed markedly, both in the physical sense and in response time. Access is no longer necessarily confined to a single institution. The idea of physical access encompasses a much broader range of resources. A small independent suburban library, for example, through its computerized circulation system which is linked to the county library system, can today call on the resources of all the libraries in the county network, and even beyond, to region and state, in support of the request of a particular patron. This was not possible five years ago.

The many forms of control that libraries of all types exercise are attempts to maintain the physical integrity, and hence the physical accessibility of items in the collection. Circulation systems, overdue notices and fines, shelving and shelf reading, antitheft devices, checkout desks at exits are all forms of maintaining physical access. Libraries invest a great deal of money and labor in such activities.

Formatting may not be thought of as a value that librarians pay much attention to. It is usually taken to mean ways of arranging text and emphasizing signals of the printed page or in a computer display. The basic idea is to make it easier for a user to access and to make choices from the body of information available. If we shift our focus somewhat and look at the library as a sort of gross text, then we can say that signs and graphics help a user move around the collections more efficiently, or use computer terminals to access the online catalog more effectively. In speaking of signs in libraries, Pollet and Haskell point out that the concept includes "building directories, wall graphics, printed library guides, maps of the building, space arrangement, displays, even information stations—in short, all visual means of helping readers find and use the services of the library" (Pollet & Haskell, 1979; p. ix). If the reader will accept the metaphor, signage becomes a way of formatting the library, hence allowing users to spend their time and energy most efficiently.

Different types of libraries will have different ways of adding value in this context. Basic forms of *intellectual access* are standard across all types of libraries: description of the physical item *(Access I)* and limited forms of subject access through standardized subject heading lists *(Access II)*. By means of highly standardized formats, such as AACR 2 and the earlier Library of Congress card, most library catalogs are much the same in appearance. That is to say that a library user can move from city to city, from institution to institution, and still find the same format in the library catalog. This uniformity may change somewhat as local diversity grows as a result of online catalogs. Unique needs of special user environments, for example a pharmaceutical research laboratory, will require more intense effort in providing Access II or even *Access III* (summarizing or abstracting) than a central city public library. Classification systems for the location of physical items, descriptive cataloging, and various forms of subject tagging are, however, common forms of added value in most types of libraries.

Most libraries perform some degree of the value we have termed *interfacing (mediation),* which ranges from standard reference assistance to highly skilled question negotiation. This can range from the small rural library with a part-time librarian to the busy reference desk of a large public library, from the online searcher who serves as merely a pipeline between requestor and the retrieval service, to the subject specialist librarian who works closely with researchers in the laboratory. It is worth noting that the part-time librarian in the rural setting may be, for that library's clientele, as effective as is the subject specialist in the laboratory. Both are effective to the degree that:

- They know the subject matter with which they work: books and their qualities in one instance, and subject knowledge in the other.
- They know their clients and the settings in which those clients live and/or work.
- They are sensitive to the kinds of problems their clients face and to some extent to the criteria they use in making choices.

These similarities are usually overlooked, frequently because of the arrogance of subject specialization, which tends to elevate the importance of subject knowledge at the expense of its communication. Both are important and in our context it is their combination which gives quality. As in great teaching, the combination is critical in librarianship and in those professions concerned with the provision and use of information.

It is worth noting that, in some cases, the actual work done in support of some of these values may be performed at a distance by an agency other than the local library, for example, cataloging and classification by the Library of Congress or by other libraries in a consortium associated with the OCLC data base. The rise of networks and library computer utilities is moving some of the functions formerly performed locally away from the individual library. Now administrators and governing boards may hail this process as a more cost-efficient way of providing service than was possible before. The anticipated trade-offs in support of a more localized and more sophisticated service, however, may not materialize. The actual costs of computerization in terms of dollars, energy, time, and commitment may eat up more of the library's resources than originally planned. The warehousing may be more efficient, but the services unique to the local clientele will suffer.

As a prime example of the mediating aspect of interfacing, the intermediary for online searching has become common in several types of libraries, especially academic research libraries and special libraries. The search intermediary, as a separate "information system" is analyzed in the value-added context at the end of the next chapter on abstracting and indexing services. This has been done on the assumption that in the eyes of the user, the search intermediary is an extension of the online abstracting and indexing systems, a form of knowledgeable and skilled access to available bibliographic data bases, not a member of the library staff. It is, however, the library that commits resources in support of this searching function, by paying the salary of the searcher. Conversely, it may be that the library will be viewed not only as a local collection of information, but truly as a switching center to information anywhere in the world. Such a change in perception will depend on local service attitudes and style.

Ordering is the value added by the activities that organize all library collections in gross ways. These are so common that we tend to overlook, even discount them. They are, however, one attempt to impose order on a physical collection, and a value in which the library invests labor, energy, and time. Such activities make the collection easier to use. Things are generally where they are expected to be. The literature of Physics is separated from that of Romance Languages; handbooks, encyclopedias, indexes, and directories are separated from other parts of the collection in a place called the reference area; children's books will be downstairs and adult books upstairs; issues of current journals will always be found alphabetically arranged (perhaps by gross subject matter) in one place. In varying degrees these will be found in any sort of library.

All libraries adapt in some degree to their environments. The activities associated with this we have grouped under the rubric "Adaptability." Different types of libraries will obviously have different kinds of levels of adaptive behavior. This is due to the diversity of clientele, to managerial style, and to the objectives the library assumes, for example, archival or educational. It should be noted that exploitation and support of some of the other added values will depend on the level of adaptation that a particular library supports.

Adaptability and its reflection in closeness to problem, empathy, and flexibility, can be one of the most important roles for librarians to cultivate. Activities such as analysis, evaluation, and interpretation will become unique and critical roles in the future of information systems whether or not they are performed by librarians. As computer and related technologies assume more of the traditional activities that librarians have performed in the past, and as the information record becomes more complex, the unique capabilities, that is, the service orientation and knowledge that librarians possess, will be critical in future adapting and filtering activities.

In discussing individual types of libraries and the kinds of value they add, we can only sample for illustration. Consequently, the descriptions of activities in academic, public, and special libraries below should by no means be considered complete. That is not the intent of the descriptions. Rather this chapter presents ways of looking at those information systems called libraries to see how their activities can be perceived as value-added processes. Once the utility of that approach is established, then detailed studies can take place.

ACADEMIC LIBRARIES

The academic library needs to be discussed in two stages: as a library in support of research; and as a library in support of education. Each serves a different environment, different clientele, and different needs. Hence these two classes put emphasis on different added values. The separation is not always clear, especially in larger university libraries where a physical separation has not been made. In such cases, because universities *are* for faculties, the research or archival function tends to dominate. As this author has written previously: "although the research user is a small proportion of even the academic population, the academic library is designed especially for him or her. Library structure reflects this bias—its catalogs, its efficiencies, its packages, and its bias for print, for literacy" (Taylor, 1975; pp. 300–301).

Research Libraries

As we have said before, the library that considers people who conduct research to be its primary clientele and the research context to be the principal information environment served will emphasize certain values over others. The degree of this emphasis will of course vary, due to institutional policies, faculty capabilities and interests, and the assumptions of library staff. In addition, it is probably necessary to divide the research context into two parts: (a) the humanities, arts, and the social sciences; and (b) the natural, physical, and engineering sciences. There are other possibly finer divisions, but these two should suffice for the academic context. The library serving the former context is labelled a Type I research library and the latter Type II for ease of discussion that follows.

This discussion uses the chart in Chapter Four (Figure 4-1) as a means of organizing the comments. In this way comments and observations can be summarized over all types of libraries at the end of this chapter. Two things should be emphasized. First, this chapter deals with typical library systems, which means that the system model assumed attempts to include most variations, but the edges and detail may be fuzzy. Second, academic research libraries do not add many of the values listed. The academic library itself is a rather gross cut of the information process. From the standpoint of the user, the values added may be limited, but they are significant and important in what they do do. It is important to remember that we are only including academic libraries here and what the librarians themselves seem to do in those libraries. Not included for example are the processes of abstracting and indexing, though their products, both print and online, may be available in or through the library. The concern here is only with the fact of their provision and their use through the library. Abstracting and indexing as a value-added process is considered in the next chapter.

Under "Ease of Use" the following added values are considered: browsing, formatting, interfacing, ordering, and physical accessibility.

Browsing in research libraries is enhanced by several activities: classification and display. Browsing supports such needs as accidental discovery (i.e., serendipity)l, the need to be informed, and the need to keep current in one's field. The browsing capability in larrge research libraries, however, will reflect varying requirements. In Type I libraries the need for browsing in the stacks is important; hence book classification, with all its faults, is a primary means of supporting that value. In a Type II library, the opportunity to scan for up-to-date information is important; hence current periodical display and associated reading space become primary activities in support of browsing. This does not mean that these two types of activities are mutually exclusive: It is rather that the emphasis will vary because of the kind of users. One of the forms of browsing that most libraries have neglected is the shelf list. After all, if the books on the shelves themselves are classified and arranged so that a user may browse in a subject neighborhood, then the listing of items in the order that they are parked may be more useful than stack browsing, because it will also show those books that are in circulation, frequently the best and the most recent books. The online catalog at Syracuse University's Bird Library supports this particular capability.

Formatting is probably of less importance in academic research libraries than in other types of libraries.

The value *interfacing* in libraries in general has been commented on above. In the research library it is principally reflected in the assistance provided through the reference service desk to patrons in making use of the catalog or of the collections. With the advent of online reference retrieval systems, the search intermediary provides an important function as a conduit to those systems, negotiating and framing a question so that effective and efficient use can be made of a particular system. This *mediation* function is an important added value of research libraries. The *orienting* side of interfacing is of lesser significance in academic research libraries.

The provision of *physical accessibility* to the research literature has been and is one of the major functions of research libraries. Comment has already been made on the change that has occurred in the meaning of physical access as a result of the growth of networks and support technologies to facilitate access among many institutions. This is especially important for research libraries. Some of the energy and labor which was earlier expended to maintain local accessibility is now being channeled in cooperative fashion to provide physical access for more researchers in more locations. Individual reprint and note files are supported by electronic information exchange systems, by the use of the ubiquitous library copier, by interlibrary loan and copying arrangements, as well as by the usual processes of reprint exchange. These are all means of providing physical accessibility for researchers. Research libraries play a major role in most of these processes.

Noise reduction encompasses the following values: Access I, II, and III, linkage, precision, and selectivity.

Access I and *II* include the traditional enchancements that libraries perform through descriptive cataloging and the provision of subject headings. Like physical accessibility, modern communication technology, cooperative consortiums, and computer utilities are reducing the investment in labor that the individual library makes in support of intellectual access. It is worth speculating whether the total investment, including dollars, time, energy, labor, has indeed been reduced. To the author's knowledge there has been no research of the real effect of these changes on the allocation of resources.

For the academic research library, especially those of Type I, the activities in support of Access I and II, for example, cataloging, classification, and, to a lesser extent, subject description, are of special importance to the research people it serves. Bibliographic description and source verification are important reference points in the production of new knowledge. The whole concept of citation indexing has been built on the research need to acknowledge related and supporting literature. Research libraries play a major role in the bibliographic verification activity. Very few activities in support of *Access III,* i.e., summarizing, are performed by research libraries. In a few cases there might be specialized abstracts of current information issued for highly specialized research interests on the campus. These may or may not be the responsibility of librarians, and would depend on local arrangements.

Linkage means active referral to and provision of information from outside the local library. This goes beyond the provision of online searching of remote bibliographic data bases, which is considered physical access. It pertains especially to personal contact for expertise. It is informational rather than bibliographic. Because of the nature of academic research, library activities in support of this value are probably unusual, built on personal knowledge rather than formal commitment by the institution.

Precision, like linkage, is dependent on the level of adaptability of the library staff to the environment of its clientele.

Selectivity, in the sense of reducing noise, is probably not a particular enhancement of academic research libraries. In fact, because of the needs of academic research, a major emphasis is placed on comprehensiveness rather than selectivity.

Under "quality" the following added values are considered: accuracy, comprehensiveness, currency, reliability, and validity.

Accuracy of the bibliographic information is of major concern in research libraries. Considerable effort is expended by academic librarians as a group in developing standards for bibliographic description through national and international activities such as Committee Z-39 of the American National Standards Institute and the development of the Anglo–American Cataloging Rules. Such standards are important inputs to accuracy, and indeed to similarity of product across many libraries.

Comprehensiveness is a major value of the academic research library. Size of library collection and depth of particular research collections are considered an important quality of a major university. Size implies comprehensiveness in the context here. This is especially true for Type I libraries, where the library itself is the laboratory. It is the principal resource for information in the humanities—where comprehensiveness may be critical.

Currency is of particular importance to Type II libraries. Considerable investment is made in maintaining currency in the collection through review of new books, new periodicals, and, if necessary, specialized reports. The currency of periodicals, especially important in support of scientific research, is maintained through procedures in periodical check-in and in the claiming of missing issues. For the user who depends partially on the library as a means of keeping current, it is particularly important. Such currency may not be necessary for experienced researchers in their specific area of interest, where they have their own personal invisible college; but library currency does become important for them in related fields where they do not have personal contact.

In the terminology of the value-added model, a user or client feels a library has the attribute of *reliability* if it is consistent, especially in accuracy and coverage. That is to say, within mutually accepted limits of the research library, the user can depend on that library. Some of this trust derives from the user's perception of staff capabilities and knowledge, the ability to provide "good" answers. Some rests on the level of shelving consistency, catalog accuracy,and currency of the data in the reference collection.

The academic research library does little if anything to enhance the value of *validity* which has to do with the truth of falsity of the data it presents. The library merely serves as a conduit for data collected elsewhere, and which appear in reference books and throughout the collection. Individual librarians may be aware of possible discrepancies and may caution users about them; but such activities are minimal in library operations.

Adaptability, as it has been defined here, depends a great deal on the knowledge and skill of the reference staff in active and sensitive support of user needs. It takes particular form in the research library and will vary by the kind of clientele (Type I or Type II). Most academic librarians have been educated and frequently hold advanced degrees in the humanities. Consequently, they have been more effective and active in Type I libraries where their subject expertise and their knowledge of the resources and bibliographic idiosyncracies of the subject matter are important. For research in the humanities, the library is the laboratory, and hence the knowledgeable librarian can become an active partner in that process. This can be inhibited, however, by the walls that have been erected around disciplines which affects the acceptance of a person with "part-time expertise"—the librarian—into the fraternity.

In Type II libraries, librarians are generally less effective for the converse of the reasons cited above. Very few hold advanced degrees in the sciences. The library itself is not the central focus for the activities of scientists as it is for the humanities. The scientist's place of work is in the laboratory, however defined. The librarian seldom participates in laboratory experiments, and hence has very little awareness of the information problems arising in these contexts. Consequently, librarians in Type II libraries are generally excluded from the critical part of the scientific process, and hence from developing a true interface.

Improvement in *response time* is reflected principally in the increased investment in speedier access to bibliographic data, both internally and externally, and in faster service for interlibrary loans, due to library networking. This is a value in which libraries over the past dozen years have invested a good deal of money and time. It has provided faster access to the information and the packages handled by research libraries.

The user of the research library may be adversely affected by the growth of computer networks. That is to say, the user may not *save costs* in terms of dollars.

As more online bibliographic searching takes place, it is doubtful that the library itself will be able to absorb the full cost, or it may do so only by sacrificing other enhancements. Individual users without research grants may have to pick up at least some of the cost of such searches. This is not analogous, as some may think, to the allocation of "free" computer time to faculty and graduate students, which is based on the movement of "funny money" within the institution. In the case of online searching, the library must pay hard cash to outside vendors. Whether or not the research library will be able to absorb these costs without severely affecting other services is a local problem and solutions will vary.

College Libraries

Libraries associated with post secondary education are principally concerned with education rather than research. Such libraries vary widely in context, intent, collection size, media variety, and campus role. Nevertheless, the principal role is that of educational support, and that objective governs most of their activities. An exception is in such cases as at Princeton and Syracuse universities where there are no separate undergraduate libraries, and where the research function tends to dominate. The Lamont Library at Harvard and the Moffitt Library at the University of California at Berkeley are examples of separate undergraduate libraries, which are supported by and are part of very large research collections on their campuses. Libraries of principally undergraduate colleges will vary from the superb book collections of Amherst, Oberlin, and Reed Colleges to haphazard collection of 25,000 volumes in small colleges hanging on by their fingernails. The shift from books alone to a broader concept of media can be seen in the learning resource centers or media centers of the community colleges and other two-year colleges. These two-year institutions may indeed be closer to the educational process than are the other types of college libraries. Despite the variety, however, the principal role of these libraries is to support the educational objectives of the parent institution; and that objective governs most of their activities. The term "college library" will be used to cover all of these varieties. Some may object because of the semantic baggage carried by the term "library." It is used as a shorthand for learning resource center, media center, instructional resources center, as well as for the conventional library associated with post–secondary education.

As has been the case with many kinds of services during the past decade, the educational mission of these libraries and resource centers have been affected (a) by the economic realities of inflation, (b) by flagging interest in innovation in higher education, and (c) by the overwhelming attention and resources given to automation. For example, the generic library at Evergreen State College, the experimenting library at Hampshire College, and other similar efforts of the late 1960s, while still active, are no longer perceived as feasible models for the college library.

What are some of the things that can be said about the educational phase of libraries, *cum* learning resource centers, that distinguishes them from other types of libraries?

- Their scope of collection is usually broader than that of the research library, and may include such nonbook media as film, video recording, audio recording, and other formats, sometimes called "the generic book."

- The librarians work closely with faculty in developing book and media support for courses, ranging from a reserve collection to the production of instructional materials in nonbook formats.
- The library may provide extensive facilities for the production of electronic media and for their transmission to other parts of the campus.
- The library usually provides extensive space for study, frequently used by students studying nonlibrary materials.

Like other types of libraries and information systems, the college library is also concerned with assisting users, in this case students, through a variety of value-added activities in making choices among the range of information available. The processes of making choices, however, have shifted from a research and problem-solving context to a context in which "making choices" is governed by the instructional boundaries of courses, term papers, assignments, public presentations, and examinations. The dream of all educators, of course, is that these boundaries will be breached by students driven by a curiosity to go beyond the needs of educational formalisms. Both of these objectives—formal education on the one hand and open-ended education on the other—are important goals both for the parent institution and for the supporting college library. What does the college library do in the context of the value-added model to support these goals?

For the college library, values added, such as browsing, interfacing (mediation and orientation), and physical accessibility, are of special importance in supporting *Ease of use*. Because of the smallness of the collection, compared to research libraries, the encouragement of *browsing* as a means of educating its users (in this case, students) can take many forms dependent on the skills and resources available. Subject displays, new book displays, exhibits relative to major current events, media display, arrangement of special collections in support of particular interests, and of course open stacks and comfortable reading spaces—these are all ways that student browsing is enhanced. We do not know very much about how successful they are in educational terms. In a way they are an act of faith: a belief that the encouragement of intellectual curiosity is an important part of education.

Formatting, as in the research library, is principally dependent on the signage used throughout the library. In the college library, however, such signs and graphics may be more extensive and more carefully planned and designed because of the educational environment in which the library exists, and the need to instruct users in the use of the library.

Interfacing is important in the educational environment because it provides various forms of *mediation* between users and system: to explain, to illustrate, and especially to relate information and knowledge to the specific user. These are significant enhancing activities if the college library is to move beyond the warehouse level. The college library places special emphasis on the *orienting* function, instructing students in effective ways of using the collections. A sizable investment is made for this purpose.

The *ordering* value, as mentioned before, is a straightforward and common enhancement in all types of libraries, with variations for specific institutions.

Physical accessibility, including the provision, control, and maintenance of study space, is a major value added by college libraries. Considerable investment and major resources are allocated to these activities. Study space is included here for two reasons. First, it is a space and an activity in which major investment is made. Second, the availability of such space enhances the student's educational objectives of meeting immediate course obligations, whether or not personal materials or library materials are used. The amenities and physical comforts built into the modern library enhance the physical proximity and accessibility of the materials. The circulation controls, shelving maintenance, and antitheft controls are all attempts to raise the probability that a student user will find the package he or she wants. The reserve book collection is a most successful attempt to locate and control information materials of presumably high use centrally. All of these activities are means of enhancing, if not assuring, physical accessibility to the libraries collections.

Among those added values grouped under the rubric ''Noise Reduction,'' three are of particular importance: Access I and II and selectivity.

The catalog of holdings represents the principal investment in support of the descriptive and subject cataloging activities which are the basis for *Access I* and *Access II*. This, however, is true of all types of libraries, though the college library may put more emphasis on subject description and subject access *(Access II).*

Access III (subject summary), *linkage,* and *precision* are of little concern to the college library.

In contrast to the effort that research libraries invest in comprehensiveness, the college library invests time and effort in those activities which support the added value of *selectivity*. More attention is paid to selecting appropriate materials for the particular educational context, the formal courses and the range of faculty subject interests that are course related. Over the past two decades college librarians have invested a great deal of effort in such activities as the several editions of *Books for College Libraries (BCL)* and the book review journal *Choice*. Though these efforts have had problems, they recognized the importance of selectivity for the college library.

The several added values listed under the criterion of *quality* are probably of less importance in the college library than they are in other types of information systems. This does not mean these are negative, rather that the college library does not make a large or particular investment in supporting them, especially true of accuracy, comprehensiveness,and validity. *Currency* may be of some importance because of the educational context and the need for tie-in to political, economic, and social trends. *Reliability,* in the sense of perceived consistency of operations and services, is important for any information system. In the college library, user perception of high reliability is directly related to the quality of the interfacing activities. Good, candid, and helpful reference service will do much to enhance the perception of the library's reliability.

As part of the education process, the college library does very little in the way of analysis and evaluation and other activities supporting *adaptation*. Its function is to help educate and train students in effective methods of finding information for themselves. Reference librarians may occasionally add value by filtering, for example, by recommending one book over another, but this is not perceived as a major function of the college librarian.

Activities in support of and resources allocated to *time savings* and *cost savings* for the user are not of particular significance in the college library.

In summary, we can say that in general the college library invests most of its resources in activities supporting the following added values: browsing, interfacing, both mediation and orientation, physical accessibility including study space, Access I and II, and selectivity.

PUBLIC LIBRARIES

One of the difficulties in discussing public libraries in the value-added context is that their objectives either are not very clear or are so diffuse as to include everything (Lundberg, 1981). The utility of the value-added model is dependent on the degree to which the information system, in this case the library, can state its objectives in terms against which we can evaluate services, even if only in qualitative terms. In the simplest possible terms, a public library's objective is to make resources available to a population which in character may cut across all interests, all ages, and all levels of literacy. Now, there are several problems associated with that statement.

The first problem is the definition of "resources." The term in this context includes (a) books and related printed materials; (b) films, recordings, video tapes, and related media; and (c) in the 1980s, the microcomputer and related software. Does the term include "information"? This is a critical question, for it implies different and varied kinds of resources. There are three levels of information in the public library context:

- information at the traditional reference book level, where the information/reference service is dependent on external collection and provision of information in book form;
- information useful to special groups, for example, business information, which requires specialized staff, extensive, dynamic, and internally generated collections, and on-line access to financial, business, scientific, technical, and demographic data bases;
- information of a coping nature, the intent of which is to help people make useful decisions about personal matters, for example, employment, education, welfare, health, rat control, crime prevention, drugs, or housing.

Most public libraries operate only at the first level. The larger libraries may have several specialized information services, some of real distinction. Very few operate at the third level at this time.

The second problem associated with the statement on objectives is how to make these resources available. Availability implies means of delivery. Public libraries have used several ways of delivering their traditional resource, the book, e.g., via branch libraries and bookmobiles. Reference services provide the means for delivering conventional kinds of information. The growth of specialized information services has been fairly rapid, but only the larger libraries have been able to justify the cost of such services. Indeed, libraries are not looked upon by the general population, even those with special interests, as primary sources of useful information. Consequently, these specialized services need to build up their clientele; there is no ready market.

The growth of for-profit information brokers is in direct competition to this form of service by the library. Indeed many information brokers make their living by intelligent exploitation of public library resources. A few libraries have attempted self-supporting services to serve business, commercial, and industrial interests. Though apparently successful, the lack of real commitment and support from the parent library have almost guaranteed failure of these operations. This poses some fundamental questions of the provision of private goods and services versus public goods and services (Getz, 1979). The assumptions of this book, however, are not particularly dependent on one's interpretation of the public–private controversy. The concern here is with the kinds of value-added activities the typical public library performs in order to provide information and services to those it believes are its publics.

The third information area—the provision of coping information—is a more difficult concern, and one fraught with controversy. The public library is uniquely situated to provide such services. It has the reputation of reliability and neutrality. It represents no special interests. It is a community agency. Librarians have the professional skills to collect, to organize, to interpret, and to disseminate information. Despite these attributes, the library is not looked upon by the general public as a source of useful information (Warner, Murray, & Palmour, 1973). There are "turf" problems with other agencies, when the library attempts to formalize information service in, for example, such concerns as consumer affairs, health, the environment, or welfare. These are not necessarily insurmountable as is illustrated by the experience of the Memphis–Shelby County Public Library and Information Center (Cronenberger & Luck, 1976) and the Onondaga County Public Library (Syracuse) with community health information (Yellott, 1982). Childers (1983) has a good review of recent attempts, successes, and problems of information referral in public libraries.

In the context of value-added activities, then, the typical public library is perceived as serving two principal functions: (a) the provision of volitional reading, and (b) the provision of information, both standard reference and, to a limited degree, specialized information. There is a third function, more visible but perhaps more subtle than the others: improvement of the quality of community life. This is difficult to discuss in value-added terms (see Powers, 1980), but comment will be made where it is deemed appropriate. For a more extended discussion of the output of public libraries see Zweizig and Rodgers (1982).

Under the rubric "Ease of Use," the activities associated with *formatting* and *ordering* are fairly standard throughout all types of libraries, though interpretations may differ. The public library may invest more in signage and graphics (i.e., formatting because of the diversity of its activities, its varying public, and the needs, for example, of non-English speakers. *Browsing* is enhanced principally as support for volitional reading through specially formed collections, displays, and reading lists.

A major investment of public libraries is made in support of *physical accessibility*. Volitional reading and, to some extent, the informational function are supported by the extensive efforts made to provide access: branch libraries, open hours, bookmobile services, and system-wide links for book loans and reference questions.

The level of enhancing activities in support of *interfacing I (mediation)* depends on the degree of commitment to special information services. Most public libraries will have some level of standard reference service; and some libraries are willing or able to support specialized information services. The amount of resources committed to this mediating form of interfacing may be increasing as public libraries begin to provide access to bibliographic, textual, and financial data bases.

Interfacing II (orientation) is not of particular importance at the adult level of public libraries. There are exceptions of course, such as literacy programs. There is an overlap here with what we have called the stimulatory value as part of the adaptability criterion discussed below. This form of interfacing (orientation) is, however, a major investment at the children's level. Story hours, summer reading programs, children's events, the maintenance of separate children's areas in the library are all designed for this special audience. These are programs quite successful for the small population they reach, and serve to interpret the context of the public library and to build a sense of comfortableness in the use of library facilities in the future.

Under the rubric "Noise Reduction," the only added value distinctive to the public library is *selectivity*. The interpretation of selectivity has special meaning for the public library. Limited resources, the range of clientele from children to senior citizens, the censoring pressures of special interest groups—all force the public library to place emphasis on its selection activities. In order to support basic ideals of intellectual diversity and the right of access (maybe even to deflect criticism) such emphasis on selection tends to make available a range of opinion and information on controversial and current topics. This concern reflects to some extent on the quality of the information in the collection, especially on the sense of trust and reliability that users—and indeed the population at large—place in the institution of the public library. This is a significant role for the public library: that the population (users and nonusers) perceive the public library as a major contributor to the quality of life. If that be too strong a statement, then at least they feel that, if the library were to close, it would be a loss to the community. In his study of the Enoch Pratt Library in Baltimore, Lowell Martin summarizes this as follows:

> Ninety-seven per cent of the total adult nonstudent population answered yes to the question: "Would it be a great loss to Baltimore if the public library were closed

> down?'' and in the case of library users this response was almost unanimous. It would not be easy to find other institutions to which there is a 97 per cent positive response from a cross section of citizens.
>
> When the question is made personal— ''Would it be a great loss to you personally if the public library were closed down?''—over half of all adults respond affirmatively. Evidently many who do not themselves use the agency still see a value to them personally in its existence, whether because they think they might want to use it in the future, or members of their family may need it, or because it has sufficient significance that not only the community but the individual would be hurt if it were not there. (Martin, 1974; p. 37)

It should be noted, in reference to the last part of the foregoing quotation that, of the total adult population, 18% of the total adult population felt that they would be adversely affected if the library were to close. This despite the fact that libraries are way down the list (1% or less) when people are asked: ''When you think of all the places you go when you go out, where do you most like to go? (Martin, 1974; p. 38). The same pattern is substantiated in a 1973 study of information needs of the general public in the Baltimore metropolitan area, in which 3% of the respondents indicated that they had used the library as a source of information (Warner, Murray, & Palmour, 1973). Despite this apparent lack of use and indeed of actual usefulness, perception of the library's contribution to community well-being remains high. How long this reputation can be maintained in the face of increased demand by a variety of agencies for limited tax dollars is debatable.

Within the criterion *adaptability,* the public library with one exception does very little to add value. It does nothing in the way of analysis or evaluation of the information in the collection. It provides no flexibility within the context we have defined here. The Reader's Advisory Service, which could be a prime example of filtering, seems to have disappeared as a formal service. Martin notes that ''guidance in reading is given . . . across the service desks every day—but more in where to locate materials than in what to locate'' (Martin, 1974; p. 41).

It is in the activities that enhance the added value called *stimulatory* that the public library makes a unique contribution as an information system. These may include a wide range of activities: provision and scheduling of space for meetings of local organizations; presentation of small concerts, poetry readings, art displays, or current book discussions; sponsorship of topical debates, special seminars, how-to-do-it demonstrations, or garden clubs. It is worth noting that for the most part, the library and its staff contribute space and possibly reading lists or information displays in support of these activities, but little more, unless there happens to be expertise among the staff. Real investment in time, money, and energy (cost) is fairly low relative to the possible benefits that accrue to the community. This is, of course, difficult to evaluate. As we attempt to define quality of life indicators, however, these stimulatory events may be more important than books circulated, magazines subscribed to, or reference questions answered. The one caveat here is that, like the other services of the library, these stimulatory events tend to reflect only the interests of the educated and professional middle classes.

Some librarians have argued the need for activist kinds of public librarianship (a) through information and referral services for public social agencies, or (b) through limited advocacy of third party intervention for those who need service/information assistance, but feel that they may not be getting it from another public agency (Cronenberger & Luck, 1976). There is, of course, a delicate line to be negotiated here, and its location depends a great deal on the social sensitivities of librarians and on the support and political acumen of the library director. Whether or not such activities are perceived as part of a library's mission will have an effect on the kinds of values that the library in fact adds (benefits) and the investment of resources (cost) that it makes to support relevant activities. An active information, referral, and advocacy role by public librarians is certainly a function which fits the intent of the adaptability criterion. As laudable as these activities may be, they appear at this time to be atypical of public library services.

In reviewing the literature on public libraries, several things are apparent which have an effect on the value-added model and its application. First a great deal of effort (i.e., resources) seems to go into the processes of defining the structure and bureaucracy of the organization. Like the technological fix, overemphasis on organizational structure tends to limit the time and attention paid to the people who presumably are to be serviced by the institution. Bureaucracy, like technology, tends to take on a life of its own, and the users, clients, and patrons are the losers.

Despite the rhetoric about users and the plethora of user surveys and needs assessments studies, librarians seem to know precious little about the kinds of problems that people have for which a particular type of book or a specific piece of information would be of help. As Martin points out:

> Librarians do not customarily think of books in the psychological terms of how they develop the reader as a person. The professional tends rather to be subject oriented; to the librarian books are usually about something. To the extent that the librarian thinks of the purposes or motives of readers, he assumes they are students or quasi-student in one form or another, persons who more or less systematically are seeking to learn about a subject. The concept of a reader motivated by a search for self-identification or self-understanding or self-fulfillment is not central or in sharp focus to the librarian, nor is it an integral part of his training, although this motive plays a strategic role in the print use of adult out-of-school readers. The public librarian usually selects materials by subject, classifies by subject, and thinks of subject when a reading inquiry comes to him. Small wonder that students are his single largest group of readers, for they are the portion of the public that reads within subjects and searches out material by subject groupings. (Martin, 1974; p. 25)

Lowell Martin's remarks are directly relevant to the approach of this book to information use environments and problem dimensions.

In summary, the public librarian seems to spend a significant amount of his or her resources in just making books and related materials physically accessible. Interfacing, as orientation, has a particular and unique importance in the programming and services for children. In a larger sense the public library benefits from the reputation that it enjoys as a neutral but reliable institution and a contributor to the quality of life in a community, despite the fact that it is not looked upon as a source of everyday information. As such its services, in systems terms its outputs, enjoy a reflected sense of quality. The stimulatory activities that the library encourages and for which it provides space are an important contribution to community life. Some may consider these efforts tangential and not central to the library's utility as an information system. These activities, however, are part of the processes of encouraging use, and hence familiarity with the library's resources and services. These activities establish a context and a mode of information delivery (both book and other media) to its clientele, and thus have profound effect on perceptions of quality and reliability.

SPECIAL LIBRARIES

The special library, as a collective term, is difficult to categorize because of the range, intent, and organizational status of its exemplars. Special libraries may range from a corporate ornament (though this is becoming much less frequent) to the special subject collection on a university campus, from extensive library resources and information networks throughout an organization to the small and highly active technical or financial library in support of research and development or financial services. The special library was recognized as a separate organization in the early part of this century. In some instances the special library has become a technical information center. This may in some cases be only a name change without basic change in function. In other situations the change has been complete, combining information resources and services with information analysis and evaluation. Though extremely diverse in subject interest, size, and operational posture, the special library now occupies a significant niche in the information spectrum (Jackson, 1980).

As in all institutions, there are wide qualitative differences among special libraries, ranging from the conventional library which passively collects and dispenses information on demand to the highly active agency that interacts well and easily with its clients in the parent organization. For the purposes of value-added analysis, the special library has the following characteristics, with a bias on the dynamic side:

- Its total collection of materials is small, but highly concentrated in subject matter.
- Its clientele and their interests, both general and specific, are known and can be described fairly accurately.
- It is part of a larger organization, i.e., private corporation or government agency, and shares and supports the objectives or mission of that organization.
- Special librarians put a premium on service to their users, and will go to considerable expense to obtain specific information or answers for their clients.
- Though special librarians may filter, or select, delete, or rank output by perceived importance, they will neither evaluate information nor produce new

analyses. (We are well aware that some special librarians may perform analytic functions, but for our purposes here we consider information analysis and evaluation separately in Chapter Seven.)

The principal functions of the special library are research support and informational, in contrast to the educational and research functions of the academic library and the support of volitional reading, informational, and community service aspects of public libraries. The functions themselves take on a different meaning in the special library because of the emphasis on the provision of answers and the frequently direct and continuing relationship between librarian and clientele.

Among the spectrum of added values under the criterion ''Ease of Use,'' the special library places highest emphsis on the mediating act of interfacing and on physical accessibility, and within varying degrees some emphasis on browsing. Interfacing and physical access complement each other. The act of *interfacing (mediation)* means finding out what an inquirer wants, how he wants it, and why he wants it. This involves skilled negotiation and an understanding of the kinds of problems and pressures that the library's clientele are likely to have. This activity obviously overlaps with the knowledge of problem context inherent in the criterion adaptability. The intent of the classification of added values presented in this book, however, is not and cannot be mutual exclusivity. The grouping of added values under each of the six criteria is offered as a way of thinking about comparable information systems and services and a way of roughly organizing data about those systems and services. The concern with question negotiation and answer provision in special libraries is a case in point, where activities in support of one added value (interfacing—mediation) meld into another (closeness to problem) and there is no discernible or useful boundary between them.

Physical access for the special library means delivery. The activities that special librarians perform to provide that access to the information needed also differ from other types of libraries. Whereas the academic research library tends to build large collections encouraging chance encounter and on-the-spot delivery, the special library, with a small highly concentrated collection, depends more on a network of personal contact, knowledge of special resources, and a willingness to pay for fast delivery when required. Physical accessibility for the special librarian means getting the right document or the right data into the hands of the client within that client's time frame, and in a useful form. For example, if the information is in Japanese, and the client does not read Japanese, and there is a high need for it, as may be the case in technical research or in a patent case, the librarian will obtain a translation or have it translated.

Browsing in a special library may be shown in a variety of activities. There may be, for example, (a) display and reading space for current journals and daily newspapers; (b) routing of title pages of current journals; (c) selective dissemination of information (SDI) in which new documents or abstracts on highly specific subjects are sent automatically to interested individuals or groups in the organization periodically. There may even be daily or weekly excerpts and review of potentially relevant external information culled from current journal and newspapers. In all of these cases the activities are means of supporting focused browsing in the current literature. The intent is not only informative, but also a means of browsing at a distance, with additional information available on demand. The computer, through such systems as electronic information exchange, will provide a quicker means for selected people throughout an organization, regardless of geography, to participate in this browsing potential. There is a very real danger, however, of overloading the client. This has become a problem with SDI systems, with the consequence that some receivers just turn the output off or throw it away. There is an important but subtle need for sensitive and knowledgeable discrimination here. This, too, edges into adaptability concerns.

The other added values under Ease of Use (formatting, interfacing (orientation) and ordering) are of lesser importance to the special library.

Under "Noise Reduction" several specific added values are of importance to the special library. For formal information products generated within the parent organization, the library provides all three forms of *access*—item identification, subject description, and subject summaries. In many cases these information chunks are confidential or proprietary in nature and will require special handling. *Linkage* to related data bases is of importance, as is *precision* among the processes of intellectual access. It is worth noting that activities in support of both of these added values are for the most part performed by human intermediaries, that is, librarians who through experience, personal contact, and personal knowledge can support the linkages and precision in providing specific information for particular situations. The technology merely supports. *Selectivity* of data and information input for the library is of particular importance, for it requires not only a sensitivity to the local information use environment, but also a knowledge of off-beat sources of collectible information, i.e., channels outside the usual publishing, document and data base providers.

Of the values added under "Quality," probably the one most common is *currency*. Because of the nature of their clientele, special librarians have a high need for up-to-date information. *Accuracy* in the recording and transfer of data and information has importance, but it is not unique to the special library. *Reliability* of services, though important, is also not unique to special libraries, though a good deal of effort may be expended in strengthening the user's perception of reliability.

The user's perception of the library's *adaptability* will be reinforced by two types of activities, and by the librarian's empathy for and sensitivity to the customers' problems. The first is the capability of performing informed filtering. That is to say, the user is knowledgeable about and comfortable with the service the librarian performs in online searching in making decisions to delete items deemed of little or no interest and/or to rank output in terms of perceived importance to the task at hand. This capability is obviously dependent on the librarian's knowledge of the organizational climate, problems of the client, and on the librarian's own subject knowledge. For the special library, the degree of adaptability is dependent on the level and quality of activities the librarian may perform *outside* the physical space called the library. That is to say, the ability to work closely with the engineers, scientists, managers, and others who make up the library's clientele, will determine the relevance of the library for its potential audience.

Dependent on personal capabilities and interests, special librarians may perform different kinds of *stimulatory* activities: speech writing and editing for executives; total document control for the organization; forms design; correspondence and records management; organization and retrieval of engineering drawings; internal consulting for different kinds of computer-based information systems; managing and presenting seminars of interest to the parent organization.

More than other types of libraries, the special library needs to "earn its way," to prove itself. The special library does not have the tradition and custom of the academic library. Though the old saw, "heart of the university," may bring derisory smiles, the phrase is still proclaimed in commencement rhetoric, freshmen orientation, and college catalogs, and permeates the unconscious level of academia. The public library, as has already been noted, seems to occupy an important niche in the popular perception of the quality of community life. The special library wears none of these haloes. On the contrary, it is usually classified as "overhead," as a nonproductive entity in the organization. Consequently, it needs to establish visibility and a reputation for quality, relevance, and indispensability. One of the major ways of doing this is through the activities included in the categories of adaptability and interfacing.

SUMMARY OF VALUES ADDED BY LIBRARY TYPE

Table 5-1 is a chart of values added by the different types of libraries discussed in this chapter: research, educational, public, special. The table presents a subjective synopsis of the chapter in scalar form. Each type of library is evaluated for each of the 23 values on a scale from 0–5 (nonexistent to intense activity). The estimates are very rough and of course highly subjective (but based on 35 years of work, observation, and teaching). The types of libraries are generalized; there will be wide variations among individual libraries.

There are several reasons for presenting this table, despite its subjectivity. First, it illustrates a way of viewing a particular type of information system—the library—which may be useful in determining its objectives and its utility. Because the values are essentially stable over time, the model provides a way the library as an institution could adapt to new circumstances, and what such a change requires in terms of resource allocation in support of certain values added—a form of metalibrarianship, if you will. Second, it is hoped that the table and its judgments will generate discussion on the value-added model as presented, and will provoke arguments on its overall usefulness, with extensions and refinements.

Third, it is hoped that particular libraries may utilize this approach to analyze how they allocate their resources—money, time, staff, space. One can be as literal or conservative as appropriate in interpreting whether a special activity does indeed add value, and whether that value is where the agency wishes to allocate a portion of its resources. Consistency of application and open acknowledgment of assumptions is of course required. The value-added approach can generate fundamental review concerning objectives at the agency level in fairly concrete terms. The model and its application may also provide a basis for early measurement.

Table 5-1. Values Added by Library Types

Value Added	Academic			Public	Special
	Research		College		
	Type I	Type II			
Ease of Use					
Browsing	2	2	3	3	2
Formatting	1	1	3	3	1
Interfacing I (Med.)	3	2	3	3	4
Interfacing II (Orient)	1	1	4	3	1
Ordering	1	1	1	2	1
Physical Access	4	4	4	4	4
Noise Reduction					
Access I	2	1	2	2	2
Access II	1	1	1	1	2
Access III	0	0	0	0	2
Linkage	0	0	0	0	2
Precision	1	0	0	0	1
Selectivity	1	1	3	3	3
Quality					
Accuracy	3	1	1	1	1
Comprehensiveness	3	3	0	0	0
Currency	1	3	2	2	3
Reliability	2	2	1	2	2
Validity	0	0	0	0	1
Adaptability					
Closeness to Problem	2	0	1	0	3
Flexibility	0	0	0	0	0
Simplicity	0	0	1	1	1
Stimulatory	1	0	1	3	2
Time Saving	1	1	0	0	3
Cost-Saving	0	0	0	0	1

Chapter Six

VALUE-ADDED PROCESSES IN ABSTRACTING AND INDEXING SERVICES

This chapter is an expansion of part of a project supported by the National Science Foundation (see Taylor, 1983) which applied the value-added model to a major activity in the information process: abstracting and indexing (A&I) services. As perhaps the most intensive, concentrated, and best defined of all information activities, the A&I process provided a useful context for the study of added value. It is a formal process, analyzed and well understood as a form of content summary and display. To complete the process from the A&I services to the end-user, two additional activities are included in this chapter: online retrieval services and the search intermediary. Librarians who are search intermediaries may think of themselves as part of the staff of a library. From the end-user's viewpoint, however, they are part of the search service, an extension of the abstracting and indexing process. This is a critical point to keep in mind, for the emphasis of the value-added approach is on the user—the person who makes use of the information—and on his or her perceptions of utility and value.

Because of the nature of the A&I operation itself, the methodology used in the study and the data collected, this chapter is organized differently than the other chapters. It looks at a particular and well-defined operation in the information life cycle and asks at each stage in that operation what value is added at that point that will aid a user in making choices. This includes its extensions in the online service and the intermediary. Though the descriptions are not complete as the reader will see, they do illustrate the application of the value-added model to a common and recognizable set of activities and operations.

The study made use of an extensive interview guide. The interview guide is shown in Appendix A, as an example of the kinds of questions that were asked. It may be of use for studies of other types of information systems. It was not the purpose of the study to develop a complete picture of the abstracting and indexing operation, but rather to see if the value-added model is a useful way of describing the operation. With some reservations, the model appears useful. This is discussed in the last chapter.

The data collected through the interviews were taped (erased at end of project because of confidentiality promised) and represent about 60 hours of interviews.

The tapes were reviewed and excerpted by the author and research assistant. The decision to excerpt was based on a judgment of whether or not the excerpted statement illustrated or illuminated a value-added process. The emphasis in the last sentence is on value-added, not on process. The need for this emphasis became apparent after a few pilot interviews, because we—all of us in the information field—tend to be systems oriented. That is to say, it was sometimes difficult to keep attention focused on the users, on their criteria for using a system, and on those steps in the system that affected user benefits and costs. Information professionals, be they systems analysts, librarians, or MIS designers, tend to look at system details as indicators of system efficiencies rather than as support for user effectiveness.

These excerpts were then grouped by question in the interview. This was not a one-to-one process. The interview was open ended. It was found that asking one question frequently elicited answers to several other questions. These excerpts were then reviewed by the project staff and by the subcontractors at the National Federation of Abstracting and Information Services (NFAIS). These were then grouped by the processes shown in Figure 6-1, and values that were felt to have been added at this point were tentatively assigned. This process was repeated several times among the four persons associated with the project in order to arrive at consensus.

These excerpts served two purposes. First, they identified specific steps in specific processes where value was added. For example, ''editing and proofing procedures'' in the Editing process provide the value of accuracy; or ''giving Chemical Abstracts Registry name'' in Citation Augmentation provides the value of linkage to other relevant systems; or ''up-posting with hierarchical vocabulary'' in the Indexing process added browsing value. Second, they identified particular values, and, by grouping them, a pattern began to emerge: where and how a specific value was added or strengthened in the total process. (See Table 6-1.)

These combinations are shown in Appendix B, which follows the order of the processes in Figure 6-1, i.e., from acquisition to dissemination. Under each process a sampling of value-added activities is listed together with the specific values that are added by that process.

In reviewing the data presented in this chapter, in its organization, and in the appendices, the reader needs to keep several things in mind. First, the intent of the study was not to develop a complete model of the abstracting and indexing operation. Rather the objective was to develop and to evaluate the utility of the value-added model, the associated definitions, and the methods of organizing and presenting data in the context of operation systems. One should not look for complete description.

Second, the data collection was verbal and the data itself was anecdotal, and the mode of collection was openended. There are dangers here of course. The study, however, was intended to tap the broad and deep expertise and know-how of a group of highly experienced professionals, and to benefit from their considered insights. The data was excerpted, extracted, and abbreviated from many hours of discussion. We tried to retain the flavor and informality of the interviews through the reduction process. There may well be differences of opinion as to which value is supported by a particular process. Through a process of discussion among four knowledgeable information professionals, we believe defensible choices were made.

ABSTRACTING AND INDEXING SERVICES

Abstracting and indexing (A&I) services have their origins in the need for cumulative and retrospective indexes to scientific journals. They first appeared in the early nineteenth century, as scientific journals, already a century and a half old, began to proliferate and as the sciences and scientific research began to expand enormously. Some of the earliest American abstracting and indexing services were *Index Medicus,* started in 1879, still published today by the National Library of Medicine, and *Engineering Index,* started in 1884. Around the turn of this century, the American Chemical Society began publishing *Chemical Abstracts,* and the H.W. Wilson Company started to issue indexes covering more popular periodicals and books, for example, *The Reader's Guide to Periodical Literature.* As the century progressed, many professional societies and similar groups began their own abstracting and indexing services: *Accountants Index* (1920); *Biological Abstracts* (1926); *Psychological Abstracts* (1927); *Mathematical Reviews* (1940). United States agencies, which were beginning to sponsor research, also began issuing abstracting and indexing services: *Bibliography of Agriculture* (1942); *Government Report Announcements* (1946); *Nuclear Science Abstracts* (1948); *Meteorological and Geoastrophysics Abstracts* (1950). Gradually, for-profit companies began to enter the arena along with H.W. Wilson Company: ABC-Clio, with *Historical Abstracts* in 1955; Cambridge Scientific Abstracts, with *Computer and Information Systems Abstracts Journal* in 1957; the Institute for Scientific Information with *Current Contents/Life Sciences* in 1956 and *Science Citation Index* in 1961.

Most of the early abstracting and indexing services tended to cover the ''hard sciences'' fields. Gradually, newer services were begun which covered social sciences, humanities, and popular literature. Most recently, abstracting and indexing services founded in the 1970s and 1980s have tended to focus on business, finance, law, government, computers, energy, and the environment. For-profit, nonprofit, and government organizations are today active publishers of abstracting and indexing services. Abstracting and indexing publishing operations range in size from a staff of four *(Social Work Abstracts)* to a staff of over 1,200 *(Chemical Abstracts Service),* annually indexing/abstracting as few as 1,850 items (Earthquake Engineering Research Center, in 1981) or as many as 890,000 (Institute for Scientific Information, in 1981). The growth of the scientific literature can be traced through the growth of A&I service coverage: in 1957, NFAIS member services indexed/abstracted about 250,000 items, and in 1981 over 3,300.000 items were covered (National Federation of Abstracting and Information Services, 1982).

The original mission of abstracting and indexing services was to disseminate the results of scholarly research to other scholars. Few fields of scholarship are so small that an active researcher can maintain currency in his or her field by reading, say five journals, so that many abstracting and indexing services founded in professional societies tend even today to hold with this *discipline*-oriented approach. More recently, however, A&I services have been started to address a *mission* such as the space sciences *(International Aerospace Abstracts)* or a specific *problem (Pollution Abstracts)*. And, most recently, the information nneeds of the more general public are being served by such abstracting and indexing services as *Magazine Index, NEXIS, Consumers Index to Product Evalutions and Information Sources,* and *National Newspaper Index*.

More specifically, A&I services serve their users by scanning a number of documents each year—documents covering a predetermined area, mission or problem, or documents found in a predetermined set of sources. *Reader's Guide to Periodical Literature,* for example, covers a predetermined set of periodicals. Indexes and (sometimes) abstracts are then prepared for these documents. As mentioned previously, some services index a few thousand documents per year, some nearly a million. Typically, these indexes and abstracts are then formatted and sold as four types of products:

- *Abstract or index journal:* A regularly issued printed index, with or without abstracts, usually cumulated every year or every few years.
- *Selective dissemination of information service, or SDI:* "The routine bombardment of each worker with an appropriate amoount of information about what is going on in his specialty." (National Academy of Sciences, 1969; p. 139). SDI may take the form of cards, printouts or printed lists, etc.
- *Bibliographic data base:* The computer-readable form of an index/abstract journal. When these were developed in the 1960s, they were searchable only in batch mode. Now nearly all are searchable interactively, online.
- *Full-text data base:* These are relatively new, but may well represent the major expansion in the future. Law (LEXIS), the news (The Information Bank), and encyclopedias and handbooks are major areas for full-text development.

The number of organizations providing abstracting and indexing services has grown enormously from 1800 to 1982, although comparable statistics are hard to locate. Manzer documents a progression from nine abstract journals published prior to 1800 to 310 at the end of 1920 throughout the world (Manzer, 1977; p. 109). By 1963, 1,855 titles were cited in *A Guide to the World's Abstracting and Indexing Services in Science and Technology,* (National Federation of Science Abstracting and Indexing Services, 1963; p. vii), including approximately 650 English language titles. In 1982, Gale Research Co. published the first issue of a three-volume directory which is expected to cover 1,500 English language abstracting and indexing services (Schmittroth, 1982). The growth of the number of "word-oriented" data bases has been documented by Williams in data base directories published over several years. The 1976 directory described 301 data bases, the 1979 edition 528, and the 1982 edition 773 (Williams, Lannom, & Robins, 1982; viii).

The abstracting and indexing process is at the lower end of the value-added spectrum (Figure 1-1): the organizing process. But then so are all the other information systems, except those that build in a human contribution at the output side and in the negotiating space. Information analysis centers are a case in point, where human interpretation and evaluation of information outputs takes place before the final client makes use of the information. In the purely processing sense, abstracting and indexing systems are highly sophisticated, built on a long tradition of the intellectual organization of knowledge and of the literature. In their complexity they far surpass other systems at the organizational stage, such as management information systems which are basically only transaction and reporting systems, or decision support systems, if indeed such dynamic systems exist in a truly operational sense. Abstracting and indexing services do not alter input. Their output—references, papers, documents—are the same as their input. What they do is provide a whole series of tangible signals and intangible values that make it easier for customers to make choices. The question of making choices may be unique to this kind of information system (including libraries) and to data-based systems of a factual or scientific nature.

Processes in A&I Services

In order to produce their data bases and index/abstract journals, A&I services must carry out a series of processes. These processes are remarkably similar from service to service although, of course, there are many differences in method and degree. Figure 6-1 shows the processes as they were organized for the study. This order of listing was a convenient way to organize the interview format as well as the data gathered. The interview guide is shown in Appendix A.

Acquisitions: Acquisitions includes defining the user, defining the scope/mission of the service, selecting journals and other documents to be covered, arranging to physically access these documents, and then selecting items to be indexed/abstracted from these sources.

User, scope, and mission issues are usually dealt with on a formal basis by management, or auxiliary advisory groups. Journal/document selection may be handled also on a policy basis, by designated staff members, or by the abstractors/indexers themselves. Physical access can be obtained through donation, purchase, exchange, or through proximity to an appropriate library. Item selection is almost always done by the abstracting/indexing staff.

1. Acquisition
   1.5. Control/Claiming
2. Citation Development
3. Citation Augmentation
4. Indexing
5. Abstracting
6. Editing
7. Formatting
8. Dissemination

Figure 6-1. Abstracting and Indexing Processes

Control/Claiming: Nearly all A&I services have an internal system in which journals and other periodic documents ordered or expected are checked in as they arrive. When such documents do not arrive, the missing items are "claimed" from distributor or publisher. Such systems range from small manual files to automated systems in which computer-generated claims are sent out.

Citation Development: The bibliographic citation uniquely identifies the item selected for inclusion by the A&I service. Always included in the citation are: title, last name of author, source identification, and some type of accession number. The citation may be developed by the abstractor, indexer, or another staff member. Each A&I service has its own format for citations; some follow established standards in choosing a format.

Citation Augmentation: Some A&I services add additional elements of information to the citation, such as: author's first name; author's address or affiliation; language of document; ISSN, ISBN, or CODEN; type of document (report, book, etc.); or they even extend the title to give additional subject access points.

Indexing: Indexing involves creating a list of terms which point to key words, concepts, or ideas within the selected item. Such terms may be drawn from the item itself (title, text, or references) and/or may be selected from a thesaurus or subject heading list. In addition, items are frequently assigned to broad subject categories which govern the arrangement of abstracts in the abstract journal. In a few files, pointers may be added to or from records in other files or data bases.

Abstracting: Abstracting is the creation of a concise summary of an item, often slanted toward the particular viewpoint of the A&I service and its clientele. Length can vary from a sentence or two to several hundred words. In some A&I services, the same person both abstracts and indexes; at others, different people perform the two operations.

Editing: When the citation, index terms, and abstract have been prepared, they are assembled into a record and edited: reviewed, corrected, keyed (typewriter or computer), proofread, corrected, rekeyed, proofread again. This cycle may involve a separate staff of experts and editors, and several iterations.

Formatting: Most formatting of abstracting and indexing products today is done by the computer, which takes the keyed-in record and automatically generates the page proofs of (a) an index/abstract journal(s), (b) SDI outputs, and/or (c) data base(s) which can be searched online. Many different products can be formatted, or "spun off" from the one data base.

Dissemination: Dissemination includes marketing, sales, user feedback, and user education. Large A&I services may have a whole division which handles these activities; smaller services, say, or professional associations, piggyback them with general organization and office operations.

From variations of the basic processes described above, come four diverse products:

- a subject index to a predetermined list of periodicals, or parts of periodicals, available in paper, microform, and online;

- an index to a large number of scientific journals using citations in references and footnotes as access points and linking mechanisms;
- An interrelated group of products, available in print and online, for example;
  a. cross-reference list of chemical synonyms, formulas, and structural data;
  b. structural diagrams of chemicals;
  c. abstracts of documents in the particular field; and
  d. bibliographic information and location of journals and serials in the particular field.
- Online data base of the full text of a number of periodicals: here, the texts are acquired in machine-readable form from the publisher; indexing is done by computer from all significant words in the text; no abstracts are produced.

A&I Services and the User Environment

Because the concept of value in this project is user based, a part of the interview (Appendix A) was directly addressed to questions concerning the perceptions of the user by the A & I service (question groups 1.1, 1.2, 1.3). In addition, single specific questions were asked concerning particular activities (e.g., 3.5.3. How do you relate your decisions on input activities specifically to user benefits? That is to say, how does the user [however defined] benefit from the decision and policies you make?) Similar questions were asked at 4.2.5, 4.5.3, 5.4, 5.6.

In a sense, the intent was to ask the services what they knew or perceived about the informatin environment within which they were operating: Who were the users? How did they make use of the service? What kinds of problems did they have, i.e., why did users use the service? What did the services think the effect might be on the user of a particular system decision or activity?

After listening several times to the tapes and reviewing personal observations of the interviews, one thing became quite apparent. With very few exceptions, the abstracting and indexing services, for a variety of quite valid reasons, know relatively little about the information use environments which they service and within which they operate. Indeed very few, if any, information systems and services of any type know their clientele in the sense delineated in Chapter Three. There are several reasons for this.

The professional society-based nonprofit A&I services traditionally sold their (print) products to libraries and to individual members of the society, in effect, a guaranteed and intuitively understood customer base. Thus, little effort was made in their initial years to identify and explore markets. As Neufeld and Cornog point out, however, ''A new awareness of economic factors . . . has led many secondary services to expand their marketing activities'' (Neufeld & Cornog, 1983; p. 161).

Second, and more to the point today, producers of abstracting and indexing data bases, in most cases, sell to the user through the online vendors, and it has been these online services who, having the direct user access, have done the marketing studies and have gathered the user information. Many producers are now trying to get direct access to information about their users: a Subcommittee of the Database Publishing Committee of the Information Industry Association has been addressing the issue of online services sharing user data with the producers. Other A&I services, such as Chemical Abstracts Service and the Institute for Scientific Information, have established their own online services, and one of their reasons for doing this seems to be the need for closer contact with users (Neufeld & Cornog, 1983; p. 158).

There are other possible reasons for the lack of knowledgeable responses to the questions about users. It may be that in the interview, questions were asked that really could not be answered at this time (e.g., 1.1.6: What kinds of user problems is the service or product designed to respond to?). Note that the referent is problems, not questions. Abstracting and indexing services respond to questions rather well. That is to say, knowledge of problem identification and the relationship of information to problem solving is still at a fairly tentative stage, especially as it may impact on system design.

This focus on problems rather than on questions was a difficult area to cover in the interview. It is also obviously a key concept in the notion of the value-added model. It was difficult to explain briefly to those being interviewed that we were interested in something beyond the conventional image of the user as an asker of questions. Those being interviewed had difficulty in seeing system response in the context of problems rather than questions. All of our training and thinking has gone toward strengthening the idea of question answering rather than problem attacking. In a sense the interview process was an education both for the interviewers as well as for those being interviewed. One person put this rather succinctly.

> One of the more interesting marketing challenges is to understand needs that people don't even know they have. There is a kind of reactive solving of an obvious problem, but there is also an interpretive aspect to market research. We are looking at ways people do their jobs, and inferring from that what their needs really are. And then coming along with something that helps them do their job better. We are not very sophisticated at this point.[1]

Many services have been developed, and indeed have a formal mandate, to cover comprehensively a body of literature concerning a particular subject or discipline. Such an approach is quite different from designing an information system from user or market attributes. In a historical sense, the idea of coverage of a subject matter has roots in the traditional academic disciplines. As such, the services have organized the printed literature for scientific research and scholarship. This appears to be equally true of those A&I services that call themselves "mission oriented." Such services are in fact disciplinary, or perhaps interdisciplinary, not problem oriented. That is to say, system design is several removes from the reality of the environment they are attempting to service. It is only recently that the idea of utility has begun to surface. Large discipline-oriented systems (chemistry, biology, psychology, medicine, etc.) were established to organize access to a total literature of a subject, so that researchers (and sometimes students and educators) would be

[1] Unacknowledged quotations are excerpts from the taped interviews conducted in the study.

aided in finding papers of interest to them. This was a perfectly valid definition of an information environment, quite appropriate under the circumstances. However, one of the assumptions of this book is that the nature of information and knowledge utilization has changed drastically in the past several decades, and that such earlier definitions of information environments may no longer be subtle enough. The questions of technological assessment, policy making, environmental impact, global economic and technical infrastructures, and techology-based legislationn and decisionmaking in all sorts of large and small situations require a deeper understanding than exists at present of real and potential use and users (beneficiaries) of the knowledge store. This is the reason emphasis has been placed on problem typology and problem contexts, where subject matter *and orientation* govern, rather than subject matter alone.

In this context, A&I systems have been designed to be expansive and comprehensive. Indeed this may be a significant characteristic of most information retrieval systems. That is to say, the assumption has been that information imparts an intrinsic benefit, so valued by the user that he or she is willing to "pay" in time, money, energy, and foregone opportunities, the cost of retrieving this information. This is not a fruitful approach because in reality the users have more information available to them than they can possibly select, let alone make use of. Consequently, users must estimate the importance of the problem to them (benefits of a solution), which, in turn, will provide some idea of the costs they can bear. This question of optimization is discussed further in Chapter Eight on information in decision contexts. The point of these remarks is that information systems need to address user costs and minimize them, and, at the same time, develop a more sophisticated attitude toward user values (benefits). If this approach is not taken, formal information systems will be bypassed for more hospitable information channels no matter what the value of the information. A point made by Gerstenberger and Allen on the choice of information channels by engineers is pertinent to this discussion:

> Engineers, in selecting among information channels, act in a manner which is intended not to maximize gain, but to minimize loss. The loss to be minimized is the cost in terms of effort, either physical or psychological, which must be expended in order to gain access to an information channel. (Gerstenberger & Allen, 1968, p. 277)

There exists considerable confusion as to who the users of an online service are: actual users of the information, that is, the end-user, who may know little about the search process; or someone in between system and end-user who interprets the questions to the system, that is, a search intermediary. This lack of clarity has an effect on how users are perceived, how user education is designed and presented, and, indeed, how the interface should be designed. In response to the question on how users were defined by that particular A&I service, the following rough definitional categories could be identified:

- by discipline (chemists, the legal community);
- by profession (students, lawyers, legal researchers);
- by organization (hospitals, museums, libraries);

- by problem/issue (earthquakes, energy);
- by capability (having a terminal);
- by experience (know about our service);
- by intermediary status (librarians);
- by corporate rank (managers, decision makers);
- as "person with a problem," or "anyone";
- don't know who user is.

The formal mandate of the service and/or perception of the market was an important determinant as to how the user was viewed. An agency that is comprehensive pointed out that "if we were narrower in our coverage, we would be talking about a different group of users." From a service that is user governed: "We operate the service for them; they are the bosses; they are the users." There seemed at times to be a separation of clients from end-users. Clients were those "who have the money for the products" or "where the terminals were located," and, consequently, end-users tended to get lost in the ins itutional maze.

Most agencies were very much concerned with the intermediary/end-user dichotomy. System protocols, command languages, terminal location, financial control, and even the cultural impropriety of a scientist to "play around with online searches" were stated as bars to end-user activity. There was a strong feeling that this would not change until "software developments and access to terminals will be based, more on who has a telephone, rather than who knows a command language."

A caution is necessary here. Even if online services become more "friendly" in a technical sense for the end-user, there may still exist inhibitions against its use by that hypothetical end-user. As long as systems are bibliography based rather than information based, an intermediary will probably be used as the systems expert and as a first filter. However, as systems move toward numeric and textual data bases, and toward better means of selectivity, *i.e.*—getting rid of the "noise"—only then might the end-user become in fact a major direct user of the system. It would be a mistake to base the assumption of a major shift toward end-user activity on techonology and software alone.

Values Added

The interview, especially through such questions as "What is being "sold"? For what purpose?", provided a means of getting at the perceptions of the services as to the kinds of values added in their processes. Though the language may vary, the responses tended to confirm some of the values added that were listed, discussed, and defined in Chapter Four.

- currency of information
- access to information
- convenience of access
- elimination of duplication of effort
- compactness

- consistency of coverage
- completeness/comprehensiveness of coverage
- cumulation of information
- pointer to information, i.e., bibliographic references
- provision of variety of access points to information
- customization (especially alerting services)
- repackaging
- information on prior research
- information
- time savings
- research service

There may be some slight differences in interpretation, but the following values (see Table 4-1) seem to be noted in the perception of the service:

Physical accessibility
Formatting, e.g., repackaging
Currency
Reliability, e.g., consistency
Comprehensiveness
Access I
Access II
Access III
Precision, e.g., customization
Time savings

In reality, as will be seen, A&I services add many more types of value in the information-handling process than they seem to be aware of.

User input to the system comes mostly through service-sponsored user seminars and, with the larger services, through special phone access to subject and system expertise. User training courses seem to be mostly directed toward and attended by search intermediaries. There is some effort to reach the end-user. ''Interaction with users through training programs also helps to offset the ''distancing effect'' of use through online vendors, and it allows for more direct user feedback'' (Neufeld & Cornog, 1983; p. 163).

The following paragraphs are a descriptive summary of Appendix B. The use of Table 6-1 is suggested as a skeleton summary of the value added processes in A&I services. It shows (a) what values are added and at what point in the entire process; (b) what values are intensified or strengthened at what point in the process; and (c) how values are cumulated at successive points in the system process.

In the *Acquisition* process, reliability, comprehensiveness, and selectivity are the major values added. *Reliability* has to do principally with consistency of input, or with known coverage of a subject. *Comprehensiveness* represents a value in those services whose mandate is total coverage of a subject, and whose clients come to value such coverage. *Selectivity* is the converse of comprehensiveness, and has value when the clients want a filtering process, and do not want coverage, but solutions. Where it was felt there was a system decision to act in a way distinctly detrimental to selectivity, the phrase "Minus Selectivity" was used. For example, as one service put it: "We include marginal items because one person's common knowledge or junk lit is another's find-of-the-year." Though such a criterion may support the value of comprehensiveness, its formal statement is strong enough, we felt, to justify the negative side of selectivity.

In *claiming,* basically an extension of acquisition, *currency* is a major new added value, and *reliability* is strengthened. The services are concerned in maintaining the current state of their data base, as well as the consistency of their coverage, so the process of claiming missing journal issues becomes a valuable contribution of the service.

In *citation development,* Access I, accuracy, and formatting are the principal new values added. The bibliographic citation is in fact *Access I.* Its standardization allows for more *accuracy* and *reliability. Formatting* in standardized ways allows users to scan and to browse quickly because they know where each relevant item of information will be in the total presentation.

In *augmenting the citation,* the service is adding or changing the state of data to help users make decisions of choice. Translating, for example, a title from a non-English language and informing customers what that language is allows customers one means to make a choice whether or not to look at the item represented. This is a form of *selectivity.* Adding subject words to title is *Access II.*

The *indexing* step is of course a very large process within the activities studied. Only a few of the activities could be sampled and listed. Additionally, as one might expect, there are many indexing activities that are similar across most of these agencies. The principal values added are browsing, precision, Access II, and linkage. "Up-posting in a hierarchical vocabulary" or "indicating clusters or related fields" allows a user to scan neighborhoods, to follow "see also's," in short to *browse* more easily and efficiently, and indeed to extend the search. *Precision* as a value is strengthened by the use of a controlled, hence wellknown and familiar, vocabulary. One can argue this point, i.e., between controlled and uncontrolled vocabulary (Syracuse University, School of Information Studies, 1982). The intent of the service, however, is to facilitate precision in searching (in our language, a value). Whether it does or does not is not the question here. *Access II* is supported in a variety of ways: for example, by segmenting compound words and hence providing additional access points, or by providing analytics for chapters in a volume of proceedings. *Linkage* is supported by providing pointers to and from other data bases.

The *abstracting* step, again, a major process with many similarities among services, provides several major values, both new and intensified. Access III, cost savings, and interfacing (mediation) are especially worth comment. *Access III* (summary or explanation of content) is, of course, the major concern of the abstracting effort. This is accomplished not only by the process of abstracting, but is strengthened, especially in technical and scientific fields, by using subject spe-

Table 6-1. Values Added, Intensified, and Cumulated (*number of times intensified)

	VALUES ADDED	VALUES INTENSIFIED	CUMULATIVE VALUES
1.0 ACQUISITION ↓	Comprehensiveness Cost Saving Reliability Selectivity		Comprehensiveness Cost Saving Reliability Selectivity
1.5 CONTROL/CLAIMING ↓	Currency Response Speed	Comprehensiveness Reliability	Comprehensiveness* Cost Saving Reliability* Response Speed Selectivity
2.0 CITATION DEVELOPMENT ↓	Access I Accuracy Formatting	Reliability	Access I Accuracy Comprehensiveness* Cost Saving Currency Formatting Reliability** Response Speed
3.0 CITATION AUGMENTATION ↓ To 4.0	Access II Access III Linkage Ordering Physical Accessibility	Access I Selectivity	Access I* Access II Access III Comprehensiveness* Cost Saving Currency Formatting Linkage Ordering Physical Accessibility Reliability** Response Speed Selectivity*

Table 6-1 (Continued)

	VALUES ADDED	VALUES INTENSIFIED	CUMULATIVE VALUES
From 3.0 ↓ 4.0 INDEXING	Browsing Interfacing II Precision	Access II Accuracy Currency Linkage Ordering Physical Accessibility Precision Reliability	Access I* Access II* Accuracy* Browsing Comprehensiveness* Currency* Interfacing II Linkage* Ordering* Physical Accessibility* Precision Reliability*** Response Speed Selectivity
↓ 5.0 ABSTRACTING ↓ To 6.0	Access III Cost Saving Interfacing I	Accuracy Formatting Physical Accessibility Precision Reliability Response Speed	Access I* Access II* Access III Accuracy** Browsing Comprehensiveness* Cost Saving Currency* Formatting* Interfacing I Interfacing II Linkage* Ordering* Physical Accessibility Precision* Reliability**** Response Speed* Selectivity

Table 6-1 (Continued)

	VALUES ADDED	VALUES INTENSIFIED	CUMULATIVE VALUES	
From 5.0 ↓ 6.0 EDITING		Accuracy Cost Saving	Access I* Access II* Access III Accuracy*** Browsing Comprehensiveness* Cost Saving* Currency* Formatting* Interfacing I Interfacing II	Linkage Ordering* Physical Accessibility* Precision* Reliability**** Response Speed* Selectivity*
↓ 7.0 FORMATTING ↓ To 8.0	Flexibility	Browsing Formatting Ordering Physical Accessibility	Access I* Access II* Access III Accuracy*** Browsing* Comprehensiveness* Cost Saving* Currency* Flexibility Formatting** Interfacing I Interfacing II Linkage Ordering** Physical Accessibility** Precision*	Reliability**** Response Speed* Selectivity*

Table 6-1 (Continued)

	VALUES ADDED	VALUES INTENSIFIED	CUMULATIVE VALUES
From 7.0 ↓ 8.0 DISSEMINATION		Browsing	Access I*
		Flexibility	Access II*
		Formatting	Access III
		Interfacing II	Accuracy***
		Linkage	Browsing*
		Ordering	Comprehensiveness*
		Physical Accessibility	Cost Saving*
		Precision	Currency**
		Response Speed	Flexibility*
			Formatting***
			Interfacing I
			Interfacing II*
			Linkage*
			Ordering***
			Physical Accessibility***
			Precision**
			Reliability****
			Response Speed***
			Selectivity*

cialists. That is to say, it is assumed that subject experts will tend to produce abstracts of higher technical quality. *Cost savings* to customers is an active decision by the service when it decides to use author abstracts, rather than generate new ones. One can, of course, argue that there might be negative values resulting from the use of author abstracts. However there are trade-offs here. If the positive side is taken, then the value of cost savings is emphasized. The abstracting operation in this review has one of the few examples of the value interfacing (mediation)—"preparing informative abstracts," which relate the work to the field and indicated data types and range, methods, and equipment. These are useful ways of presenting nonsubject aspects of a paper to clients to facilitate choice.

The *editing* step is principally concerned with maintaining a level of *accuracy* in the product. This is an intangible value, but one of critical importance to the clients, who must be assured and feel certain that what they are getting is accurate in its details. Citations must not lead to nonexistent papers. Indexing terms and descriptive abstracts must be as accurate as the art allows. Authors' names need to be correct.

The process of formatting, of course, supports the value of *formatting*. The function of this step is basically to allow a user to be more efficient in using the product, by placement in display or by highlighting important parts with bold-face type and other attention grabbers.

The final step, *dissemination,* is the culmination of the whole process as far as the abstracting and indexing services are concerned. The principal value intensified at this point is *physical access* to the service: by providing document delivery, by allowing downloading, or making access a little simpler by providing user-friendly hardware and software. The opportunity to download, when available, allows some *flexibility* at the local level, because the information can then be manipulated by software adapted to local needs.

It is worth comment here that one quality value not found in the A&I process was *validity,* that is, the provision of signals about the degree to which data or information can be judged as sound. Surprisingly, there were no instances of the production of critical abstracts. Such abstracts would comment critically on research methodology and sampling procedures. It should also be noted that, aside from a few instances of flexibility, A&I services generally are not designed to be adaptable in the sense used here. They are content based. Hence, as has been discussed before, users and their problems have not played much of a role in A&I design and operation. The hotline employed by a few agencies may begin to provide a better interface for the user (usually an intermediary). They are, however, for the most part designed to help answer questions, not to solve problems.

To most professionals in document-based systems, these activities and the values added may seem mundane and commonplace: And indeed they are when considered only simply or only from the system point of view. Two things are of importance here. First, the user-driven approach to the assessment of value is critical. Despite the rhetoric about clients and markets, designers and managers of information systems of all kinds do not appear to know much about the users of these systems, nor for what purposes they use information systems. The value-added approach implies a fundamental shift in attention from cost-efficiency on the part of the system to cost-effectiveness on the part of the user of that system. That is to say the latter, not merely the former, should be the basis for internal system decisions.

The second point is that the A&I operation, like any extended information process, is a cumulative process of adding value in a series of related formal activities. Given appropriate cost accounting methods, this approach provides a structure for deriving dollar costs and assigning those costs to a set of specific values. An agency, for example, could decide what set of values it wished to emphasize, that is to say, where it felt its clients would be best served. The activities where those values were added or intensified could be identified, isolated, and costed. A form of cost-effectiveness measure would result, for example, it cost X dollars to support the addition of this particular value in a given system. More important than dollar costs, which change over time, would be a method and rough algorithms for the collection and analysis of data. Through this process, the agency could derive baseline data useful in costing those values deemed of high utility to its clientele, and for pricing the services that provide those values.

The Management of Costs and Values Added

In the study just described, there were several concerns with costing and management information systems. First, we wished to see if it was possible to associate systems costs with specific values added. If successful, this would provide the link between *values added* as used in this report and *value added* as commonly used in economics. Questions (3.6, 4.6, 5.7, 5.8, 6.7, 6.8) in the Interview Guide (Appendix A) were intended to elicit such information. The interest here, of course, concerned the utility of the value-added model as a planning and management instrument. Certain classes of users may find higher utility in certain kinds of values in the system's outputs. Hence, by identifying those activities that add or support those values and by costing them in system terms, the agency could provide a product better attuned to its users. At the same time, the agency could have a better and more rational control over its costs and the possible trade-offs.

Second, by means of the questions in Section 2.0 of the Interview Guide, we tried to obtain a picture of the management information system (MIS) itself as a value-added system. Every abstracting and indexing activity has an MIS, whether it is recognized as such or not. That is to say, there is, in every organization, some formal structuring of operational and cost data which allows, in some degree, decisions to be made and control to be maintained. Those questions in this part of the interview (2.0) were asked in the belief—a justifiable belief, it was thought—that the value-added model is an appropriate model for such information systems. That is to say, the model (a) can encompass and describe all the processes, (b) can, within limits, isolate subprocesses where more processing may be required and possible, and (c) can point to and relate the information needs of the system clients, in this case, the managers of A&I services, to the processes and the values added by those processes.

These attempts were not fully successful. Our perceptions of the reasons for that lack of complete success are discussed in the summary and evaluation in Chapter Ten, because they reveal not only something about the generalizability of the model and about our approaches to information systems, but, more importantly, of differences among information systems.

One observation may be useful at this point. From the standpoint of organizational size, A&I services are rather small, ranging from three or four people to about 1200 persons. Their production lines are highly structured and easily describable (see Figure 6-1). Their products are fairly straightforward, and, despite earlier caveats, their customers or users are in general definable within the total market structure. In addition, the labor involved usually consists of highly trained professionals. There is a sense of dedication and service. In some cases, the abstracting and indexing operation is part of a larger operation, especially true in government and professional societies. This has an effect on the way management data may be generated, structured, and interpreted. That is to say, because of the smallness and cohesiveness of these organizations, management and supporting information systems are set in a fairly personal context, where discussion and decisionmaking can frequently be done face-to-face or in small groups. Such an ambience, of course, does not preclude the need for good process, flow, and market data. However, these for the most part are control, transaction, and financial data delivered in fairly traditional formats. This level of management information system is not of much use beyond operating and control levels. That this is a more general state of affairs can be attested to from the cries of anguish from managers in many different kinds of business about information overload and irrelevancy of information reports (see, for example, Rockart, 1979; p. 81).

A brief summary of some of the points made by those interviewed will serve to highlight certain aspects of these processes. In general, it should be noted that formal management information systems ranged from nonexistent to well-thought-out systems. One of the problems that affects the abstracting and indexing industry was stated most succinctly by one of the agencies, we suspect with tongue in cheek:

> We are probably one of the few manufacturing industries that doesn't know about its raw materials, where they are coming from, how much, or what the quality is going to be.

This statement was made by a person from one of the A&I services that is comprehensive in its coverage. It implies that it is difficult to plan, because one does not know quantity, quality, or timing of input. But this is true of all services, information based or not. For information services, the user-driven model, tempered by experience and professional know-how, can provide a significant way of organizing, evaluating, and interpreting data for estimation and planning. The older industrial models, based on linear process and physical product, are not longer relevant as models for systems evaluation. The value-added model is especially appropriate for information systems because of the peculiarities of information and its provision, be they library or decision-support systems.

In only a few cases did the interviews reveal any comprehensive or analytic concern with managerial data. As was pointed out before, this indeed may not be necessary because of the cohesiveness and professionalism present in A&I services. However, one might suspect that better information control over operations will provide benefits to managers, with eventual pay-off to the users of the services.

In the design of data and reports, the interviews seemed to reveal a decision to "count everything," just in case that data may be needed. This approach begs the question. It is expensive in two ways. First, collecting and maintaining data that are not particularly useful has costs that the profession has not even begun to calculate. Second, providing data to managers that may not help them in the decision process, or that, because of poor presentation, require too much effort to interpret and to make use of, is a very expensive process. On the other hand, there were, in a few cases, deliberate efforts to develop and to provide different types of reports to different levels of management.

Most of the agencies interviewed are concerned about productivity and the most efficient ways of using personnel without sacrificing quality. Quality of output remains high on the scale of service criteria. Approaches to productivity range widely. In one case, a management-by-objective (MBO) approach is taken, where abstractors sign a performance agreement and are evaluated on that basis. In one very real sense, however, because of the professionalism and collegiality, A&I services have long had built-in "quality control circles," an approach to productivity that is only beginning to penetrate American industry at this time. This is an important intangible that should not be sacrificed in the name of efficiency.

In the process of costing specific value-added activities in A&I processes, there were varying results. In most cases it would seem that costing such activities accurately would be difficult. Elias (1979), in presenting hypothetical costs for the production of bibliographic data bases, implies that at least gross costing is possible. In rough figures, 7% of the costs were allocated to acquisitions and control/claiming; about 7% to citation development and augmentation; 15% to "intellectual processing to install access characteristics for later retrieval use," or indexing, but it is not clear if this includes abstracting. He assigns about 19% to data entry which we have called editing. About 9% is allocated to "system computing"—the figure is not broken down further. "Support" receives about 19.5%, which we interpret as overhead, though it probably could be allocated at least partially to various processes. He estimates nearly 25% for "output," which we would characterize as formatting and dissemination. Though Elias never explicitly states it, we have assumed that these are at best rough estimates by an experienced professional. It does seem possible that these costs for A&I services could be allocated to the nine processes (plus overhead), and a beginning could be made toward estimating the costs of specific value-adding activities. As one interviewed agency put it: "We can cost out the process of doing all the features but not specific features. Best that can be expected is an average. Augmentation can be costed; but not finding the cost of a single index term."

It may be that, at this time, the processes are changing too rapidly due to automation and that the marketplace is being altered by a rising information literacy and information accessibility, for accurate costing. Indeed it may well be that the basic operation of indexing and abstracting will undergo fundamental system changes in the next decade as numeric, text, and natural language systems become more available. Such potential changes, however, do not preclude the necessity for isolating, understanding, and costing value-adding activities. A fundamental assumption of this book is that the added values which were identified and defined are permanent features of any information system or service. Paying attention to those values is critical because, despite system and process changes, the values will remain and their analysis will provide a continuing base for evaluation and costing.

ONLINE RETRIEVAL SERVICES

Online retrieval services are organizations, usually private companies, that provide computer and supporting services for a number of data bases which are usually created by other organizations, such as data base publishers. Data base publishers normally include the A&I services that have been analyzed here, as well as numerical data bases, for example, financial, demographic, scientific, and credit, and a growing group of text data bases. The concern here is principally with bibliographic data bases generated through A&I services. Online services handle and provide access to multiple data bases, sometimes more than a hundred such files.

Online services were first envisioned in the early 1950s (much of this section is derived from Bourne, 1980). It was not until the early 1960s that a formal service became operational. The delay in development during these two decades was caused by the lack of appropriate technology—computer time-sharing, remote terminal equipment, and communications equipment. In 1964 a batch search service was instituted by the National Library of Medicine using MEDLARS tapes. Though a batch service, this was the first publicly available, retrospective, large-scale, computer-based search service.

There were a number of experimental and demonstration online search projects developed during the early and mid-1960s. These were for the most part production services for limited constituencies. Lockheed for the National Aeronautics and Space Administration, for the Oak Ridge National Laboratory, and for the Educational Research Information Center (ERIC); System Development Corporation (SDC) for the US Air Force at Wright–Patterson. These projects helped develop the early versions of DIALOG (Lockheed) and ORBIT (SDC). The Biomedical Communications Network was developed by the State University of New York (SUNY) in 1968 to provide online searching of the MEDLARS data base.

By 1970, data communication networks were needed in order to provide service to large and geographically scattered audiences. This capability began to be available in 1971–1972. For the online services as we know them now, this was the final link. By 1980, there were numerous bibliographic search services throughout the world. The number of data bases, especially numeric, literally exploded. There are now well over 100 bibliographic data bases, and very possibly several thousand other types of available data bases. The bibliographic data base is now a regular and accepted service in most research and special libraries and in some public and school libraries.

These online search services provide added value processing which increases or enhances the value of the original product. They operate at several levels in a value-added sense:

- with individual data bases
- with clusters of data bases
- with all the data bases in the service
- with systems design, including telecommunications links
- with systems software, i.e., with interfacing software
- in training users of the online services
- by developing special data bases to extend coverage in a particular subject area.

The diagram in Figure 6-2 shows the data flow process of an online service in dealing with a single data base. It is difficult to classify the values added by the data flow because at one point a particular value may be isolated and a decision made (planning and design of file treatment), at another point this value will be implemented (program conversion and load file), at another point it is tested (testing) and at still another point it is documented (documentation). It is worth comment because these processes are so dynamic and because the processes are not as rationalized nor as linear as in the abstracting and indexing process that isolation of points in the process where specific value is added is somewhat difficult. This says something about the value-added model itself and will be commented on in the last chapter. It is also necessary to add that the following analysis is by no means a complete picture of online services. It identifies and discusses what appears to be the major values added at each of the steps in the process. Those activities that appear to add value are discussed, using the diagram as a touchstone for the process.

Selection and acquisition of a data base implies a choice. Such choice are based on several criteria: anticipated market; how the data base fits into the online service; and the amount of reprocessing necessary to bring the data base up to the standards of the service. At this stage, the values added are *comprehensiveness* and *physical accessibility*. Selecting a new data base adds value by making the file accessible to a broader set of users in a variety of locations than the printed version might be. In some cases, there may be no printed version, only the machine-readable form, where the online service provides the only access to that data base. The acquisition may provide a more comprehensive coverage of a subject, either by itself or in combination with other files in the service. In some cases there are more records and more index terms in the online version than in the print version. In addition, the online service may produce its own data base where none existed before, but where there is a felt need. The School Practices Information File of Bibliographic Retrieval Services (BRS) is an illustration of this.

After a data base has been acquired, that is after the rights to the data base have been negotiated, the file goes through a number of processes before "going public." As one online service put it: "Our major effort in value added is putting stuff into the record that was not supplied to us in the record." Examples of these enhancements are discussed below.

1. "Consolidation or provision of more search access points than were practically available in the original product." (Bourne, 1979; p. 2) For example, search can be made on words in the abstract or on parts of the bibliographic citation, such as date or language, in addition to the standard index terms. (Values added: *Access II*.)
2. A new file may have certain types of codes, such as the Standard Industrial Code (SIC) of the US Bureau of Labor Statistics. The online service may provide a table look up to convert the numerical codes into text equivalents so

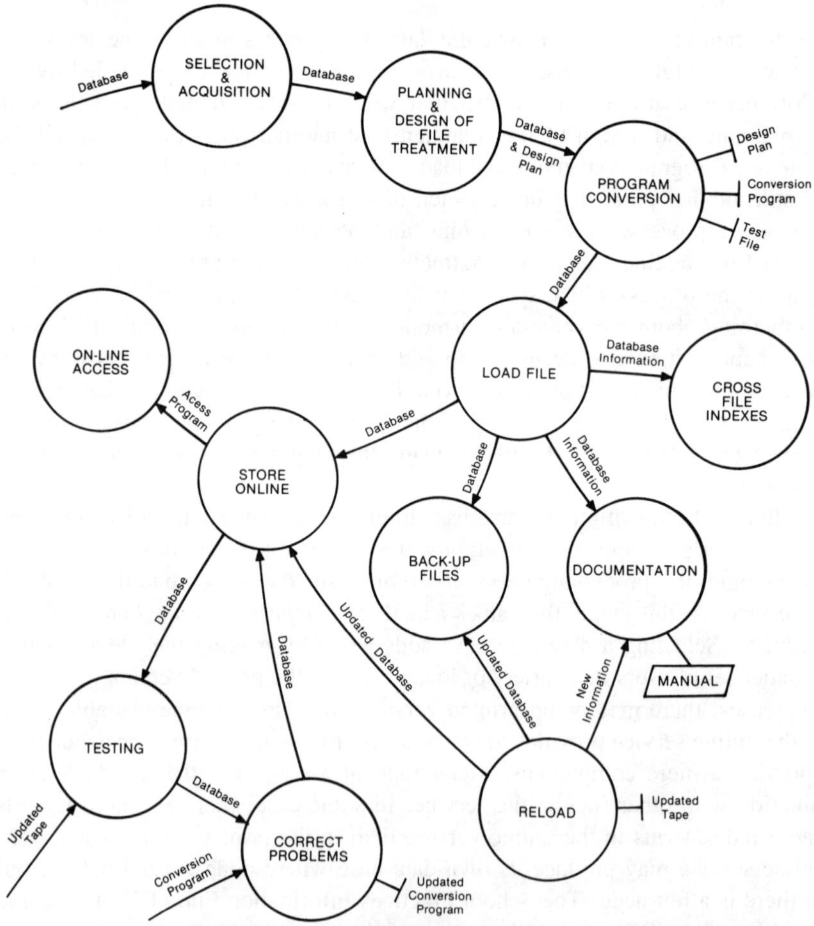

Figure 6-2. Data Flow Diagram: Online Services

that records may be retrieved through several means and, indeed, can be related to other records that do not use the codes but use equivalent descriptors. (Values added: *Access II; Linkage; Browsing.)*

3. In some cases an online thesaurus for a particular data base may be incorporated into the online system, or the capability of exploding terms may be included. This allows the user to scan for subject-related terms, for example, broader than, narrower than, or synonyms. (Values added: *Browsing; Precision.)*
4. Some data bases were created from the input to the printing process. The online service receives them in this form. In such cases, tapes are often dirty, in nonstandard formats, and typesetting codes are present. Such files must be cleaned up for input in standard online formats. (Values added: *Accuracy; Reliability.)*

In the processes of loading the file, testing, and providing a backup file the online service enhances the quality of the product. Testing, for example, is a form of quality control, assuring accuracy, consistency, standardization, and reliability. It is worth noting that these are intangible values, qualities the customers cannot see or feel: they trust the system to be reliable and accurate. The system itself must invest time, money, and energy in providing these attributes. Providing a backup file, though this might be considered normal or mundane, assures continuity and reliability of service. (Values added: *Accuracy: Reliability.)*

When the data base is ready for public use, documentation must be prepared for customers. Such documentation interprets the system for clients and provides them with information on how to make best use of that particular data base: how the file is structured for searching; what access points can be searched; file peculiarities. In this sense, documentation affects all added values; but, specifically, it makes it easier for the clients to use that particular file, because they have some form of instruction and orientation in hand. The problem of cross data base searching, however, is not alleviated. The difficulty, as one online service put it, is "that the user must learn the idiosyncracies of many different files." On the assumption that knowledge about how a system works makes it easier to use, then the value added here is *Interfacing II* (orientation).

The process of updating the file merges current data supplied by the data base producer to the file already in storage. This may occur daily (as with newspapers), weekly, monthly, and so forth. In each case, the new file must be reprocessed according to the program conversion developed when the file was initially put into the system with whatever changes may have been added since that time. The amount of work here will vary widely, depending on the data base. This process assures currency and file integrity. Worth noting is that file structure, and hence mode of access, for a specific data base may vary among different online services, and is dependent on the structure at the time of the original acquisition by that particular online service. (Values added: *Currency; Reliability.)*

At various times during the life of a data base, it may need to be reloaded. That is to say, because of changes in the data base, it becomes necessary to restructure and rewrite the original program conversion. There are two types of reloading. In a few cases, the data base producer makes a major revision, and does it retrospectively. The new file is a new version, replacing the old. It requires a new program conversion and may require changes in documentation for the customer. In the second case, the online service may itself reload the file because of the cumulation of minor changes over a period of time. In such instances it is necessary to go through the process from the beginning, in design and program conversions, and in documentation. This basically maintains the *reliability* of the file. Such ongoing maintenance is frequently overlooked in value-added considerations, but without these processes, the file would deteriorate rapidly. As one online service pointed out: "This is a costly process. There is no incentive for us to do it unless we thought that there were good reasons for doing it. . . . Generally it makes a user happy because it makes for a more useful file, more consistency, easier to learn, and it generally adds more search capabilities than were there before."

Beyond the single data base there are other enhancements that pertain to the total online service. A sampling of these are discussed briefly below.

1. All the services provide various means, for example, dictionary files of varying structures and capabilities, for intellectual access across data bases. These enhancements help clients orient themselves among the complex variety of data bases available. For exaple, DIALIST, a merged term frequency index developed by Lockheed, allows a searcher to compare data bases by frequency of terms. CROSS (BRS), DataBase Index (SDC), and DIALINDEX (Lockheed) provide indicators across data bases, and are intended to help a client decide which data base to search first. (Values added: *Browsing, Interfacing II.)*
2. There is a gradual standardization of field names across all data bases, for example, AU for author, TI for title, DE for descriptor. There is some degree of standardization among the services, more by chance than by design. This is inhibited by fears of antitrust actions and concerns about restraint of trade. Where it has happened, these forms of standardization have in gross ways, made it easier for the client to access the file effectively. (Value added: *Access I.)*
3. All online services offer several forms of instruction in the use of the services, typically one- or two-day seminars. Swanson (1982) has reviewed and assessed various types of such instruction, including those offered at universities by schools of library and information science. Within the online services themselves, there are attempts to make the service more accessible (a) by hotlines, which are a mediating process for quick and informed assistance on search problems; and (b) by presenting user seminars, to orient users and make them more adept in the use of the online services. In the latter case, the students are usually search intermediaries not end-users. At the present time, one search service estimates that "one intermediary is "worth" about 20 end-users." There are varying degrees of success for these seminars, but they do require a large initial investment and continuing reevaluation if they are to be useful. (Values added: *Interfacing I* (mediation) and *Interfacing II* (orientation).

4. Several online services offer a means of ordering documents whose references have been retrieved by search and which are of interest to the user (Gibbs & Laszlo, 1980). We need to remind ourselves constantly that, from the user's point of view, the retrieval of a bibliographic reference may only be the beginning of a process. (Value added: *Physical Accessibility.)*

This then is the face the online service turns to its public: physical access via computer terminal to a comprehensive collection of data bases in many fields. To assist users in utilizing this collection effectively, browsing and orienting mechanisms have been built in for access across data bases; some form of mediation is supported by hotlines; intellectual access is supported by standardization and broadening the number of search access points available; quality of the files are maintained by updating for currency, by reloading for consistency and reliability, and by testing for accuracy.

THE SEARCH INTERMEDIARY

The *search intermediary* (librarian, searcher, or information specialist) is the final step in completing the cycle from the selection of input into the A&I service to the delivery to an end-user of items, usually bibilographic references, that may be of use. There are basically three levels of search intermediary.

- Those who serve only as a pipeline between client and online systems, transmitting requests as submitted by the client and giving that client the output of the search.
- Those who negotiate the question with the client. This may range from determining the right set of search descriptors to an attempt to understand where the client is coming from, in other words, what the problem is that generates the question. In some cases client and searcher may do the search together, with consequent feedback and readjustment of search as it proceeds.
- Those who not only negotiate the question as stated above, but who also analyze and filter the output.

This is a continuum, and the three levels noted here may merge into each other. They present merely a convenient way of discussing the intermediation process in value-added terms (see also Fenichel, 1981).

In the first case above, the "pipeline" model, the only role served by the intermediary is to make the system more accessible. There may be some minor negotiating, for example, ascertaining time frame or data bases to be searched. Basically, however, the intermediaries only provide physical access because they know the process of getting into a system and the search protocols of different systems and different data bases. Very little, if any, independent judgment is exercised by the intermediary. (Value added: *Physical Accessibility.)*

At the second level, the degree of presearch negotiation depends a great deal on the interviewing skill, the subject expertise, and the experience of the searcher. Meadow and Cochrane have stated that the process is to help "make the transition from *first* to *best* question'' (Meadow & Cochrane, 1981; p. 25). The implied definition of ''best'' here is that, as a result of the negotiating skills of the intermediary, (a) the client is able to specify his or her requirements more precisely, and (b) the statement of the query matches the vocabulary and search constraints of the data base, what Taylor has called the ''compromised question'' (Taylor, 1968).

In a project which examined the presearch interview process by analysis of videotaped negotiations, the task has been broken down as follows (Cochrane, 1981):

- Description and tutorial activity
  - User description
  - System description
  - Data base selection
  - Tutorial activity
- Clarification of request
- Request negotiation
- Vocabulary construction for search
- Search strategy formulation

In the presearch interview project, 82 interviews (69 usable) were videotaped. The content of the interviews was encoded and analyzed within the framework outlined above. The following results of the analysis are useful in considering the value-added process:

- Little time was spent in asking the users about themselves:
- Descriptive and tutorial tasks occurred only infrequently.
- A major activity in the process was that clarification was requested by the intermediary and not offered by the client.
- Another major activity was itemization of output restrictions, for example, date and language.
- In most cases the client spent time discussing the vocabulary or search terms to be used.

It would appear from the results of the Cochrane study that the presearch interview is for the most part taken up with designing a searchable question. It does not appear that the searcher attempts to understand why a request is made, that is, what the problem space from which the question comes looks like. In one of the interviews, in the NSF study, the intermediary put it this way: ''We rephrase the question in terms of what we think is searchable.'' In this sense, the intermediary acts as an interface between client and system, and the degree of added value in that activity, beyond that of providing physical access, depends in good part on the skills and knowledge of the intermediary. The critical question here is: What differences does the intermediary make in the search; in other words, what value is added? At an elementary level, we can say that searchers provide physical access because they have knowledge about the system that the client does not have and probably does not want to have. In a way, the searcher is part of the system, but provides a human (and friendly) interface. The degree of personal negotiating skills, systems know-how, indexing knowledge, and subject expertise will determine the amount of value added here. (See Crouch, 1979, for a good review of the information interview.) In our terminology, those added values are *physical accessibility, interfacing I, Access II,* and *Selectivity*.

At the third level of this process, the filtering level, we begin for the first time to move out of the basic stage of organizing processes in the value-added spectrum (see Figure 1-1) and into the analyzing level. It is here that the intermediary will exercise judgment and analyzing capabilities, dependent of course on that person's skill and knowledge, and on the ambience of the surrounding organization. These processes may run all the way from formatting the printout, for example, underlining or boldfacing key phrases to make scanning easier, to ranking outtput in terms of perceived importance to the client's problem. One of the interviewed intermediaries, a subject specialist, said concerning output: "We print out the abstracts so users can make selections, but I also look up papers which I think most relevant to the query and send copies along."

It is at this stage that the process begins to move from answering questions to responding to problems. Up to this point, as in the abstracting and indexing operation and online services, the values or enhancements are external to the information itself. The original content of the information message has not been altered. However, by saying "these are more relevant to your interests than those (ranking)," or "I have deleted those I don't believe you are interested in," the searcher has begun to alter the output. In the value-added terminology, this step of filtering intensifies certain values already present, especially *Interfacing I,* and *selectivity,* and it certainly implies some degree (understanding) of *closeness to the problem*. The next step is to move into the information analysis operation where the output is different from the input. For example, one of those interviewed pointed out that he might "write succinct summaries in which answers to questions are specifically detailed." This is a most important step in moving from the physical and intellectual access values of the system as supplier to the values of adaptation to user needs and problem space.

The role of the search intermediary has come about principally because, at this moment, it is the intermediary who possesses knowledge of the online process. That is to say, they know what systems to search, how to access them, and how to design and perform efficient searches. The primacy of this form of cabalistic knowledge may not remain entirely theirs for long (Fabisoff & Hurych, 1981). When the novelty wears off, the true costs of effective (versus merely efficient) searching, become apparent, and when users themselves learn the rules of the game and have a terminal at their desks or benches, then the online services will become but another form of reference service. Making use of information is hard and painful work. As Calvin Mooers has put it in what has come to be known as Mooers' Law:

"An information retrieval system will tend *not* to be used whenever it is more painful and troublesome for a customer to have information than for him not to have it" (Mooers, 1960).

The intermediary has learned the intricacies and efficient means of searching the system. To maintain this position in the future, the intermediary will need to develop an understanding of the problem contexts in which he or she works and toward which the information is directed. This situation will force a choice on the intermediary: either to retreat to being an efficient pipeline, with frills, between user and system, or to move boldly and with confidence and appropriate preparation into the area of information analysis.

SUMMARY

This chapter has presented a useful way of looking at a specific document-based system within the value-added framework in concrete and systematic terms. One needs to be reminded that at the beginning of the abstracting and indexing process, there is an immense and disorganized mass of papers, documents, court proceedings, books, news articles, legislative debates, numerical data, maps, and charts. In addition these are of varying quality and validity, in different languages, of varying length, of widely different levels of sophistication, and on every subject matter under the sun (and some not under the sun). The value-added processes just analyzed are, despite the caveats, an example of a remarkable set of complex intellectual and practical activities that bring order out of this chaos. They are representative of the first major phase in the value-added spectrum (Figure 1-1)—the organizing processes.

1. By selection and gross ordering, the myriad of recorded messages have been divided into large collections of similar subject matters or form divisions. Chemistry is separate from social work; engineering from biology; current news from medicine; art from law.
2. Through a variety of subject indexing and linking mechanisms, intellectual access to these many different subject collections is available to those who need and want information from those graphic records.
3. Summaries, called abstracts, of increasingly high quality, are written to aid those who need to know more about a particular record before committing time and energy to reading and analyzing that document.
4. These indexing, linking, and summarizing mechanisms are organized into coherent systems which provide access to users either through print or, via terminal, through computer networks.
5. Computer access to these data bases is available at any time, from anywhere, to anyone with a terminal, a telephone line, and the money to pay for searching.
6. Because of the intricacies of the interface between user and system, however, a new information skill has grown—the search intermediary. The level of value added through this skill depends on the capability of the intermediary to adopt to the context served.

These organizing processes do not alter the input to the information stream. They organize and display. The output is the same as the input. That is to say, the same scientific paper that comes into the system goes out in response to search and document delivery. It has had a bunch of tags attached to it in the process, without which retrieval would have been impossible. As an aside, it is worth noting that the technology may alter these processes so that output from these systems may indeed be different from the input of graphic records. In any substantial sense, however, we are not there yet. At present, the next step is to go beyond the organizing and retrieval of graphic records to those activities necessary for filtering, analyzing, and evaluating the information in those records for use.

Chapter Seven

VALUE-ADDED PROCESSES IN INFORMATION ANALYSIS

I don't want you coming back and telling me that what we need is more data. Every time there is a problem, people come back and say, "The answer is for us to purchase additional data." We've got information coming out of our ears and what we need now is some way to make sense of it.
— Chief Executive Officer of Major Company to his data processing manager.[1]

John, I can't make a damn thing out of this tax problem. I listen to one side and they seem right, and then God! I talk to the other side and they seem just as right, and there I am where I started. I know somewhere there is a book that would give me the truth, but hell, I couldn't read the book. I know somewhere there is an economist who knows the truth, but I don't know where to find him and haven't the sense to know him and trust him when I did find him. God, what a job.
— President Warren G. Harding to a friend.[2]

So much raw intelligence on possible terrorist threats poured in that, after a while, the marines stopped taking all of it seriously. The problem in Beirut was notinsufficient intelligence, but a lack of trained analysts to evaluate it.
— New York Times, December 11, 1983[3]

But, if our experience of the rich tapestry of community life seems somehow less intense than the Lynd's, our surveys were more thorough and more numerous and they were linked to a computer technology that permits extensive analysis. We are not at all sure that we understand the community as well as the Lynds did, but we have more information about it.
— T. Caplow commenting on 1982 study of Middletown and referring to earlier (1929, 1937) studies of same community by Robert and Helen Lynd[4]

"That's absurd," objected Milo. . . .
"That may be true," the Dodecahedron acknowledged, "but it's completely accurate,

[1] *Computerworld Extra,* September 1, 1982; p. 6.

[2] As quoted by R.F. Fenno, (1959). *The President's Cabinet* (p. 36) Cambridge, MA: Harvard University Press.

[3] *The New York Times,* December 11, 1983; p. 49.

[4] From Theodore Caplow et al. (1982). *Middletown Families* (p. vi). Minneapolis MN: University of Minnesota Press.

> and as long as the answer's right, who cares if the question is wrong? If you want sense, you'll have to make it yourself."
> —*The Phantom Tollbooth*[5]

There are a number of words, phrases, and insights in these quotations that are relevant to the concerns of this chapter.

- information coming out of our ears
- more information, less understanding
- accurate information, right answer, wrong question
- lack of trained analysts and evaluators
- making sense

These quotations and their extractions serve to point up the critical importance of the processes of information analysis and some of the concerns that underlie that criticality.

The first and primary point to be drawn is that more data and more information are not a solution, but in fact may be the problem. Though we are well aware of this truism of information overload, by now almost a cliche, we continue to act and to plan as though it were not real. Today we can collect and store more data than ever possible before. Indeed, our civilization demands more data, as we attempt to face and to alleviate social, economic, and environmental problems caused by unregulated industry, war, and the debris of exploding populations. The assumption is that by collecting more data and information and measuring more phenomena, we somehow will find solutions to these problems. This is fallout from Lord Kelvin's remark that there is no real understanding without measurement.

> I often say that when you can measure what you are speaking about, and express it in numbers, you know something about it; but when you cannot measure it, when you cannot express it in numbers, your knowledge is of a meager and unsatisfactory kind; it may be the beginning of knowledge, but you have scarcely in your thoughts, advanced to the stage of science, whatever the matter may be.[6]

It is not that this may not be a valid course of action, at least in certain restricted realms. Mere measurement and collection of data, however, is not enough, not by a long shot. The real task is information analysis, evaluation, synthesis, and judgment: of making sense of the data collected. These processes cost money and are only partially amenable to technological fixes (Dosa, 1983).

THE FUNCTIONS OF INFORMATION ANALYSIS

In terms of the value-added spectrum (see Figure 1-1), we are concerned in this chapter with the processes labeled "Analyzing" and "Judgmental." Though they are shown as two levels, they are in reality a continuum of activities which perform

---

[5] From Norton Juster. (1964). *The Phantom Tollbooth* (p. 175). New York: Random House.

[6] Quoted in R. Lehrer (Ed.) (1983). *White Collar Productivity* (p. 25). New York: McGraw-Hill.

significant and fundamental operations on data and information, and on the ways they are processed and displayed. The total process will be referred to as "Information Analysis."

Though information is processed and analyzed continuously by human beings, we are concerned only with formal structures which have evolved to perform certain kinds of operations called "analysis" on data and information. In the terminology of this book, these are information systems, formalized sets of processes which add value in a variety of ways to the data and information accepted or selected as input. Because of their nature, they are intensively human activities, though they may be supported and assisted by computer systems.

In system terms, information analysis is made up of those processes that have "the capacity to manipulate information in such a way that it is recognizably different after the manipulation" (Knight & McDaniel, 1979; p. 19). In the context of added value, the manipulation must also result in an output that has more value to users (hypothetical or real) than the original input. This addition of value to user is the principal and, arguably, the only function of an information system. The phrase, "recognizably different" implies not mere physical change, but rather a substantive change through the processes of information analysis (Hall, H., 1983). This contrasts with the accepted value-added processes of libraries and A&I services in which the output is the same as the input.

In our information-rich world this is where difference is going to be made: analysis and evaluation. It is an intensely human and intellectual operation, and will be for some time to come. To assume, as some do, that this process is to a significant degree amenable to technological fixes anytime in the near future—and to build operating systems on that assumption—is an invitation to disaster. Technology can deliver the information, can display in several forms, can search on word tokens and their identifiable synonyms. Technology can provide the means for manipulating the data, can compare data and tell you which is higher or lower, and can inform you of the statistical significance level. But it cannot put the information together in meaningful ways in response to the needs of a person or a group of persons sitting in a particular situation with particular problems, be those problems well or ill defined. The danger, of course, is that many people believe that technology *can* respond automatically and directly to these needs.

The basic concepts of information analysis are as old as is human awareness of the cumulation of knowledge, and of the need for formal ways of reducing the growing mass of knowledge into manageable and usable chunks.

> One of the diseases of this age is the multiplicity of books; they doth so overcharge the world that it is not able to digest the abundance of idle chatter that is everyday hatched and brought forth into the world.[7]

Sound familiar? This complaint was voiced in 1613 by Barnaby Rich, soldier and

[7] As quoted by Derek J. de Solla Price. (1963). *Little Science Big Science* (p. 63). New York: Columbia University Press.

author, one of whose works was the source for Shakespeare's *Twelfth Night*. This was a half century before the publication of the first periodical, *The Philosophical Transactions* of the Royal Society, one of the purposes of which was to extract and summarize new scientific knowledge. We have been extracting and summarizing by various means ever since. The encyclopedists of the eighteenth century carried this process further. By the early nineteenth century, scientists, especially chemists, found it necessary to extract, analyze, and summarize current knowledge of specific substances and elements. In 1817, L. Gmelin in Germany introduced a system "whereby a skilled specialist took on the job of reading the existing literature on behalf of all his colleagues, extracting the main ideas and summarizing all knowledge gained in this way" (de Grolier, 1979; pp. 63–64). The "handbuch" era of scientific information was born.

By the end of the nineteenth century, recognition of the degradation of the quality of data led to the preparation of the *International Critical Tables* after the First World War. The effort required more than 10 years and produced seven volumes of carefully selected and evaluated chemical and physical data (Simpson, 1962). The problems of currency and accuracy in the growing mass of data resulted in the mid-1960s in the development of the National Standard Reference Data System, coordinated by the National Bureau of Standards. In the 15 years that this program has been operational, its published compilations occupy more than 16 feet of shelf space, in contrast to the nine inches of the International Critical Tables published between 1920 and 1930 (Lide, 1981; pp. 77–78). We are indeed awash in a sea of information and data, which because of its sheer mass and widely varying quality can only be made useful (given value) through activities such as analysis, evaluation, synthesis, and judgment.

Because of the wide diversity of information and data, the explosive growth of highly specialized needs and requirements, and the need for highly specialized and evaluated knowledge, there has been a rapid growth of special information analysis centers (IAC). It is difficult to determine the exact number of information analysis centers, partly because of the disagreements on definitions and partly because of the large number of such centers in private corporations established to support proprietary interests. There were about 13 such centers in the nineteenth century. By 1961 there were reported to be more than 200 such centers (Simpson, 1962; p. 45). The principal concern here is not with the number of centers, but rather with the actual functions that take place in these centers and in similar operations. These functions or processes seem to include: evaluating, analyzing, condensing, comparing, compiling, extrapolating, synthesizing, and repackaging (Carroll & Maskewitz, 1980; pp. 151–152). One major definition of IAC's by the Committee of Scientific and Technical Information (COSATI) in 1967, included "acquiring, selecting, storing, retrieving" on the list of processes (Carroll & Maskewitz, 1980; p. 151). Within the model of value-added processes these four activities are considered the function of libraries and were discussed in the previous chapter. The presumed division (see Weinberg, 1964) between libraries and information centers is not important in this discussion except as conventional divisions. If particular libraries or librarians analyze, evaluate, and synthesize as discussed in this chapter, then they add the values under discussion. Division by institutional entities is only a convenient means for organizing material and dividing by chapter. The purpose of the value-added model is to span such divisions by observing what different processes actually do to help a user to make choices, make decisions, clarify problems, or make sense of a situation. These are the critical desiderata in the model, not who does it. This allows discussion to proceed along rational lines, rather than on the protection of turf. Indeed one of the prime advantages of the value-added approach is to break down old divisions and perceptions, and begin to move the discussion to different, more fruitful, ground.

INFORMATION ANALYSIS SERVICES

In order to provide a useful setting for the consideration of information analysis, and beyond that to the judgmental processes, it is worthwhile taking a brief look at several specific, but quite different, active information services.

- The Center for Information and Numerical Data Analysis and Synthesis at Purdue University.
- The Engineering Materials and Processes Information Service of the General Electric Company.
- The Congressional Research Service of the Library of Congress.

Each of these agencies is unique in the kinds of data and information it handles. They all, however, analyze, compare, evaluate, manipulate, organize, and display information dictated by the kinds of information handled and, to varying degrees, by their sensitivity to the kinds of problems their users have. In addition, we will briefly examine the growth in the past three decades of knowledge centers in the modern organization, and their very significant role as information processors in adding value. Indeed, the major growth of information analysis and its formalization in organizations and its impact on modern life may be outside the scientific and technical information context in business, industry, and government. This impact of nonscientific data and information is explored briefly in the discussion of knowledge centers below, and in Chapters Eight, Nine, and Ten.

These descriptions of the agencies and centers are of necessity superficial and brief. They serve however, to focus attention on a broad range of organized formal activities that play a significant role in the information processes that add value.

The Center For Information annd Numerical Analysis and Synthesis

The Center for Information and Numerical Data Analysis and Synthesis (CINDAS) at Purdue University[8] is a specialized center for the identification, compilation, critical evaluation, analysis, and synthesis of numerical data on the physical prop-

[8] The information on CINDAS has been derived from Ho and Touloukian (1977) and from Powell and Touloukian (1973).

erties of materials. There are 45 persons on the staff, including 16 senior researchers. The Center's aim is the generation of evaluated data for worldwide dissemination. As of 1976, CINDAS covered "14 thermophysical properties and 21 electronic, magnetic, and optical properties of nearly all materials in all physical states and at all temperatures and pressures." Between 1957 when it started and 1976, CINDAS "had compiled more than 100,000 sets of experimental data from the literature, in addition to performing data evaluation, analysis, and synthesis to generate reference data."

Unfortunately, property data reported in the literature are in many cases "conflicting, widely divergent, and subject to large uncertainty. It is, therefore, imperative to critically evaluate the validity and reliability of the literature data and related information, to resolve and reconcile the disagreements in conflicting data, and to synthesize the often fragmentary data to generate a fuller range of . . . internally consistent values." There is a potential range of systematic error that normally contributes to unreliable results and these must be examined, evaluated, and compared. Sources of such systematic error include: unsuitable experimental method or poor technique, poor instrumentation, and poor sensitivity of measuring devices; mismatch between theoretical assumptions and experimental boundary conditions; specimen contamination and stray heat flows; and possible errors in the reduction of the data and even errors in drafting, typing, and printing.

The value-added processes demonstrated here are considerable. They have to do principally with the quality of the information, with synthesis, and with establishing standards so that data generated in the future will be of higher quality. In addition, because of the nature of the center's objectives they have not only made the data more reliable, but also more usable. Because of their work of synthesis, new data are generated, new knowledge is created. Of importance also is that, through their investigations, areas of present ignorance are revealed where future work should take place. By their work they also establish standards, by pointing out potential sources of systematic error so that future investigations will provide data of higher quality.

Engineering Materials and Processes Information Service, General Electric Company

A more highly focussed type of information analysis operations is embodied in the Engineering Materials and Processes Information Service (EMPIS) of the General Electric Company.[9] EMPIS, now over 50 years old, is part of the Materials Information Service of the company.

EMPIS supplies GE personnel worldwide with authoritative information on the char-

[9] The information on EMPIS was derived from Westbrook (1981a), from the *Newsletter* of October 1981 of the Materials Information Center of the General Electric Company, celebrating the 50th Anniversary of EMPIS, and from interviews conducted at the EMPIS location in Schenectady, NY in March 1982.

acteristics, behavior, identification, availability, and methods of test of a broad range of raw and semifinished materials, commercial hardware (mostly fasteners), and applied finishes. In terms of materials, its scope includes metals and alloys, ceramics, chemicals, plastics, papers, textiles, rubbers, and laminates; in terms of application area, these materials include those incorporated in product components, those used in processing operations, those used in packaging, and those used in maintenance and repair; in terms of types of information collected for these materials, EMPIS embraces properties, specifications, data for ordering, test methods, processes, and finishes.

The information is packaged in some 23,000 pages in 50 loose-leaf volumes, or in microfiche. There is a staff of 12 professionals. The system is presently being shifted to a computerized data base, so that eventually it can be accessed online. There are three basic series in the system: properties, specifications, and data for ordering.

The properties series is made up of information for the engineering designer "who must evaluate alternatives, select materials and processes, and carry out a detailed part design." The data going into the system receive "informed technical scrutiny," so that a certain level of reliability can be assumed by the user. The materials are coded to provide a gross ordering, for example, nonmetallic, metallic, or chemical materials, intended "to group similar materials or subjects for ease in locating information." The kinds of information on these properties sheets are selected in anticipation of the kinds of problems that design engineers in General Electric might be faced with: chemical composition, for estimating potential characteristics of the material; reaction of material to different environments, such as electrical or vibrational stress; atmospheric variations; processability (the ease of working the material and manufacturing items from that material); trade-offs, qualities versus properties, economic trade-offs; dimensions and tolerances of the particular material; possible alternative materials and cross references to industry standards; weaknesses and necessary precautions in handling.

Specification sheets are "prepared and issued for the procurement of materials, parts, and finishes and for the use of inspection and laboratory personnel who are responsible for the acceptance and control of incoming materials. The specifications establish the means by which the materials may be tested in case of dispute."

The data-for-ordering part of EMPIS basically provides the kinds of information necessary for those who procure materials for the company. It informs the buyer what specifically should be on the purchase order and who the sources of supply have been. This is a fine example of standardization of routine information processes, simplifying what could be a complex process.

It is worth noting that the EMPIS system is built on a good knowledge and anticipation of the problems and information needs and their contexts for three kinds of information use environments: design engineers; inspection, laboratory, and testing personnel; and those who purchase or otherwise procure materials for the company. In contrast to CINDAS, just described, the EMPIS staff are highly sensitive to their users' environments and to the kinds of problems they face. There is a high level of feedback from users of the system, which generates not only new information, but new structures and formats better adapted to the specific use environments.

The information in EMPIS is updated as necessary. It is a system that draws its information from a wide range of sources: the literature, testing procedures and results; from experience; from company expertise; and from vendors. These varied sources provide information that must be compared and evaluated, digested, summarized, and then displayed in the several formats just described. The nature of the information may require alteration and review by others to assure precision in the data and descriptions, in terms of the engineering, processing, testing and procuring of the materials in question.

One of the particular needs for a file of this sort is to be able to search on a combination of properties for a material suited to a particular situation. This is not easy under the present loose-leaf system. Computerization of the file, one would think, is a natural development, and would support those particular kinds of search needs. There are, however, several difficulties, and those difficulties, in a way, underline the problems of converting a file that is useful precisely because of its complexity and variety (Westbrook, 1983a). These problems occur because of "the large size of the file, the diversity of materials and properties covered, the unstructured nature of the file, and the fact that such of the information is textual or graphical." A computerized file requires precision and structure. The paradox is that it may be these qualities (diversity, lack of structure, and variety of display format) which, together with the human interface, give the file its value.

The EMPIS system is the information base for a number of services within the Materials Information Service of the company. Specific reference publications are compiled and issued. Special courses (3–5 days) are offered by EMPIS staff for company personnel on topics of interest, for example, bearing materials and technology. Extensive internal consulting is performed because of the knowledge contained in the data base, as well as the individual expertise of the professional staff. Because of the need for a wide variety of contacts both within and outside the company in maintaining the data base and servicing the clients, the staff also serves as a sort of switching center to expertise.

From this brief review, it can be seen that EMPIS, together with its surrounding activities, adds value in many ways. It collects and organizes data from a wide variety of formal and informal sources, and provides physical access to that data. The information is analyzed, compared, evaluated, and repackaged in a variety of retrievable display formats, designed to be useful for specific types of problems and contexts. Because of their knowledge of materials, the EMPIS staff provides consulting, short courses, interpretive reference, and referral services in extension of the data base. Their knowledge of materials, combined with their sensitivity to the kinds of problems in the organization where such information is relevant and useful, is critical to the value of the information system.

The Congressional Research Service

The Congressional Research Service (CRS) is a department within the Library of

Congress which "under its statutory charter, works exclusively as a reference and research arm for Members, committees and staff of the United States Congress."[10] The CRS currently responds to nearly 420,000 inquiries a year and has a staff of 858, of which 583 are research and information specialists. Though there may be differences over its specific functions, there is no question about the role and responsibility of CRS. "Congress uses the Congressional Research Service as its own, in-house group of experts. They focus on *legislative* responses; their replies should be tight, action-oriented statements that are related to ongoing legislative activities" (Goodrum & Dalrymple, 1982; p. 211). Because of the peculiarities and the special nature of the legislative setting, there are several rather important characteristics of the work that it performs. Not only must the information be timely, accurate, and responsive, but it must be objective and nonpartisan.

> To assure quality in CRS responses, every written product must go through at least two levels of review. At the divisional level, a report is checked to see that it is accurate and thorough in its handling of the subject. Then the Review Section of the Office of Policy, Planning, and Review assesses the report for compliance with CRS's rigorous standards of balance and objectivity. It is the responsibility of these reviewers to look at a paper for fairness, responsiveness to the request, lack of bias, the absence of advocacy, and disciplinary blind spots. Even personal writing, written on a staff member's own time, must be cleared if it is being submitted for publication and treats public policy issues related to the employee's field of specialization in the Service.

The range of interest, as one might suspect, and in contrast to the very specific mission of EMPIS, is as broad as the Congress perceives its legislative responsibilities and interests to be. Inquiries may range from a simple factual data request, such as the population of Chicago, to the need for a study of the possible ways of providing medical care for the aged. One required a few seconds; the other six months of work by three analysts.

There are seven research divisions which are comparable to academic disciplinary departments. They are staffed by nationally recognized experts: American Law; Economics; Education and Public Welfare; Environment and Natural Resources Policy; Foreign Affairs and National Defense; Government; and Science Policy Research. There are also a number of senior specialists, who because of their careers and experience, provide a depth of knowledge and interpretive assistance to the Congress. There is also a Congressional Reference Division which handles about two-thirds of all the requests the CRS receives, principally those for general factual information and bibliographic support.

The range of interest may best be illustrated by a selected sample of titles of recent CRS output which have appeared in Congressional committee prints, in the published hearings of committees, and in the *Congressional Record*.

---

[10] Information on the Congressional Research Service, unless otherwise noted, has been derived from Lindley (1984), from the *Annual Report* of the Congressional Research Service for the Fiscal Year 1983 to the Librarian of Congress, and from *CRS Studies in the Public Domain* (November 1983), all publications of the Congressional Research Service.

Animal sciences: advances in reproductive and health technologies (1983, 76 pp.)
The changing capacity for U.S. steel-making capacity (1983, 26 pp.)
Compensation for victims of water pollution (1979, 372 pp.)
Background data on physician reimbursement under Medicare (1983, 109 pp.)
Computer and communications systems: Policy considerations in a technological age (1983, 2 pp.)
The Hispanic population of the U.S.: An overview (1983, 198 pp.)
The implications of the nuclear arms freeze for the U.S. economy in the short run (1982, 24 pp.)
U.S. Science and engineering education and manpower: Background; supply and demand; and comparisons with Japan, the Soviet Union, and West Germany (1982, 258 pp.)

The CRS develops and publishes what are known as *Issue Briefs,* analyses of topics deemed relevant or potentially relevant to Congress. These briefs, which are maintained in computer form for access and updating, consist of a definition of the issue (e.g., Food Stamps: Funding Crises and Appropriation Ceilings); background and policy analysis; congressional initiatives in the past; an analysis of the options; summary of concerns by such offices as the General Accounting Office and other governmental units; state government and private sector interests; relevant legislation presently in force; congressional hearings and other references sources on the subject. These are available online through some 2,000 terminals to the 20,000 legislative employees in congressional offices and committees through SCORPIO, the Library's automated information system. Because of their computer format and storage, these *Briefs* can be updated as quickly as changes occur. Indeed "during the Iranian hostage crisis . . . the basic *Issue Brief* was updated three or four times a day to keep track not only of developments in Iran, but of State Department Announcements, Congressional hearings and briefings, et cetera" (Goodrum & Dalrymple, 1982; p. 133).

CRS staff also presents special seminars, workshops, or institutes to its congressional constituency. It may also work closely with committee staffs in developing information of use in specific legislation.

The major function then of CRS is to process an enormous variety of information into chunks that are useful to their clients: Members, committees, and staff of the U.S. Congress. These processes require (a) the extensive collections and capabilities of the staff of the Library of Congress in providing support services; (b) the capability to filter incoming inquiries and to design appropriate responses; (c) information analysis in all its forms by knowledgeable subject experts; and (d) close liaison with the clients and users of the output of CRS with consequent sensitivity to their specific information needs.

In the value-added context, one of the principal concerns of CRS is to provide objective and balanced information, and "to describe and analyze the range of alternative choices available to Congress *without* advocating any particular policy, bill, or point of view and to maintain a confidential relationship with each congressional inquirer.'' Though the subject matter is very broad, the constituency is finite and well defined, and the relationships and context understood.

In summary then, the CRS is concerned with several major categories of added value. Of these, the most important is the analysis of large bodies of information and their synthesis into chunks useful for a specific set of clients, with defined information needs. One may argue the question of objectivity and nonpartisanship as limits to the value of information. However, the point is that the Congress and its various staffs is a defined constituency with specific kinds of needs. The constraints and conditions imposed by that body of users become the context within which the value of information is defined by those clients. This is very clearly a user-driven model, in contrast to the content-driven model of, for example, CINDAS. This understanding of the user environment is basic to the value-added model. Of the three services briefly described here, it is worth noting that CRS seems to go farthest in presenting options and alternatives, what in the value-added spectrum (Figure 1-1) have been labeled judgmental processes.

These very brief descriptive notes are not meant to imply that there are no problems with such an operation as CRS, serving a political body like the Congress, with many points of view, powerful interests, competing demands, and various ways of applying pressure. Nor does this discussion imply that we know very much about the role of information in the legislative process. We don't. It is, at best, an act of faith that something approaching objective knowledge, analyzed and evaluated, with options presented in unambiguous terms will provide the basis for better legislation.

INFORMATION ANALYSIS IN ORGANIZATIONS

Two of the three information analysis organizations described in the last few pages are part of organizations: EMPIS and CRS. As such, they work within specific frameworks and share the objectives and constraints of their parent organization: the General Electric Company and the United States Congress. More importantly, they evolved in response to specific information needs within a particular environment. Consequently, they work closer to problems and closer to the people who have problems for which information might be applicable and helpful. Each has grown in response to the growth and complexity of the modern organization, of the environment in which the organization sits, and of the consequent need to filter, standardize, and synthesize the information relevant to that organization's well-being. That ''need to filter, standardize, and synthesize'' has meant the growth of a wide range of personnel, specialized in their knowledge and expertise—persons whom Drucker has called ''knowledge professionals.'' They essentially epitomize the information society.

> But the real growth of middle-rank people in management jobs has been in manufacturing engineers and process specialists; in tax accountants and market analysts; in product and market managers; in advertising and promotion specialists. It has been

> in a host of functions which, a generation ago, were hardly known. The new middle managers are the knowledge professionals.
>
> The traditional middle manager is essentially a commander of men. The new middle manager is essentially a supplier of knowledge. . . . (Drucker, 1974; pp. 447–448)

Mintzberg has divided this middle management growth into two parts: (a) the technostructure made up of "control analysts who serve to effect standardization in the organization;" and (b) support staff who reflect "the organization's attempt to encompass more and more boundary activities in order to reduce uncertainty" (Mintzberg, 1979; pp. 30–32).

The technostructure is made up of

> . . . three types of control analysts who correspond to the three forms of standardization: work study analysts (such as industrial engineers) who standardize work processes; planning and control analysts (such as long-range planners, budget analysts, and accountants) who standardize outputs; and personnel analysts (including trainers and recruiters) who standardize skills. (Mintzberg, 1979; pp. 30–31)

The second group are the support staff groups, including the individual internal consultant, which are located at all levels of the organizational hierarchy. These include such concerns as public relations, economic analysis, and legal counsel; industrial relations, pricing, and research and development; and, closer to basic operations—payroll, the cafeteria, mailroom, and so forth (Mintzberg, 1979; p. 32). With the exception of the latter few operations, the principal intent is to filter, to analyze, to standardize, and to synthesize information so that the organization can be more effective. It should be noted that all of these processes stop short of the actual use of information. There may indeed be many reasons that information is disregarded or "bent" at the point of use, in order to fit the political, personal, organizational, or symbolic needs of the situation, or just out of sheer inertia and resistance to change. The provision of information, no matter how valid, does not guarantee its actual use. The value-added processes of analysis and judgment only give that information a potential for use. Our assumption is that the potential for use is higher than if the processes had not been performed. Worth noting is that persons in the technostructure work mostly with information that is generated internally; those in the support staff work, as filters and interpreters of external information, at the boundary of the organization. In traditional management terms these positions are staff rather than line positions. Persons occupy these positions, not because of particular managerial ability, though they may have that skill, but rather because of their specific expertise and their ability to select, evaluate, and interpret information that is presumed useful to the organization.

Within the technostructure, information processes are concerned with finding patterns in the internally generated information so that what were formerly complex processes can now be standardized and made routine. There are dangers in the processes of standardization, to be discussed later.

With all due regard for the necessity and excellence of the processes described in the previous chapters, the critical steps in the value-added process are those associated with the analysis, evaluation, synthesis, and judgment of information. In the modern organization, these knowledge centers in the technostructure and in the support staff are probably the most important input of evaluated information to major decision making. Typical corporate knowledge centers are the legal counsel, the research and development operation, the data processing group, the marketing department, the strategic planning staff, and the controller's office. Each of these centers is made up of highly knowledgeable people who either process internal information or who monitor the external environment, and adapt and interpret external information in the context of internal information and decision needs. These knowledge workers, though without line responsibility, have a direct and major impact on the performance and direction of the business. Among other examples, Drucker calls attention to the tax accountant in a company.

> The tax accountant . . . has no command, can give no orders, and often has no one reporting to him. . . . Yet, in effect, he has a veto power over even top-management decisions. His opinion on the tax consequences of a course of action often determines both what a company can do and how it must do it. (Drucker, 1974; p. 449)

Some of these centers might be called "quasi-firms," that is they almost lead a life of their own and could in some cases be independent entities. As Marc Porat has pointed out, in the context of his study of the economics of information:

> Each unit has a well-defined technology—with recognizable inputs and outputs and can be conceptualized as a "quasi-firm" embedded within a noninformation enterprise. Its information producing, processing, and distributing activities are *ancillary* to or *in support of* the main productive activity. . . . These quasi-firms (e.g., electronic data processing) have direct analogs in the primary information sector. In many respects, the economics of the quasi-firm are indistinguishable from those of an established data-processing vendor selling its services.
>
> Some information quasi-firms are extremely well defined as cost-centers within the enterprise. . . . The enterprise is paying the opportunity cost on the resources committed to the quasi-firm, and only continues supporting the quasi-firm if its imputed rate of return is higher than would be experienced with alternate forms of investment. At the very least, the quasi-firm must be competitive with the primary sector substitute. (Porat, 1977; I, pp. 147–151)

In a sense, decisions concerning these quasi-firms inside the larger enterprise are "make or buy" decisions. Small firms, for example, instead of having their own accounting department will contract out their accounting, or will use outside computing facilities and expertise, outside marketing analysts, or outside legal counsel. There are intangible and not very well-articulated reasons for having these quasi-firms within the organization. The need for effective control, accountability, communication, and elimination of time delays are the more obvious. Less obvious are those directly relevant to the information environment of the organization: closeness to problems, awareness of political criteria, and sensitivity to organizational and proprietary interests.

One of the richest types of knowledge centers in the modern corporation is that of strategic planning, the function of which is "the formulation of long-term goals and objectives for the company and the selection of strategies to achieve these goals and objectives in light of an uncertain external environment in which the firm must operate" (Naylor, 1980; p. 7). Note there are several phrases here, the implications of which are relevant to the discussion of information analysis. First, it is future directed, and therefore has certain levels of uncertainty and risk. Second, it requires a knowledge of the "uncertain external environment." Third, it requires a "selection of strategies." Fourth, though not stated explictly, there must be some control mechanism for comparing results against the plan, for without control and evaluation one is just whistling in the wind.

An assessment of the external environment requires the collection and analysis of data covering a variety of factors: rate of inflation; changes in public opinion (e.g., the change in public attitudes about nuclear energy after the Three Mile Island accident); migration patterns; major social change (e.g., the civil rights movement); environmental impacts; competitor's financial strength; at the international level, the effect of changes in government on nationalization policies (Naylor, 1980; pp. 116–120). The obvious purpose here is to be able to anticipate events, to reduce uncertainty to a manageable risk. In the former case, that of uncertainty, it is not possible to assign a value to the probability that a particular event will happen. Hence, we are dependent on "what if. . . ." scenarios. Within the context of risk, there can be a "believable set of estimates" for the probability that such and such an event will occur. Estimates are made from the best data and analysis available, especially for such quantitative variables as rate of inflation, energy costs, of market share. In very large organizations, these estimates of relevant external environmental factors and the assessment of potential impact may be sent to divisions and departments, where they can be used to formally assess opportunities and problems relevant to that particular unit and their potential effect on the organization as a whole. The quality of data, the correctness of evaluation, interpretation, the assessment of probabilities, and the eventual mode of presentation of the data are critical steps in the process of information analysis.

In the process of planning, a set of questions are posed (e.g., What are manpower and capital requirements for a certain course of action?) for which analytical tools, usually quantitative and computable, are developed and which require decision on what variables to consider—their range, duration, interrelationships, and relative importance. These planning models encompass many types of information—financial, and marketing. They are formal attempts "to generate alternative scenarios and business plans based on varying assumptions about business unit policies and assumptions about the external environment of the businesses" (Naylor, 1980; p. 83).

The strategic planning process sketched above is a rich example of information analysis, evaluation, and synthesis. It is an information system which makes use of a range of value-added activities, ranging from analytic models to scenario building, from data validation to data reduction. These processes, in value-added terms, reduce noise—which may pose other problems to be considered below. They are quite flexible and adaptable, allowing different assumptions to be built into the models, creating a range of scenarios which support a greater freedom of choice. They help to define the kinds of questions that can be asked, or problems that can be posed and, hence, prescribe the kinds of information that is appropriate for the decision and control contexts that are the objective of the whole planning process.

INFORMATION ANALYSIS—CONTEXTS

It becomes obvious that as one continues up the ladder in the value-added spectrum (Figure 1–1) from organizational to analytical to judgmental processes that the benefits and costs of good or poor information, and its interpretations, are more complex, more dramatic, and more heavily based on human processes. There is more risk associated with value-added processes at these levels. The cost for wrong or inaccurate information, including its modeling and interpretation, can be frighteningly high. The cost of not understanding or of not being clear about the assumptions behind the modeling processes can cause gross misinterpretation as to applicability. In contrast, however, the rewards for good information, appropriately evaluated, synthesized, and presented, can be highly gratifying. Additionally, data and information have become significant ways of sanctioning actions and decisions.

> Using information, asking for information, and justifying decisions in terms of information have all come to be significant ways in which we symbolize that the process is legitimate, that we are good decision makers, and that our organizations are well managed. . . . Decisions that are viewed as legitimate will tend to be information-intensive. Decision makers who are persuasive in securing acceptance of decisions will request information, gather information, and cite information. The behavior is a representation of appropriate decision making. (Feldman & March, 1981; pp. 178–179)

Paradoxically, information has developed a value in and of itself, *sui generis*—esteem value—worn like jewelry, because it gives the wearer status and even power. This is an important factor in any attempt to describe information use environments, though it may not conform to rational processes. We make note of it principally because it is a factor frequently overlooked, even ridiculed, in the contexts that benefit from the value-added processes of information analysis.

The reflection of values added in the system, that is, actual enhancing activities, may be somewhat different from those encountered in document-based systems. It is, however, more a difference in emphasis and objectives, for all are information systems concerned with the delivery or display of data/information/knowledge in usable and useful chunks. In information analysis, the system activities in support of these criteria are affected by several parameters which require varying assumptions about users and about the kinds of things that can be done with and to data and information in order to enhance their utility.

- closeness to the problem
- characteristics of the data/information
- standardization

The way these parameters are perceived, and the assumptions built around those perceptions, will influence the relative roles of technological and human processes and will affect the benefits that the ultimate users will gain and the costs they will incur. There is a primary assumption underlying the discussion of this chapter: that most of the truly valuable processes of information analysis and judgment are human activities, supported in varying degrees by applied technology. The human activity is, however, dominant. Not everyone will agree with this; or at least though they may agree in principle, their activities belie that belief. This poses some rather fundamental problems concerning our attitudes toward information and hence for the value-added model. This will be discussed in the last chapter.

ANALYSIS: WHERE ONE STARTS FROM

The degree of closeness to the problem harks back to the earlier discussion in Chapter Three on the user-driven model and the content-driven model. The assumptions made about the data; the setting itself, for example, scientific, managerial, or political; and the assumptions made by the analyst about the context—all of these will have a critical effect on the utility and shape of the resultingg analysis. Where the analyst starts from: assumptions about the data and the context in which they will be used colors the whole process of analysis and complementary processes.

On the one hand, the analyst may start from the data. That is to say, the body and characteristics of the data define the process of analysis. This is especially true in the physical sciences and in the quantitative social sciences, which are based on "hard," that is, factual and numerical, data. In this case, the purpose is to clarify, to define, to compare, to validate, and to interpret through various "re-expressions" a body of data so that users, unknown to the analyst, can make sure of those data more effectively and presumably with greater benefits than if the analysis had not been made. The end-product is a new synthesis of evaluated, tested, and validated information; one may even call it new knowledge. Because of this synthesis, or, in John Tukey's phrase, "re-expression" (Tukey, 1977; pp. 57–96), something is known or perceived that may not have been known or seen before. The work described above of the Center for Information and Numerical Analysis and Synthesis, and that of similar scientific information analysis centers, are examples of this form of analysis. They start from the data. Their principal concern is with the quality, validity, accuracy, and presentation of the data. The data themselves are the determinants of the analysis process. How they may be used is not a primary concern of these processes. The user must reinterpret that product or those data. Indeed the user may need to combine these with other data, even newly derived data, in order to apply them to his or her situation or problem. Further, the user may need to weigh the advantages and disadvantages of the options implied in these combinations.

On the other hand we may have an entirely different form of analysis—one that starts from the problem and its context, *including the bias of the information user*. The intent of that qualifying phrase—the bias of the user—is not necessarily to imply that users are biased in a pejorative sense. Rather it implies that users, because they sit in particular situations, have unique criteria by which to judge the utility (value) of the information.

Data-oriented analytic processes are content driven. Their intent is to establish and verify the quality and validity of the data in hand. *Problem-oriented analytic processes* are user driven. Their intent is to assist in solving a problem in making a decision, or in clarifying a situation. The difference is critical in the process of analysis. Each is necessary. Each complements or supplements the other.

The analyst, when starting from the user, needs to put data—sometimes seemingly disparate data—together to form a new synthesis, one dictated not by the data but by the situation and the problem. The data in such contexts will include hard and soft data, certain fact and uncertain prediction, single choice or many options. The analyst in this case will indeed perform many of the same value-added processes as does the data-based analyst, but the criteria of utility and the nature of the product are different. Indeed the problem-oriented analyst will be the beneficiary of the value-added activities and products of the data-based analysts. The utility or valuableness of the product of problem-oriented analysis, however, may be partially based on grounds other than validity or accuracy: situations where, for example, ambiguity may be a necessary concomitant to solving a problem, because the nature of the process is to change the situation in such a way that it is no longer a "problem." As Lindblom and Cohen remark: "Problem-solving interactions change what has to be thought about, what has to be analyzed" (Lindblom & Cohen, 1979; p. 27).

Data Analysis: Nature and Problems

In discussing "data" (hardness, softness, and other qualifiers and attributes) it becomes painfully apparent that there is no unambiguous definition of the term. Indeed as Dolby and Clark point out in a footnote in their report on *The Language of Data:*

> In 1973 Dolby and Tukey published a cumulative index for books in the field of statistics which included some 600 definition entries; not one was devoted to "data". . . . The word "comparison" is equally ignored within the discipline of statistics, as are "table" and "graph." Thus we are faced with a situation in which the fundamental object of study, the fundamental operations on such objects, and the fundamental forms of communication are essentially undefined. (Dolby & Clark, 1982; p. 4)

Like Saint Augustine who, when asked what time was, replied "I know so long as you don't ask me." In this sense we will need to take "data" partially on faith, as symbols "that designate the state (conditions) that characterize an entity at some point in time" (Dunn, 1974; p. 78).

The problems of data quality are very real as Lide (1981) points out, and our dependence on valid data ever more critical as we attempt to deal with, among other concerns, global environmental problems: depletion of the ozone layer; causes and effects of acid rain; benefits and costs of the usage of EDB, and so forth. Unfortunately, "the quality of the data preserved in the literature leaves much to be desired." Lide calls attention, for example, to the recent study on the thermal conductivity of copper as a function of temperature. Systematic retrieval of relevant literature showed some 200 different measurements of this property. The scatter of these measurements resulted from such causes as the level of impurities in the samples upon which those measurements are based, and the failure to specify such information as sample purity (Lide, 1981; 1345–1346). A question in biological and medical research which is only beginning to surface is that of chronobiology (the timing of the body's internal rythmic cycles), which may affect everything from blood pressure to decision making (Hilts, 1980). The results of some previous drug and cancer research are now in doubt because of the failure to realize the influence of time-of-day on the effects of toxic agents, experimental substances, and the measurement of bodily functions. Both of these examples are indicative of the need for data analysis and evaluation of high level and for a better understanding of data quality by the producers of data, so that decisions made on the basis of those data can be based on more solid ground.

There are in general terms three broad classes of quantifiable data (Lide, 1981; 1343–1344).

> *Class A* (hard data): repeatable measurements on well-defined systems, for example, "traditional physical and chemical data resulting from measurements of well-understood properties of systems of known composition."
>
> *Class B* (semihard data): observational data, for example, "the results of measurements that are dependent on time or space and cannot be checked by remeasurement;" includes much of the data from the geosciences and environmental monitoring.
>
> *Class C* (soft data): statistical data, for example, demographic, chemical production records, energy consumption figures, and health statistics.

This range from hardness to softness is, of course, based on the capability of measurement and consequent quantification. In our culture, quantification of data seems to imply that, just because they are quantifiable, the data are more reliable representations of reality. This unfortunately may or may not have anything to do with their accuracy or their validity. The halo surrounding numericity tends to fortify the reliability of data expressed numerically and to deflect questions concerning their validity. We need constantly to remind ourselves that data are but symbols representing reality, not reality itself. These observations are intended to point up, indeed to emphasize the need for competent data analysis, and an understanding of the processes that give the resultant data their value (Westbrook, 1983b).

With the advent of very large computer memories and highly sophisticated number manipulating capabilities, the function and status of data may be changing. That is to say, it will be necessary in the future to take data management schemes into consideration, for they may have an effect on the quality and reliability of data. As Dolby points out:

> Thirty and more years ago, most data analysis was done on relatively small data sets using pen and paper with an occasional assist from mechanical devices. Large-scale mechanical assistance was mainly restricted to sorting, selecting, and aggregating through the medium of punched cards. For the most part the analyst was able to keep in mind what the data *meant* while trying to discover how it could be used to confirm, refute, or extend existing knowledge. It was natural then to look to the computer for assistance in the various number crunching activities common to data analysis—a tendency that was encouraged by the development of programming languages most suitable for crunching numbers.
>
> By now, of course, we are long since accustomed to the availability of statistical packages that include not only the standard number crunching procedures, but also many of the newer ones. We also have access to more and more sophisticated number management schemes operating over larger and larger sets of data. However, there comes a time when any analyst finds that it is no longer possible to keep in mind the meaning of each and every datum, not to mention the meaning of the several analyses that have been tried over, perhaps, a substantial period of time. (Indeed it has been suggested that a "larger data set" is one that cannot be completely absorbed and maintained in one head.) The problem gets worse as data and methods are revised and as more and more users interact with the same database. (Dolby, 1983; p. 1)

It would appear that data itself is now confronted with the problem of naming. This is a tertiary level, and one which librarians and information retrieval people have been struggling with for a long time. How do we name (label or tag) specific text or body of data? How do we control that vocabulary of names (descriptors)? How do we relate one descriptor to another? How do we search those descriptors? Today with linguistic text, we are moving toward complete text search for word tokens. Such a step is obviously not possible with numerical data— they must be labeled with a natural language descriptor. Dolby, Clark, and their colleagues in the Language of Data project (1982) are one of the few groups concerned with this problem.

Standardization

One of the results of information analysis is in the processes of standardization of information, that is, the mutual agreement to accept a specific level of data and modes of practice in specified situations. In its best sense standardization is a broad-scale effort to bring order out of chaos, to provide an acceptable and common information base from which products can be designed and tested and upon which decisions can be made and understood. Of interest especially to our concerns here is that a formal technical standard is an information output, the result of an extensive process of analysis, synthesis, *and compromise,* and that its impact on manufacturing processes, for example, can be costed.

A recent example of the need for a formal data base with validated and reliable information has to do with the lack of complete and unified phase diagrams, a necessity for nearly every metallurgical or materials engineer working with metals alloys. According to the International Nickel Company, at least 250,000 man-hours are lost in that company each year due to the lack of reliable phase–diagram data, which they estimate amounts to $5,000,000 annually. The National Bureau of Standards, together with the American Society of Metals, has now established a phase–diagram program and expect it to be self-sustaining by 1986.[11]

The process of standardization is a necessary base in the larger context of information synthesis, for standardization "minimizes disadvantageous diversity, assures acceptability of products, and facilitates technical communication" (Westbrook, 1981b, p. 32). In the value-added context, standardization not only facilitates the transfer of information, because receiver and sender both use a specific term in the same way, but its existence has an effect on benefits and costs.

> The costs and benefits associated with standardization are determined by direct and indirect effects. A proper assessment depends on having suitable baseline data with which to make a comparison. Several surveys have shown typical dollar returns for the investment in standardization in the range of 5:1–8:1 with occasional claims made for a ratio as high as 50:1.
>
> Savings include reduced costs of materials and parts procurement; savings in production and drafting practice; reduction in engineering time, e.g., design, testing, quality control, and documentation; and reduction in maintenance, field service, and in-warranty repairs. . . .
>
> From the customer's point of view, there is an optimal level of standardization. Increased standardization lowers costs but restricts choices. Furthermore, if a single minimal-performance product standard is rigorously invoked in an industry, competition in a free market ultimately may lead the manufacturer of a superior product to save costs by lowering his product quality to the level of the standard, thus denying other values to the customer. Again, excessive standardization, especially as applied to design or how the product performance is to be achieved, effectively can limit technological innovation. (Westbrook, 1981b, pp. 42–43)

In organizational terms, we seek to make complex processes routine so that those processes can be performed with dispatch, that decisions can be based on predetermined norms, and we can get on with the work. Without such standardization, a great deal of the world's work would grind to a halt. This has worked splendidly in many cases, especially when the situation has been of such a nature that could take standardization and when those who applied it knew its limits. History, however, records infinite instances of the failure of standard solutions in the face of changed circumstances. They failed because they were convenient, easy, and because of the attitude reflected in "this is the way we have always done it."

There are several dangers in such routinization. The first is that these processes tend to grow until the standardization controls the organization, and it becomes a frozen bureaucracy, unable to respond except by prescription. In stable times and in normal situations, such organizations are extremely efficient, able to react in standard ways to what have been predefined as standard situations. The difficulties, of course, are in the variations that the system does not recognize because they fall outside the standardized version of reality. One of the unfortunate results of such

---

[11] From Phase-diagram project underway. *Materials Engineering, 95*(1), 10–11 (January 1982).

frozen bureaucracy is that the real objectives of the organization tend to become lost, and the rules, regulations, and standard operating procedures begin to govern totally. An extreme and almost comical example of this may be seen in a recent newspaper report from the Midlands of England:

> Complaints from passengers wishing to use the Bagnall to Greenfields bus service that "the drivers were speeding past queues of people with a smile and a wave of the hand" have been met by a statement pointing out that "it is impossible for the drivers to keep their timetable if they have to stop for passengers."[12]

They forgot what the bus service was intended to do—to transport people. Though extreme, this has a sort of reverse parallel in the information field where, for example, reports are generated and distributed to persons who have no need for them and, in most cases, dump them in the wastebasket. This is partly caused by our inability to deal with an information-rich culture—the result of an explosion of information relevance, of indiscriminate application of computers to information handling, and the inability as yet to define in useful ways the information environments of clients and customers.

A second danger of these processes of standardization is the tendency to label as important those things that can be done, or measured, and as unimportant those things that cannot be easily done or measured. Knight and McDaniel cite personnel tests as a case in point.

> Personnel tests received emphasis because they can be administered, despite the fact that they might not be good predictors of future job success. It is the fact that the test can be given and scored that makes it important, not the fact that it is closely related to the potential employee contribution to the job situation. (Knight & McDaniel, 1979; p. 101)

These perceptions are of course not new. The point here, however, is that if these processes and decisions had been built around the value-added model based on user criteria, then the benefits and costs of such standardization or routinization might be more carefully scrutinized and weighed. The paradox here, of course, is that the user or his organization demands quick and easy methods of making personnel decisions, on the assumption that such traits can be measured; and the information person responds. This is one of the anomalies of information analysis and its related processes: that the expectations and indeed the demands of information clients are higher than the system can in fact deliver. We tend to expect too much and, as information professionals, we perhaps have oversold our wares. We need to constantly remind ourselves that the processes of information reduction, be they mathematical, analytic, or advisory, exact a price—the loss of variety—while at the same time they add the possibility of informed choice. It is in these trade-offs that the informed use of value-added processes in analysis will find their primary role.

---

[12] As quoted by Patrick Ryan in *Smithsonian, 8*(6), p. 140 (September 1977).

VALUES ADDED IN INFORMATION ANALYSIS

Information analysis is the process necessary to produce, transmit, and present evaluated information to the point of use. That point of use may range from the laboratory bench to the managerial desk, from a vote on a bill in Congress to a decision to give up smoking. As Weisman and others have pointed out, historically there have been many forms of information analysis: the monoliths at the stonehenge, the oracle at Delphi, the shaman of primitive tribes (Weisman, 1972; p. 138). Our concern, however, is with modern contexts, and with formal processes and the values added in those processes. Information analysis, as Wallin remarks, "is an *imperative* because it is so firmly linked to decision making. As an imperative, it *must* be performed and *will* be acted upon, whether competently and thoroughly, or just the opposite" (Wallin, 1982; pp. 1–2).

It was pointed out earlier in this chapter that there are several concerns in discussing analysis in the value-added context. The first asks *where analysis starts from:* the data or the problem. Though the processes of adding value are substantially the same, the intent in each case is quite different. The second concerns the *nature of the data*. On the one hand, we deal with several classes of quantifiable data; on the other hand, with information based on undefined probabilities and even irrational behaviors. The third concern is with *standardization*—a natural result of much of the analysis process—and with its effect on information use and organizational behavior. Though these concerns are important, they probably have little overall effect on the analytic processes themselves, but more on those processes labeled judgmental, where the principal concern is with presentation of options.

Of the user criteria described in Chapter Four, the analyzing and judgmental processes seem to focus principally around (a) those that *reduce noise,* (b) those that enhance the *quality* of the data, and (c) those that *adapt* the data to particular contexts and to the problems associated with those contexts. In reviewing the extensive but unorganized literature on information analysis, in particular Carroll and Maskewitz (1980), Mason (1979), Wallin (1982), and Weisman (1972), a number of substantive terms and phrases (usually undefined) are used to describe processes and values of concern here. This literature is mostly concentrated around the scientific information analysis center, and consequently has some limitations. These terms and phrases have been compiled and distilled into brief discussions, together with comments on the resulting benefits, under the six user criteria (a process akin to information analysis). This is by no means complete. It is rather an ordered and suggestive presentation of the processes of information analysis, and the resultant values. Not included in any of the comments below but worth noting, is that one of the results of information analysis is the production of new knowledge and new insights. In the context here, it is hard to put a value on this—in a sense, it is invaluable! (A curious word—it's all backwards!)

Ease of Use: The principal processes here are those of repackaging and compiling scattered data and presenting them in orderly formats, which may include online forms. Handbooks, tables, and graphs are outputs of scientific information centers.

Issue Briefs, as published by CRS, are examples of repacking diverse data into more usable formats. The data and information (the content) in these new packages are only as valuable as the other processes, commented on below, will allow.

Noise reduction is achieved principally through organizing, classifying, and "increasing density." The first two, of course, are the result of (a) bringing like things together, so that nonrelevant information can be identified and excluded at that point; and (b) relating information internally to potentially relevant information. Increasing the density of information is the result of ruthless exclusion of nonrelevant material in any form or shape. The use of graphs and charts, for example, may convey and present information more efficiently than discourse. One of the faces of such efficiency is density of information. The whole question of enhancing the use of data by its graphic and tabular presentation is ably presented by Clark (1983) and in a chapter entitled "The Syntax of Tabular Data" in Dolby and Clark (1982).

The level of *quality* of data and information is one of the major and most important values produced by the analysis process. Mason's study (1979) of perceived benefits of information analysis centers showed that the quality of information was most important to scientific researchers. On the other hand, Gerstenberger and Allen (1968), in their study of R&D engineers, showed that technical quality ranked behind ease of use as a criterion for channel choice. These differences, however, are based on different settings. As we have argued in Chapter Three, it is the elements of the environment that will define the criteria of use. Nonetheless the quality of data and information is a critical characteristic of almost any result of information analysis: accuracy, comprehensiveness, currency, reliability, and validity. The last one—validity—is probably the most critical of all these values, and the one upon which, correctly, the most attention is focused. Validity has to do with the soundness of the data, and with an open understanding of the assumptions and weakness associated with the data.

Adaptability is a reflection of how close the processes of analysis are to the actual and specific problems of users. This has been discussed above. It is merely necessary to note here that such closeness is a critical part of adaptation, and colors all the other criteria and added values. Flexibility becomes especially important, as discussed above in the section on strategic planning, in the capabilities of the modeling and simulation programs in allowing a client to make various assumptions about the data, and hence to construct different scenarios. Both these software programs and the options presented in the CRS *Issue Briefs* build on and go beyond the analyzing processes to those of judgment. It is precisely this ability to present viable options to the client which represents the intent of activities associated with flexibility as used here. Simplicity is an intangible value, which may or may not be present, dependent on the particular abilities and sensitivities of the formal processes of analysis and judgment. The level of simplicity is a value that can only be ascertained in particular instances.

Time Savings: The example of the International Nickel Company noted above is a prime instance of the effect of the lack of a specific information analysis operation can have on the efficient use of professional manpower. It should be noted that we are not talking about the inability to retrieve information, but rather about the specific lack of analyzed information (phase diagrams) and their impact on one company. There are undoubtedly many more such examples.

Cost Savings: Mason's (1979) study of information analysis centers found that cost considerations (dollar costs to the user) ranked fourth among four criteria in importance to IAC users. We don't really know, in the larger social sense, or even within organizations, what the true costs of information analysis are. As implied above, intuitively we feel that the processes of analysis are probably the most important in the information process—and in all likelihood the most expensive.

VALUE-ADDED PROCESSES IN INFORMATION ANALYSIS

The processes in support of these values are myriad, complex, and, as we will see, ill defined. They can only be touched upon here. One of the problems is with words and their use and misuse. Of particular concern is the word "analysis." To compound the problem in this book the word is used in two senses. Up to this point, "analysis" has been used as a sort of portmanteau word to cover everything from original filtering of information to its synthesis and beyond to the presentation of options. Now we will use the word in its more precise sense. What indeed does "analysis" mean in this more precise sense? From the *Oxford English Dictionary,* we find that the origins of the verb, "to analyze" stem from those meaning to loosen, to untie, to break up. For "analysis," the dictionary expands on this: "the resolution or breaking up of anything complex into its simple elements, the opposite process to synthesis; the exact determination of the elements or components of anything complex. In logic: the tracing of things to their source, and the resolution of knowledge into its original principles. . . ." From *Webster's Third Unabridged Dictionary:* "a detailed examination of anything complex in order to understand its nature or to determine its essential features" Thus for our purposes, analysis means breaking up something of high complexity into simpler elements in order to ascertain how these elements fit together, that is, to better understand, and in order to compare them with other "similar" elements, and hence to evaluate their role, function, and validity. Questions of similarity, discrimination, and differentiation are too complex to be dealt with here. Eventually, however, we will need to examine (analyze!) all of these operations in order to understand these highly useful processes that add so much value to information in the processes from system to user.

In the literature we've cited and examined, the following process terms (other than *analysis*) seem to be important when people discuss and describe information analysis. It should be noted that none of these process terms are defined in the literature, or even specifically described. They seem to be merely parts of lists or casually mentioned within a sentence. The purpose of this chapter has been to identify these processes, to label them, and, if possible, to comment briefly on them so that future discourse might be a little clearer and more lucid.

The term *evaluating* is frequently cited. Basically it is defined in *Webster's Third New International Dictionary Unabridged* as "to examine and to judge concerning the worth, quality, significance, amount, degree, or condition of" and the dictionary, as an example of usage, quotes Havelock Ellis: "It is not enough to count, we must evaluate." Evaluation is obviously a principal value-adding activity. It provides the basis for the values of accuracy, currency, and especially of validity. But there is a hint of something more here: nonquantitative worth, something that states that though a datum or chunk of information is accurate, current, and valid, it may be trivial, of little worth. That indeed is a critical and sensitive value, for it reduces noise in an unorthodox way by saying "that is not worth your time, though it is correct." As are all analytic processes, evaluation is also dangerous because it can be subjective. Evaluation, in the best sense, would also include the assumptions, biases, and validating methods to back up its assertions.

Comparing and *correlating* are terms which imply setting data side by side, seeking for resemblances, similarities, differences, and analogies (relationships). This process looks at data which, though they measure the same phenomena, are quantitatively different—and asks (a) the magnitude of that difference, and (b) why this is so; which one might be a better representation of reality (be more valid) and under what conditions are the data valid. These activities might be part of the process of evaluation, but they seem important enough as separate activities to merit notice.

Filtering is akin, of course, to selection; but within the context here it is a much finer mesh. The process of filtering basically asks which data among a body of data are related, comparable, and amenable to useful evaluation; and then extracts those data that match its predetermined requirements of relevance, similarity, or utility. The activities associated with filtering may make choices of data on the basis of problem requirements; or it may make choices on the basis of data compatibility and similarity.

Digesting, a peculiar word, crops up rather frequently. It seems to mean that, analogous to the physiological process, it breaks down the information into pieces upon which certain processes (enzymes?) can perform certain operations (extraction of glucose?) so that the resultant product is more useful or, perhaps, usable. In this sense, digesting seems to cover almost all of the processes we have been discussing here, without providing any useful insights, except as a familiar analogy. It is suggested that the word be dropped from this vocabulary.

Extrapolating is the process through which, from present data (a) new data can be derived: (b) future scenarios can be projected; and (c) better interpretative models can be structured. Many specific processes can be involved. Its principal value is to provide the means for estimates of future constraints and opportunities.

Synthesizing is the putting together of the results of all the processes of analysis, filtering comparing, evaluating, and extrapolating. Because of the processes which have preceded it, a new combination of data and information can be composed, with insights and relationships not apparent before. In Renan's well-known phrase, you need years of analysis for one minute of synthesis.[13] Synthesis is the culmination

[13] Quoted in de Grolier (1979; p. 68). Joseph Ernst Renan (1823–1892) was a French philologist and historian, and a leader of the critical school of philosophy in France.

of many processes in combination with the sensitivity and expert knowledge of many people.

Interpreting are those activities that (a) provide ways of understanding the data presented, and (b) attempt to make sense of the information presented in the context of the problem it is intended to address. This description is so stated because it relates directly to our earlier question as to where the analyst starts from—the data or the problem. If the former, then the interpretation is concerned with the assumptions in back of the data, their meaning, and structure. If from the latter, the problem, then the interpretation is concerned with fitting the data into the problem space of the client or user. The product of the interpretive process would (a) delineate ways the information is specifically useful, and (b) present options, with advantages and disadvantages, for client decision or action.

Chapter Eight

INFORMATION IN DECISION CONTEXTS

This chapter is based on two premises. The first is that the making of decisions are the means by which organizations—and indeed individual human beings—adapt to changing environments, allocate scarce resources, and maintain their well-being—in short, survive. Decision making may be defined as "the conversion of information into action." (McClure, 1978; p. 382). Though human beings may in fact be reluctant decision makers, as Janis and Mann (1977) argue, decisions will continued to be made, whether or not we really want to make them. Indeed, it may be the case that no decision *is* a decision. The second premise is that processing of information is a vital aspect of human behavior. In the context of this chapter, information—in all its guises—is a critical input to the decision process. As McDonough states, "information flow is the material handling of the managerial function" (McDonough, 1963; p. 29). How and under what conditions information is transferred and used (or not used) and what the attributes of that information are is of concern here. These statements will be refined, modified, and, perhaps, even basically altered in the pages that follow.

The focus of this chapter is with the nature of the information systems that exist to support decision making, and with the formal information processes that may or may not add value to information in the making of decisions. As context for this we are consequently interested in an understanding of several factors:

- the environment within which decisions are made;
- the quality of decision processes;
- the level and nature of decisions;
- the role of information in those processes; and
- the formal processes of information provision and whether or no they are of use in decision making.

There are two general approaches to the concern with decision making. On one side is the engineering or systems approach, including that of the economist, which is concerned with the design of rational systems and with models of optimal decision making. The other side of this coin is what might be called the behavioral approach, which is concerned with how people—real people—behave in problem and decision contexts, and how they search for and make use of information in those contexts.

It should be quite obvious by now that this book is built on behavioral assumptions, in the belief that such assumptions, though certainly messier, allow us to come closer to reality. The value-added approach based on the user-driven model is a behavioral approach, for it assumes that value is in the eye of the beholder, the user of that information. Our principal concern, then, is with the nature, delivery, and use of information in the process of decision making, and with "actual human encounters with information" (Feldman & March, 1981; p. 171). These remarks are not meant to imply that that formal models of decision processes are not useful. They are useful as long as we understand and allow for the constraints within which they operate. They are useful as a sort of "ideal" metaphor, within which we can begin to structure and to understand the benefits and costs of information provision in the decision-making process. They are not useful in their insistence that they represent the reality of decision making, which of course they do not.

A great deal has been written about decision making. It is not our intent to make any critical summary of this body of literature. Rather we will attempt to thread our way through and extract portions we think useful for the discussion and analysis of value-added processes in those information systems which seem to support the making of decisions.

We are concerned with consequential decisions—the making of choices that affect the welfare of a family, a group, an organization, a community, a nation. We are not concerned about the formation of opinion or with the minor routine decisions that a person faces every day. Consequential decisions imply that there are real rewards or penalties for good or poor decisions, however defined.

THE INFORMATION ENVIRONMENT OF DECISION MAKING

Decisions are made because problems are perceived which human beings sitting in certain environments believe need resolution. That simple statement carries hidden assumptions and qualifications within it which need some explication. First, there is the assumption that decisions in a formal sense are indeed made. Some observers of the managerial process question that assumption by saying that most decisions are the result of incremental steps, few if any of which are significant enough to merit the label of A DECISION. Instead, these steps are "geared to policy—putting out fires—rather than selecting the superior course of action" (Janis & Mann, 1977; p. 33). Lindblom (1959) calls this the "art of muddling through": The phrase is not used in a pejorative sense (except by those who believe in highly formal decision structure), but rather to indicate that, in the real world, societal and organizational decisions evolve in small steps through personal and coalition power, risk avoidance, and compromise. In an information context, however, each of these factors are but constraints on the way information will be used or not used and how it will be interpreted. That is to say, information will play a role regardless what model of the decision process is presented.

The second comment about the statement above has to do with the nature of the goals of decisions and the strategies used to meet those goals. Most models of formal organizational decision making assume that decision makers actively desire to select a course of actions which promises the highest payoff. That is to say, decision makers wish to optimize, seek, and implement the best solution possible, however defined. This is an expensive process in time, money, and energy, for it assumes that all viable alternatives will be considered and tested in terms of expected benefits and costs, and that all relevant information will be gathered and evaluated as it affects those alternatives and concomitant probabilities. Not only is optimization, or maximization as some call it, a costly process, but as Simon points out, human beings do not have "the wits to maximize." Instead, as Simon argus, most decision makers "satisfice." This is related to our earlier discussion of the criteria that engineers use in selecting among information channels: "they act in a manner which is intended not to maximize gain, but rather to minimize loss" (Gerstenberger & Allen, 1968; p. 277). Simon summarizes the context for the concept of satisficing.

> In the real world we usually do not have a choice between satisfactory and optimal solutions, for we only rarely have a method for finding the optimum. . . . We cannot, within practicable computable limits, generate all admissible alternatives and compare their respective merits. Nor can we recognize the best alternative, even if we are fortunate enough to generate it early, until we have seen them all. We satisfice by looking for alternatives in such a way that we can generally find an acceptable one after only moderate search. (Simon, 1969; pp. 64–65)

Sutherland argues, however, that unless we keep the ideal of optimality as a guiding criterion, then solutions tend quickly to become poor ones. In a sense, there is a sort of Gresham's Law at work: Poor decisions will tend to drive out good decisions. "Optimality," he writes, "does not demand that the decision maker always be right in the actions he takes; it means, rather, that he takes pains to reduce, to the fullest extent possible, some appropriate expected error function" (Sutherland, 1977; p. 2).

A third comment has to do with the role of information in organizational environments. If we accept a straightforward decision process in which problems are analyzed, all alternatives defined, and all relevant information sought and evaluated, then information has one role—as valuable input to problem-solving and decision-making tasks. This is certainly a function of information, but it is not the only one. This is not, as some might suspect, an attempt to belittle the role of information in decision making, but rather to strengthen that function through a better understanding of the total life of information in organizations. By understanding these factors better we can design and manage information systems that are more relevant to the needs of the organization. At this time, this understanding can be only fragmentary; but it is possible to list and discuss briefly a few of these factors.

1. Managers (decision makers) do not like to be surprised. For this reason, the external environment is continually monitored by themselves and by personnel within the organization—lawyers, financial experts, specialists in governmental regulations, and tax accountants. The function of these knowledge professionals is to produce a steady stream of information to the organization. Their position and corporate existence may indeed depend on how much new and presumably relevant

information they can feed into the organization. Without further filtering, such information tends to serve special interests in the organization and to overload the information channels.

2. There are a number of reasons why people in organizations look at information products, very few of which have to do with the making of decisions in any formal sense.

- They fear not being informed, because they believe information is the currency of power, even though the information may have nothing to do directly with their responsibility.
- A certain status may exist in receiving a particular information output, and, therefore, the recipient feels obliged to spend time with it.
- It is required of them because, if there is a certain threshold in that information, then they must act. This trigger may be either automatic or judgmental.
- There may be a conscious need to be informed in order to assess the effects of one's own decisions or to anticipate the decisions of others.
- There may be an articulated need to know in order to carry out one's own responsibilities.
- There is a need for the information input for a new package of information for other people.
- There is a direct need for specific types of information in order to make a decision of consequence.

We need constantly to remind ourselves that the real function of a manager is to get things done. That is to say decisions must lead to action. Information supporting those decisions is received in many ways, including via highly informal channels. A great deal is accomplished or affected, for example, by the passage of gossip, by the discovery of information in odd corners, and by the exchange of information in highly informal and unstructured ways.

3. An individual in an organization strives not only for an increased salary, but also seeks to expand his information privileges (Starr, 1971; p. 469). In formal terms this is what job enlargement is all about—to be able to produce and to receive more information. Information becomes a form of currency; to know more about the environment surrounding one's position provides both power and security. The result is that more people have a need to know. Such expansion tends to increase the amount of lateral information transfer. Interdepartmental memoranda, information copies, committees and their reports proliferate. Strassmann points out that "information amplification factors" of 40 to 1 are not uncommon. That is, for every formal act, such as an order, there may be as many as 40 internal messages generated "to keep the various functional units apprised of what's going on" (Strassmann, 1980; p. 60).

4. Information in a formal sense is gathered at a different point in the organization than where it is used. That is to say, "the costs and the benefits of information are not all incurred at the same place in the organization" and "incentives are modest for gatherers to avoid overloading users" (Feldman & March, 1981; p. 175).

Because we know very little about the amount and kind of information relevant to a particular decision, we tend to overload. "It is better from a decision maker's point of view to have information that is not needed than not to have information that might be needed" (Feldman & March, 1981; p. 176). The closer the information gatherer is to the problem the better he or she is able to filter and to adapt the information—to add value—for the particular decision process.

In a sense, information in organizations has a life of its own, and affects the decision process in ways we are not quite clear about yet. The factors discussed briefly above, as well as others, both constrain the passage and enhance the value of information in the decision process. There are possible opportunities here for better design of value-added activities in information systems.

QUALITY OF DECISION PROCESSES

Janis and Mann (1977) in their extensive review of the decision-making literature discuss the difficulty of objectivity in assessing whether or no a decision is successful. Subjectively of course a decision can be evaluated—and often is by one's supervisor or peers or, indeed, by one's own post-decisional regret or self-congratulation. Though we cannot objectively assess the results of decision making, Janis and Mann suggest that there are seven major criteria which can be used to determine whether decision-making procedures are of high quality. This is an expansion on our earlier remarks on satisficing and optimality. It seems plausible, they write, "that decisions satisfying these seven 'ideal' procedural criteria have a better chance than others of attaining the decision maker's objectives and of being adhered to in the long run." The decision maker, to the best of his or her ability and within the decision maker's information-processing capabilities:

1. thoroughly canvasses a wide range of alternative courses of action;
2. surveys the full range of objectives to be fulfilled and the values implicated by the choice;
3. carefully weighs whatever he knows about the costs and risks of negative consequences, as well as the positive consequences, that could flow from each alternative;
4. intensively searches for new information relevant to further evaluation of the alternatives;
5. correctly assimilates and takes account of any new information or expert judgment to which he is exposed, even when the information or judgment does not support the course of action he initially prefers;
6. reexamines the positive and negative consequences of all known alternatives, including those originally regarded as unacceptable, before making a final choice;
7. makes detailed provisions for implementing or executing the chosen course of action, with special attention to contingency plans that might be required if various known risks were to materialize. (Janis and Mann, 1977; p. 11)

It seems necessary, in order to complete the process, to add one more criterion on these seven, at the beginning of the process. It is necessary to ask at the very beginning just why a decision needs to be made at all. To fit the pattern of the list from Janis and Mann, it comes just before #1:

O. Carefully analyzes the problem which requires the decision to be sure why the problem exists in the first place, what the nature of the problem is, and indeed if the right problem has been identified;

A problem may arise from (a) external factors (reduction in market share, new government regulations); (b) perceived opportunity (new product possibility, a potential research breakthrough); or (c) internal factors (personnel evaluation and decision, loss of product quality). In each case the function of problem solving is to reduce the difference between a present situation judged undesirable and a future situation thought to be more desirable. Decision making involves those processes of evaluating relevant information and choosing among various alternatives on the way to devising a new more desirable situation. Analysis of the original problem context establishes the frame of reference for decision choices and indeed may govern the level of success of the solution. Problems, however, are not static. We tend to think ''almost exclusively on closed-form problems in which there is only one correct solution and the nature of the problem is immutable'' (Frischmuth & Allen, 1969; p. 63). The nature of the problem may well change as new information is analyzed, evaluated, and combined with other data. New data may reveal that the problem is not as pressing as originally thought. New data may cause a problem to be perceived differently and consequently one may be able to accept a solution to a different problem which would favorably affect the original problem.

These eight criteria are a way of judging and controlling the decision process. Each one might be considered on a scale, for example, 0–5, low to high, and failure to meet some threshold on any one of the criteria constitutes a defect in the particular process. The more defects, the more likely the decision maker will make a poor decision. When a decision maker meets all criteria, Janis and Mann (1977, p. 12) characterize this orientation in arriving at a choice as ''vigilant information processing.'' The sense of this is to provide a way of viewing the process on a rough scalar basis, providing a sort of checklist for assessing the likelihood of an optimal decision.

For convenience sake and for general discussion in the rest of the chapter, we divide these criteria into five process steps.

- problem: how it is perceived;
- alternatives: exploring possible solutions;
- information: evaluating the alternatives;
- decision: choosing among the alternatives;
- implementation: getting things done.

Because these are listed in linear fashion does not necessarily mean, as will be seen, that they are perceived in reality as recognizable steps by decision makers. The assumptions here, of course, are that managers who make decisions and implement those decisions consciously perform these activities and reflect on the steps. The opposite is probably closer to reality (Kotter, 1982). This will be commented on below. To overtly analyze this process might have unforeseen, indeed, unhappy effects on the performance of the subjects.

The centipede was happy quite
Until a toad in fun
Said, "Pray which leg goes after which?"
That worked her mind to such a pitch,
She lay distracted in a ditch,
Considering how to run.[1]

The perceived importance of the problem and the resulting decision making will affect the amount of time, energy, and resources that will be committed to the process. How much will be invested (cost) in seeking some satisfactory level of quality of solution (benefit)? This itself is part of the decision process and will influence the amount, type, and provenance of the information to be acquired and processed.

LEVEL AND NATURE OF DECISIONS

Our principal concern here is to provide a means of classifying decisions so that we can discuss in useful ways the value-added processes of information systems and how those processes benefit (or do not benefit) decision making. In terms of organizational function, Anthony (1965) posits three categories: operational control; management control; and strategic planning. Though suggestive, this categorization does not appear especially useful. First, it tends to group people in hierarchical fashion by their assigned function. Second, the model does not provide sufficient insight into the roles of information in decision processes. Third, the three levels do not account for the information roles that people play. To be sure, by extension the three levels can be interpreted as one goes up the ladder to mean more complexity, less routine, and increased risk, each of which can be translated into information terms. But the model says nothing about the nature of the problems faced, the decisions required, nor the information necessary.

Simon (1977) has presented a typology of decisions as programmed and nonprogrammed, which is more appropriate to the context here. This classification relates directly to the discussion in Chapter Three on problem dimensions, and specifically to the discussion of well-structured and ill-structured problems. These are essentially exchangeable terms. Programmed (well-structured) decisions are routine, repetitive, and can be based pretty much on rules, standard operating procedures, and simple computational methods. The level, amount, and scope of information can in general be anticipated. Information needs are routine and well defined, for the most part quantitative or specifically factual. Thresholds, the points where the decision mode moves toward the nonroutine and judgmental, can be more easily identified and affected by a different set of rules. Conventional accounting, inventory, and production control systems are examples of systems that provide information in programmable situations. They are essentially transaction based, and such transactions can be counted, measured, or otherwise quantified.

[1] Mrs. Edward Craster, *Pinafore Poems*. (1871). As quoted by Starr, 1971; p. 71.

It is when we begin to employ these routine approaches to other types of situations, on the assumption that they are predictable and programmable in the same way, that trouble develops. Service operations, for example, are a contrast to the more formal and quantitative activities of manufacturing and finance. In such operations information will tend to be qualitative, though it may be routine. Service operations, such as complaint departments, ambulance dispatch services, and even counseling services, are often treated as routine and programmable. Service operations, however, are dependent on nonquantifiable and, sometimes, more ambiguous information, often needing interpretation and judgment to ascertain what kind of response is required. Though in many cases responses can be routine, thresholds are harder to define and, when breached, the form and nature of the response becomes more uncertain, where other than programmed response may be required. The determination of the threshold between programmable and nonprogrammable decisions has implications for the type, variety, and acceptability of information in those systems supporting those decisions. In our drive toward efficiency, we may tend to make overly ambitious attempts to make routine that which is not routine, principally because the information requirements have not been carefully analyzed, nor have the costs and benefits to recipients of the services been fully considered.

This discussion of service operations and routine decisions has been made principally to emphasize the need to look at the routine/nonroutine dichotomy with care. Indeed it may be necessary to construct a different frame of reference for information processes and decision making in service operations. Decision-making literature has been primarily concerned with corporate, military, organizational, and, sometimes, personal situations where structure and decisive behavior are assumed, and where costs and benefits, even if uncertain, are apparent as something to be dealt with. This concern has something to do with the way we view information and its role as a valuable resource in decision processes. It is, however, not the intent of this author to pursue this interesting, indeed significant, question further. It has been mentioned principally to emphasize caution when attempting to routinize a decision process.

As we move from programmable to nonprogrammable decisions, one major characteristic is the rise in the level of uncertainty and the risk involved in making decisions. The two words—"risk" and "uncertainty"—are frequently used in combination, as though they were synonymous. For clarity and better insight, it is worth distinguishing between the two. "Uncertainty" implies a lack of any knowledge of or control over the outcome of a decision or an action. It implies an inability to usefully distinguish potential benefits and probable costs. In common parlance, such a decision may be based on a "guesstimate," that it is made "off the top of the head," that you "fly by the seat of your pants." It is interesting that our culture has spawned so many idioms to describe uncertainty, and this may tell us more about our culture than we care to hear. To be sure, some situations requiring decision may indeed be highly uncertain, and will remain so, with decision resting on the sensitivity and general problem-solving experience of the decision maker.

Though such contexts will not disappear, it is possible by risk assessment to get better control over some of the variables, and begin to place rough values on alternatives and likelihoods. Such a process will also define better the kind and characteristics of the information needed.

This is risk assessment and as Donald Schon points out "a corporation cannot operate in uncertainty, but it is beautifully equipped to handle risk. It is precisely an organization designed to uncover, analyze, evaluate, and operate on risks."[2] Risk assessment is essentially the reasoned application of odds or probabilities of the correctness of a particular hypothesis or assumption. An experienced gambler, in an honest blackjack game, has a good sense of what the odds are in getting a good card in the next draw. He or she has assessed the risks of betting on the next card. Without a sense of those odds, a gambler is operating in an uncertain situation and probably should not be playing for very high stakes.

One of the major areas of uncertainty for the modern corporation is in research and development, where investment of resources may be very high and probability of return on investment very uncertain at inception. A chairman of a major corporation has stated that "decisions that determine what research we do and don't do and what our priorities are constitute the most complex and difficult decisions general management faces" (Roussel, 1983; p. 154). This problem is exacerbated by the inability of management to communicate with research personnel. The same barrier seems to be true of the relationship between management and information systems/computer personnel. The languages are different; the assumptions about benefits and costs are different; and attitudes toward uncertainty on the part of the research scientist and computer personnel are almost cavalier. The process of converting uncertainty to risk, however, is a major function of any organization and is a fundamental process in the making of consequential and nonprogrammable decisions.

Because of the large areas of uncertainty in research and development, where large sums of money need to be committed for a number of years before full results are known, it is important to have a complete diagnosis of the problem and the development of feasible steps where review can take place and new decisions made. This requires an examination of scientific assumptions, hypotheses, and theories whose approximate correctness is critical to success. Each of these has its own level of uncertainty, which with skill and careful analysis can be converted to risk probabilities. Because these problems are so complex and the potential investment is so large, it is necessary to break the process into a series of plateaus, where progress can be reviewed and new areas of uncertainty isolated and risk probabilities approximated. For example, if, under conditions A, x is true, then y is likely to happen. In this case it is necessary to place a probability on the truth of x under conditions A, and indeed on how stable the variables of condition A are. Then, given that probability, what is the likelihood of y happening. Roussel (1983) has

---

[2] Donald A. Schon. (1966, November) The fear of innovation. *International Science and Technology*. As quoted in Roussel, 1983; p. 155.

an excellent brief description of this process. He describes a hypothetical case of a large chemical company faced with the opportunity to develop a bacteria-based nitrogen-fixation process for farming which could replace the application of chemical forms of nitrogen with considerable economic and social benefit. The investment would be large and the commitment of personnel considerable; but, if successful, it would be profitable and there would be visible social gains.

Managers who make the commitment in cases like these may be two or three removes from the actual decision processes by the bench scientist, which is where the basic alternatives will be considered and decided upon. Managers obviously cannot operate at this level. In fact they probably do not have—and cannot have—intimate knowledge and control over the variables. They can, however, with effort and some luck, know the right questions to ask. Managers are dependent on the experience and candid estimates of probabilities by scientists closer to the problem. This dependence on technical expertise (i.e., information) and the distance from the actual problem is representative of very complex and important types of decision making and problems of power diffusion in both public and private organizations (Sabatier, 1978; Moore, 1981).

INFORMATION FOR DECISION MAKING

Management is usually defined in the literature as those activities concerned with the efficient and effective acquisition and allocation of resources of an organization so that the objectives of that organization can be accomplished. This bland sort of description may conceal more than it reveals. The definition really describes but one end of the spectrum of management activities. Decisions associated with the allocation of resources will tend to be nonprogrammable, though they may be supported by inventory, optimization, and forecasting models, as well as other useful simulations. At this end of the spectrum, managers are concerned with control in a short-term context, three to six months or less. Emerging management information systems, as they move beyond straight transactions systems, and decision support systems are designed to provide assistance at this managerial level. The acquisition and allocation of resources takes place, however, within the constraints of organizational plans and strategies, and depend a great deal on the skill of a manager to work with and through people. Information in this context comes in many shapes and forms, both formal and informal.

Kotter (1982), in his study of successful executives, points out that such managers spend time early upon assuming their position in (a) establishing an agenda for future action (more formally a set of objectives) and (b) building a network of cooperative relationships among people who can help them in implementing that agenda, and who may be sources of useful information.

> Effective executives develop agendas that are made up of loosely connected goals and plans that address their long-, medium-, and short-term responsibilities. The agendas usually address a broad range of financial, product/market, and organizational issues. They include both vague and specific items. (Kotter, 1982; p. 160)

These agendas are where the major decisions are made, for they (the agenda items), despite their probable shifts over time, establish the strategies, plans, and criteria governing managerial actions in the future.

Though agenda setting may have similarities with what is called "strategic planning," there are significant differences, and these differences frequently have to do with how information is perceived. Managers—the persons who "gets things done"—will make use of their extensive network, not only to gather information, but to "solve" the problem. Information is perceived as a means of achieving an agenda: It is both informing and instrumental. It is frequently verbal and informal. Strategic planners, on the other hand, see information as support for a decision. They are not action oriented, bur rather are oriented toward establishing a frame of reference for decision. The information is not instrumental; rather its function is to inform, to help others make decisions. Information is acquired and is cumulative. It is usually formal, whether on paper or in computer storage.

Management is concerned with getting things done by working with other people. The best managers "ask, encourage, cajole, praise, reward, demand, manipulate, and generally motivate others with great skill in face-to-face situations" (Kotter, 1982; p. 163). Information, frequently highly informal and unstructured, is but a frame of reference in that process. As Mintzberg, Kotter, and others have recognized, "managers strongly favor verbal media," and from their standpoint "the strategic data bank of an organization is not in the memory of its computers but in the minds of its managers" (Mintzberg, 1975; p. 52). Information exchange is continuous and crucial, but, in any conventional terms, it is unstructured, except in the mind of the manager. Information derived from usual information systems is probably minimal and may frequently be secondhand. Formal information systems serve principally to maintain overall cognizance of operations and to provide an early warning signal of problems—though in the latter case, informal channels are probably faster but not as precise. There probably is a continual need for information specifically defined and interpreted to meet needs at a particular moment. However, as direct assistance for a manager's work, information systems may well "hinder effective performance."

> They impose a rigid "number crunching" requirement on GMs (General Managers) that often does not require much strategic or long-range thinking in agenda setting and which can make network building and maintenance needlessly difficult by creating unnecessary stress among people. Indeed, some systems seem to do nothing but generate paper, often a lot of it, and distract executives from doing those things that are really important. (Kotter, 1982; p. 167)

High level decisions which entail major commitment of resources or a major shift in direction by the organization are strategic decisions, important and of consequence. These are nonprogrammable decisions. The situations which require decision are novel, complex, and open ended. As Mintzberg and his associates point out: "This is not decision making under *uncertainty* of the textbook, where alternatives are given even if their consequences are not, but decision making under *ambiguity,* where almost nothing is given or easily determined" (Mintzberg, Raisinghani, & Theoret, 1976; p. 251). Alternatives are neither readily apparent nor clear cut, and they may undergo subtle change of interpretation as new information or new players make their impact. However, Mintzberg and his associates, in their study of 25 discrete strategic decisions and their review of a rather sparse literature, argue that, though the decision process may be very complex, it does not necessarily have to be unstructured. The decision processes analyzed lasted for periods of less than a year to more than four years. They tentatively posit three phases in the strategic decision process, which includes seven routines (Mintzberg, Raisinghani, & Theoret, 1976; pp. 252–260).

Identification Phase

Recognition: of problems, opportunity, or crisis.
Diagnosis: dimensions of the problem; organizing known data; establishing need for new data.

Development Phase

Search routine: to find ready-made solutions.
Design routine: to develop custom-made solutions or to modify ready-made ones.

Selection Phase

Screen routine: eliminating what is infeasible; reducing noise.
Evaluation–choice routine: evaluating consequences of different alternatives, and choosing among them.
Authorization: necessary when the decision maker does not have authority to commit organization.

The total process, according to Mintzberg and his associates, was underlain by three supporting activities. The first is decision control, which though informal and flexible, appeared in such forms as timetables, decision on who would do certain things in the process, the size of commitment in resources to be made to the decision process, and control over meetings, participation, and public announcements. The second major pervasive activity was communication, which dominated every phase of the process. This included such things as developing a data base, focusing on special purpose information, either through search or research, and developing and organizing evaluation information on alternatives. Mintzberg and his associates isolated four types of search.

- memory search, i.e., of organizational resources;
- passive search, i.e., serendipity, "solutions looking for problems";
- trap search, i.e., letting specific persons such as a supplier, know that one is looking for alternatives;
- active search, i.e., direct seeking for alternatives, implying comprehensive search.

These searches took place for the most part through informal, verbal channels of communication, *not* through formal information systems of any type. The third factor underlying the process was political. Influence, power, consensus, and relative position seemed to be significant factors in the total decision-making process.

INFORMATION VALUES IN DECISION CONTEXTS

It is necessary here for clarity sake to reiterate a caution made earlier about the use of the term "value." Management literature and decision models generally use the concept, "value of information," as one based on cost calculations of the assumed difference in having or not having the information, such as a marketing study. As one management scientist defines it:

> The *value of information* is equal to the difference between the net expected payoff from the decision made without the information and the net expected payoff from the decision made with the information. (Huber, 1980; p. 127)

Such a "value" is determined by estimating probabilities and costs of the alternatives at various stages of a decision process, and answers the question: Is the utility of knowing a particular piece of information worth the cost of gathering that information? It is worth comment that the answer to that question may be influenced, indeed prejudiced, because of poor experiences in the past with information systems, because of the perceived irrelevance of past information provided, and consequent lack of trust in the reliability of such systems.

Though we have an interest in the answer to the question posed above, the real concern of the value-added approach is to seek ways of assuring that the system, however defined, does indeed deliver data and information of value to the decision process. In the value-added approach, the following question is asked: What are the attributes of information useful in decision making in a particular context and what are the enhancing processes of the systems that deliver that information? In first person terms: What indeed am I getting for my investment that will be of use in making my decision? What level of quality, validity, and currency will the system provide? How will the information be organized and displayed so that it will be easy to use? Will the data be consistent and comparable with related data? How relevant will the information be to the kind of problem or decision faced? Why indeed should I use the system? Once it is settled that an information search is necessary, then other criteria become the controlling parameters: ease of use, relevance, quality, and closeness to the problem. Decisions based on poor, invalid, out-of-date, and inappropriate information are legion. Our concern is to begin to find out what it takes to provide useful information.

From this review can we draw some tentative conclusions concerning the kinds of information value that decision makers find useful? It does seem likely that this is possible, as long as we understand that the values are suggestive and would need empirical verification. They seem to fit what we know about the decision-making process, both intuitively and factually. We need first, however, to recall the earlier discussion of programmable and nonprogrammable decision processes.

Programmable Decisions

Programmable decisions are routine: They are repetitive and the criteria for decision are known and predictable in most cases. They are frequently dependent on simple computational methods. There are well-defined information channels and structures: management, financial, and production information systems generally satisfy these decision needs. These are operating and control decisions concerned principally with monitoring current processes to detect differences with predetermined estimates of desired performance. When differences between actual and desired performance become significant, however defined, then a nonprogrammable problem may be generated that requires nonconventional information support. Programmable decisions would seem to require the following value added properties in the information deemed useful.

- *Formatting:* Comparable data need to be displayed in familiar ways over time so that the user does not waste energy in using the reports.
- *Physical accessibility:* Relevant data need to be available; if they are not easily accessible, they will tend not to be used.
- *Precision:* One must be able to obtain the kind of data needed in a particular situation. This is easier said than done, because data structures have in the past been derived from and have accommodated particular applications. Hence it is difficult to break out new configurations of data for different orders of problems.
- *Accuracy:* Data input, whether human or automatic, must correctly transcribe from one form of data to another; software providing any computation must be accurate models of applicable processes, understandable to the user.
- *Currency* of data will vary, depending on the particular need and context. In an airline reservation system, data must be in real time; other situations may be less dependent on real time information, but, nevertheless, have a need for a certain level of currency.
- *Reliability* is basically the level of trust decision makers feel they can place in an information system's consistency, accuracy, and other intangible values they deem of use.
- *Validity:* are the data in the system indeed good representations of reality? If not—and this may be the case of proxy measurement—why is this so and what adjustments in interpretation are necessary? Information people seem to fudge on this question of validity, as though afraid to admit that the data provided may not be quite what it seems. This is exacerbated by the fact that managers expect more from information systems than may actually be there. A case of chicken or egg!
- *Response speed* depends a great deal on the individual user and on the context of the decision. One might suspect, however, that the quicker a system can respond to an inquiry or a need the more useful the delivered data will be. In control situations speed of response may be of particular value. There is obviously a trade-off in benefits and costs here, more apparent here than perhaps with other values.

No one person handles only programmable or nonprogrammable decisions all the time. The higher one goes in the organization, however, the more likely a person is faced with unstructured problems and with nonroutine information needs. Indeed if such is not the case, it may be that that manager is a prime example of the operation of the Peter Principle[3] and should be demoted.

Nonprogrammable Decisions

Managers whose position and responsibilities require decisions of the nonprogrammable type will tend to reflect quite different criteria for judging the value of information and of the modes of delivery. This is due to the uniqueness of the problems faced, the lack of predictable structure, and the heuristic techniques needed for solving the problem, that is, making a decision. Much of the information input for such decisions is informal and verbal. This is so not only because managers may be intuitively more comfortable with verbal information, but also because formal information systems for the most part can only respond to structured and formal requests. There are some exceptions to that statement, as will be apparent below. The following discussion, substantiated in part by the studies reviewed above as well as by other studies, is meant to be suggestive of the nature of the criteria which affect the value of information in nonprogrammable decision contexts. In many cases, when applied to present formal information systems, they reveal reasons why such systems are inconsequential or even impediments to decision making. Though only suggestive, the values listed below may indicate some useful areas of concern, even opportunity, in the development of more responsive information systems. It is worth comment here that none of these values exists in isolation. They are interconnected and intertwined in ways we are not entirely clear about. However, empirical analysis may indicate that some are more important than others in a given type of context.

Interfacing, especially *mediation,* may be of particular importance for managers using, for example, certain kinds of modeling and simulation software. Will the system negotiate with the manager in determining what program would be best for his or her purposes? Or, will the system provide sufficiently detailed descriptive information in a mediating mode so that the manager can decide on the appropriateness of the applications package for the problem? This may indeed be a human interface, and the complexity or hassle of using it may inhibit use of the system. In this regard, it would be wise to assume that most decision makers are relatively infrequent users of the formal system; therefore the interfacing mediation might have a high value.

Physical accessibility may not be particularly important for unstructured decision making, becuse too many other information traits, discussed below, may be more critical. That is to say, putting a terminal on an executive's desk is not very useful

---

[3] "In a hierarchy every employee tends to rise to his level of incompetence." From J.J. Peter and R. Hull. (1969). *The Peter principle*. New York: Morrow, 1969.

if the information and software available are not directly relevant to the executive's concerns, or if there is too much noise in the system.

Noise reduction, as one might suspect, has some peculiar properties when it is discussed in the context of decision making. Yes, we all wish to reduce that excess of seemingly irrelevant information when we are in the process of deciding a course of action. Yet, as has been discussed above, we are not sure if we have enough information— "Have I covered all the bases?"—to make the best decision or even a satisficing decision. Hence we encourage overload—noise. We simply do not know at what stage we have enough information. An assumption in the decision-making literature implies that there is only one decision in process at any one time. As any manager or decision maker knows, there are several, if not many, problems calling for attention at any one time. Information gathered for one decision may have an oblique impact on another. Having said all this, however, should not deflect the major objective of this criterion: to reduce the amount of irrelevant information the system delivers to a decision maker. Formal information systems of any type have tended to place more emphasis on expanding the amount of information and data available, rather than reducing the amount. Supplying information is easier than withholding, because in the latter case hard choices need to be made. Systems designers will need to concentrate more effort in providing the means whereby managers can negotiate easily, in other words, "play" with the amount of information they think are needed in any given situation. This may be part of the process of developing information literacy, i.e., raising the level of managerial awareness of the role and kinds of information available in making decisions. As managers become more sophisticated, not just in using the technology, but about their own decision processes, the more rigor (and less noise) they will demand of the system. This means that *selectivity* and *precision* become especially important added values. As was discussed in Chapter Three such values are based not only on subject matter but on the dimensions of the particular problem.

The *quality* of data seems to be a criterion to which managers have not paid sufficient attention. Or perhaps better said, they are ill served by their failure to realize the importance of data quality, even though they may have been burnt in the past by poor data. The tendency in such situations is to pass it off as a unique occurrence. There are several reasons for this. First, information labeled fact or data presented in numerical form seems to be accepted as high quality by its very existence as fact or number. These give a magical cloak of quality which when examined carefully may not be deserved. Related to this is the lack of concern with the conditions surrounding the collection of the data: assumptions made, qualifications necessary in interpretation, comparability of longitudinal data (especially a problem with economic data). Managers should—and will as they become more information literate—insist that some indication of data validity and the conditions of provenance exist in the system. It is likely that little will be done from the systems side without managerial recognition of the importance of data quality and consequent pressure for its inclusion in the system.

The lack of *adaptability* in formal systems to the specific problem and decision needs is a primary reason why managers turn to informal and personal information sources. *Closeness to the problem* would appear to be a key factor in determining the usefulness of information in the decision-making process. That is to say, sensitivity to political nuance and to the style of the manager, as well as to the contextual specifics of the particular problem, are key factors in judging the value of information. One of the major (though probably unconscious) reasons for the growth of knowledge centers and their placement near the top of the modern organization is to have access to expert knowledge in the general proximity and organizational level at which decisions are made. These knowledge centers may indeed be the true users and beneficiaries of the more formal types of information systems such as decision support systems and library/information centers.

Systems, as presently conceived, despite the soubriquet ''user friendly,'' seem to have very little to do with real decision concerns and processes. They are support for staff who recommend decisions, but don't make them. This is a critical difference, and it should have an effect on how systems are perceived and defined. If this is indeed the case, then the concern of formal information systems should be not with decision making, but with decision formation. Legislative information services such as the Congressional Research Service have as their principal concern the members of Congress, but their major users and audience are the staff, those who filter, repackage, and interpret information for committees and individual members. CRS pays a great deal of attention to those staffs.

THE FORMAL PROCESSES OF INFORMATION PROVISION

The following discussion is written in full cognizance that a great deal of significant information critically relevant to decision making is acquired through highly informal channels. Such channels have existed since human beings first began to make choices affecting a group. Such informal means exist today because they still satisfy critical functions. They will take a long time to replace, if indeed that ever becomes the case (Keen, 1981). Our formal information systems are only a few centuries old, and computer-based systems but a decade or two. Nevertheless, our concern in this section is with formal information systems of the type discussed in Chapters Three, Five, Six, and Seven, which add value to items being processed. These are the formal information resources of an organization and can be divided into four discrete categories.

- data processing operations,
- office information resources,
- information centers and libraries,
- knowledge centers.

These are not mutually exclusive; rather they represent a convenient division in information terms, and they are recognizable organizational units. There is overlap among them. Indeed, the first one (data processing operations) because of its technologies, will have an increasing effect on the others. The listing also represents a sort of rough linear continuum from hard data to soft data.

Data Processing Operations

In the large organization these operations are used principally in four areas. This division into four classes is used primarily as a means to identify outputs. The first is financial data which includes sales, distribution, accounting, and budget. The second is production data including inventory, manufacturing, parts, materials, and quality control. The third class are scientific and engineering data, including materials testing. The fourth class are the simulation processes, including such processes as computer-aided design and incipient decision support systems. Input data for these four systems are, almost exclusively, internally generated and, for the most part, are quantitative in nature.

The data in the first two represent what should be the organization's data base. In most cases truly comprehensive and usable data bases do not exist (Martin, 1981; pp. 3–19). Reasons for this state have been alluded to before. The principal reasons are historical and are important because assumptions and attitudes toward data held many years ago have determined what our data bases look like today. Data was gathered by specific departments, for example, production, sales, accounting, and personnel, for their own use. These departments ''owned'' the data in the sense that they were the collectors, designers, and users. In many cases the data were organized for batch use, for example, the weekly accounting report, the daily production or sales record, the biweekly salary check. Data structures, data definitions, and programs were established and controlled by these particular applications. Requests for use by other departments or suggested changes in content and format were filtered through the owning department; if new applications were generated the results were frequently inappropriate without extensive further manual work. The files of one department were discrete. There was very little attempt to standardize data across different files. In fact, the same data—or almost the same data—may be collected and owned by different departments, but labeled differently, structured differently, and have different rates of updating. The notorious reluctance of programmers to document their work has made it extremely difficult to understand complex progrms. This is especially true where several programmers may have contributed to a program at various times, and where several of those programmers are no longer with the organization and have left only a few confusing records of their work.

These are major problems in developing an organizationwide data base independent of the programs that use them, and in creating logical and comparable data structures necessary for the newer combinations of information being requested by a wider range of end users. Both the maintenance of current systems and the changeover to such a data ''reservoir'' are expensive. Martin points out that in some installations, 80% of the programming budget is spent on maintaining or modifying past programs and data (Martin, 1981; p. 16). King and Kraemer cite an extreme case in a military system "in which the cost of development was approximately $75 per line of code but the cost of maintaining the system over its usable life was about $4,000 per line of code" (King and Kraemer, 1981; p. 103).

More concern will need to be focused on the roles of the outputs of management information systems: what can be done to make the output more useful, that is, what values can be added to the data base? As we have noted, the outputs of MIS seem to have very little to do with nonprogrammable decision making, but are useful, indeed essential, in control and monitoring processes. To play a larger role here will require more sophisticated approaches to the relationship of MIS to the decision process (Hansen, McKell, & Heitger). The data processing profession up to now has been dependent on slogans and various forms of myth. It is now necessary to understand the role and effect of information. It is unfortunately the case that most approaches to information support for decision making are usually based on the assumption that computer-based systems provide (or in the near future will provide) all the relevant information for the organization, including planning and decision making. They essentially insist that computer-based systems *are* the information-providing systems of the organization. This is an unfortunate assumption, for not only is it not true, but if it were actually the basis for action, it would probably be disastrous for the well-being of that organization.

This should not be misunderstood. Computer-based systems are a part of the information resources of the modern organization, but they are only one part. They are excellent for routine transaction systems. The present corporation in all its complexity could probably not exist without such systems. More sophisticated attempts, however, to provide information for less well-structured management operations are for the most part still experimental—and will remain so for some time. To be sure, computer-based systems will be able to provide a variety of information in the variety of forms; but almost without exception, such information will be unusable in the form in which it is delivered. To go beyond this—to make the information usable—requires human beings who will filter, delete, analyze, and combine the data delivered by the system with noncomputable information in order to make sense out of it.

Office Information Resource

This is the traditional information resource which every organization has had since it was founded. Though the systems are being altered by technologies, such as word processing systems and various forms of office automation, the resource and its role in the corporation will remain basically the same in the future. There are six categories in this resource.

1. *Messages* into and out of the organization. Traditionally these have been written responses to external requests, or correspondence. This category is expanding to include memos or more direct records of telephone conversations, and human-to-human computer messages through information exchange networks.

2. *Internal memoranda* and correspondence, nontechnical reports, aggregated reports, newsletters, minutes of meetings, etc.

3. *Standard operating procedures:* the policies and formal routine processes that the organization has collected and codified over time as a means to assure that routine decision making at all levels will conform generally to accepted and tested patterns.

4. *Personnel records* of all persons associated with the organization, including evaluations, and salaries.

5. *Communication systems:* These are included here because of their impact on office systems, especially their facilitative nature. Included here are phone, facsimile, telecommunications, and internal mail systems used to move messages into, within, and out of the organization.

6. *Printing, publishing, and copying systems.*

All of these systems are natural language based. They are widely scattered. That is to say, the resources are localized by office or department. They frequently have security constraints, that is, access must be controlled. There are two primary concerns here: file organization for future retrieval, and the development and implementation of a records management program. In some instances these files may be very large and their maintenance may be required for tax, regulatory, and possible litigation purposes. This resource, by the way, is the formal memory of the organization: what has happened; how it operates; and how it is related to the outside world.

Generally the office has been looked upon as a place where information is produced, stored, acted upon, and processed in a variety of ways. This is the conventional view of the office. It is not wrong; it is merely incomplete. An office is also, and more importantly, a place where decisions which control that department or, indeed, the total organization are formulated and made where planning for the future takes place, where the progress of the unit and its personnel are evaluated, and where choices are made. The only function of an office, including its systems and resources, is to support those decision processes and to provide the trigger for ongoing everyday activities. Sometimes this important role tends to get lost in the concern for efficient records management.

Present office automation systems are being imposed on top of manual systems, such as correspondence and filing systems, that have taken 300 years to evolve, and were designed for a much lower rate of information messages. This means that the faults existing in the older systems will not only be frozen in, but will probably be magnified. It is the secretarial and clerical systems that are being automated with very little attention paid to the managerial work for which the office exists. Up to now office information systems have essentially been content driven, that is, the records themselves have dictated how they will be stored and retrieved. With a technology-driven system the objective will be to design a "paperless office," rather than a decision support and communication system. Again, a slogan seems to dictate design. Its purpose should be the improvement of managerial effectiveness, rather than just the improvement of secretarial and managerial efficiency. The realization of the potential for such improvement will be dependent on several factors:

- the level of understanding of the office as an information processing, value-adding activity;
- the degree of imaginative planning invested in the change;
- the willingness and ability to make informed decisions early as to file retention, retrieval mechanisms, indexing techniques, and so forth.

The critical factor in this process will be the ability and willingness of management to devote time and decision energy to careful planning and, for some initial period, to ongoing evaluation and operational testing. By no means must management relinquish complete design to technicians, programmers, or systems analysts. Managers must constantly be reminded that all office processes, manual or automated, are designed and operated to support organizational goals as reflected in their offices and in the planning and decision making within their purview. The systems are designed for the manager's use. To miss this point in making a changeover to word processing systems will adversely affect the hoped-for improvement in true productivity.

Information Centers and Libraries

This class of information resource and support systems represents the principal formal link between the organization and formal external information sources. Elements of this resource may also handle such internal documents as technical reports, laboratory noteboks, engineering drawings, and audio and videotapes. These centers may range from a formal collection of books and periodicals, as in a conventional library, to dynamic online access to alpha–numeric data bases anywhere in the world. Some centers may acquire data from outside sources and analyze, evaluate, and repackage that data for internal corporate use. General Electric's Materials Information Service, discussed in Chapter Seven, is an example of this type of system, servicing GE units throughout the world with internally developed handbooks, product specifications, materials properties data, and short courses. All of these various kinds of centers serve many different information functions with a wide range of outputs. Information centers and libraries are prime examples of the value-adding processes in information handling activities.

Their role in the decision process, like decision support systems, seems to be at the decision formulation stage where alternatives are examined and evaluated. In contrast to DSS, however, is that there is usually a human interface between user and system. The skill and the extent to which that human expertise operates is essentially a measure of the system's adaptability to the user's situation.

There are three types of library/information centers, classified by the level of human expertise necessary to provide their output. At one end is the *conventional library* which acquires, organizes, and circulates information packages. In this case, the output is basically the same as the input, nothing or very little is done to alter the packages in the system. At the other end of the spectrum are the *information analysis centers,* such as EMPIS of the General Electric Company. In between are a variety of services which provide varying degrees of human filtering between data input into the system and output to the customer, which can be labeled "information services.'' These were discussed extensively in Chapters Five, Six, and Seven. Basically the level of value added will be dependent on the level and quality of human input.

Knowledge Centers

Knowledge centers, though usually not perceived as information systems, are perhaps the most important source for analyzed and evaluated information to those in top management positions, with more input to major decision making than any other information resource. These were discussed in Chapter Seven, with special attention paid to the strategic planning function. In that chapter, attention was focused on the information analysis activities of these centers. The present chapter extends those activities to the decision process. As has been pointed out, the staff of the knowledge center do not make decisions in the organizational sense; rather they formulate, evaluate, and recommend choices of action to those who do make decisions. They may be the real but unrecognized beneficiaries of the data processing systems and library/information centers. In this sense, they are the intermediaries between system and decision maker in the decision process. On one side, they are an extension of the other formal information systems. On the other hand, they interpret and reflect managerial needs to the system. Their role of information intermediary is a critical one in the decision process.

The values that knowledge centers add to information in the decision process are considerable. Those values are principally centered around the processes of adapting the information to the precise needs of the problem and to the style and perspective of the decision maker. These are prime values at the end of the process and perform things that cannot be done at present by any other nonhuman system. The current excitement for so-called expert systems is a kind of response to this need (Gevarter, 1983; Waldrop, 1984). In this author's opinion, however, while the research on expert systems will reveal many interesting and useful things about human information processing, it will be a long time before they replace the sensitive adaptation to specific context that is the prime value of good information analysts and knowledge experts. To assume that they will is a mistaken application of the technological solution to something that humans do better. By the end of the century, such expert systems may be able to give significant support to the process of formulating a decision, but not in making the decision in the context of political interest, personal ambition, or personal and system weaknesses and biases (Feldman & March, 1981; 172–174; Churchman, 1975). The knowledge gained in this research will help in the design of better information systems. The propensity, however, in our culture to oversell and to delude ourselves with technological fixes may undercut the utility of the knowledge gained, because we expect more than can in fact be delivered.

SUMMARY

In organizational terms, there are several observations which may help to clarify the role of information and its provision in the decision process.

1. We can say that it appears that present information systems do not specifically serve decision makers per se, but rather serve the staffs of knowledge experts who formulate and recommend decision. This is a two-step process. More attention should be paid to the role of the knowledge center in the decision process and to the kinds of useful information support they need.

2. Information in all its forms is a major investment of the organization, in some cases perhaps the largest investment. Yet, very little attention has been paid to the idea of return on that investment. In part this is because the costs of information, its systems, packages, staff, expertise, have been hidden throughout the organization. Information processes and the support systems have been looked upon as overhead and, as Peter Drucker points out, ''the very term (overhead) reeks of moral disapproval'' (Drucker, 1974; p. 69), and consequently an activity that should be shunned as ''nonproductive.'' This disapproval is the result of three factors and illustrates directly our failure to consider the information context:

- our insistence that muscle labor is the only kind of productive labor;
- our inability to perceive many functions and activities, such as the office, as information-intensive processes related to managerial performance;
- our failure to see information products, systems, and services as resources that can be controlled and managed productively.

3. To help to overcome these impediments to the productive use of information, we need to provide a structured way of looking at information processes in an organization. This has come to be known as Information Resources Management (IRM). The basic IRM approach can be stated in capsule form as follows:

> *Who* acquires, organizes, and transmits *what information?*
> By *what means?*
> At *what cost?*
> To *whom?*
> To *what effect?*

Conventionally, only the first three questions have been included in any discussion of the management of information resources. This is no longer enough. Though it may be difficult, even messy, it is necessary to ask the last two questions, and develop a practical framework for providing some kinds of answers:

> To whom?
> To what effect?

Without these, the exercise is meaningless, and any data generated will merely strengthen current information overload problems, increasing the costs of information and, more than likely, reducing the benefits. The problem is not just containing costs, but also deciding what kinds of information and what kinds of information support and delivery systems are necessary for the well-being of an organization.

The ultimate goal of the IRM process is to put in place mechanisms to enable the organization to acquire or produce, and transfer, at minimum cost, data and information of sufficient quality, accuracy, and timeliness, necessary to support organizational goals. If this is thought to be an appropriate goal, then the organization

- must recognize that information is not a free good;
- that it is, rather, a costly and valuable asset;
- and that it must be treated with the same management concern as is done with such resources as money, personnel, and materials.

In a sense, because of the increasing importance of information processing and information provision in the modern organization, the IRM function can be a catalyst for strategic planning. The IRM planning process asks some rather fundamental questions about (a) organizational objectives and direction; (b) investment in expensive information resources, people, and systems; (c) accountability for information resources; (d) access to information; and (e) centralization and autonomy. The IRM approach may well have a profound effect on the distribution of power in the organization, because it deals with a fundamental resource—information. The process of change, however, is already happening as a result of information and its technologies. The IRM approach provides a means of understanding and managing that change.

Chapter Nine

INFORMATION AND PRODUCTIVITY

The last 10 years have seen a significant rise in public concern with productivity and its alleged decline in industry and government. What is usually said at this point is that one of the reasons for this drop in productivity is that there has been a massive shift in the type of employment in industrial countries, and especially in the United States, from the highly productive areas of manufacturing to the less productive areas of information handling and office work, that is, bureaucracy. Indeed, in the United States this has already happened, as we have previously discussed. United States Labor Department statistics are usually cited to the effect that industrial productivity rose by 85% during the 1970s, while there was only a 4% increase in productivity among white collar workers, despite large outlays for data processing equipment (Goldfield, 1980; p. 129). This does not necessarily mean that there has been a large drop in manufacturing jobs. Rather it means that most of the new jobs created in our society have been in the service area, especially in information handling—government agencies, company offices, education, research and development, and telecommunications. There is a very real concern whether our approaches to productivity are useful, indeed meaningful, when applied to information processes. It may be appropriate to ask if we are measuring the right things—whether productivity measures designed for an industrial society are appropriate for a society based on information and knowledge (Giuliano, 1979).

There are several aspects of this question which should be stated at the beginning. We are not so presumptuous as to think that we will be able to answer or even clarify them to any great extent, for they imply some fundamental questions about our society and the role of information in that society. What we hope to do, by exploring this domain, is to separate out and to discuss ways that the relationship between information and productivity might be fruitfully examined during the next few decades.

WHAT IS PRODUCTIVITY?

Productivity is usually defined as the ratio of what is produced to what is required to produce it, that is, output over input. Thus productivity can be increased by producing more output for the same input. Similarly the measure of productivity drops when input costs, such as labor, increase with no increase in the quantity of product. This, by the way, says nothing about the changes in quality of the product that may be the result of new information. The evolution of an information-based society, especially within the context of welfare economics, begins to impose a different set of standards and questions. It begins to ask questions about quality of product and about the level and quality of services, many of which are information based.

The question of how *output* is defined in information terms is a significant one and a portion of this chapter is concerned with it. Is it a product, such as a book, a software package, a weekly accounting sheet, a graphic terminal display? If this is the definition of output, then it can be handled in the same way economists count and measure baby diapers, carburetors, beer, and steel ingots. We suspect, because of the intellectual nature of the product, that it is more than a steel ingot. We, therefore, need to ask questions about its effect on the recipient of the information product. Indeed the value-added approach demands that these questions be asked, even though the answers may not be very clear. When the output of an information activity is a service—a consultant's customized report, a reference question answered, a computer program altered on request—then the problems of defining output become somewhat more complex.

The other part of the productivity equation—*input*—is important also, but of less concern in this chapter. Traditionally, input has been limited to labor and materials costs only, that is productivity has been defined as output over the costs of labor and materials necessary to produce that product. No account has been taken of capital investment, overhead, research and development, and other fundamental and frequently large costs of production. The costs of performing a service pose additional complications. Because of this failure to include all costs of input, productivity measurement tends to provide highly distorted views of reality.

We need to remind ourselves that productivity measures are made from the point of view of the producer not the consumer. This starting point tends to underplay the role of the consumer of information, an approach which affects the value-added model in curious ways. If we shift our focus from the producer of an output, be it product or service, to the consumer, then we begin to pose entirely different questions. As Milton Moss has pointed out in the NRC study on productivity: "Economic production is an input to consumption, leading to a broader outcome, which may be called welfare" (National Research Council, 1979; p. 276). Moss rightly insists, however, these two measures (the term is used loosely) should be kept separate: outputs and outcomes; producer efficiency and consumer (user) effectiveness. Because of the nature of information, this separation is sometimes difficult to achieve. However, we do need to make the attempt.

The accepted dichotomy between producer and consumer may indeed be breaking down entirely. The growth of what Alvin Toffler has labeled the "prosumer," the do-it-yourselfer, is based in good part on information products (Toffler, 1980; pp. 282–305). One of the major functions of the public library today is the provision of books on how to paint a house, how to repair a car or a refrigerator, how to detect symptoms of ill-health, how to grow vegetables, or how to program a personal computer. This whole new economy ("new" is perhaps a misnomer, for it may be the oldest economy of all) is not included in production or productivity figures. The US Bureau of Economic Analysis, which prepares GNP estimates, is now beginning to develop estimates of the value of home production (National Research Council, 1979; pp. 9–10). How soon this can become a part of productivity estimates is a moot point. One may suspect that it may be a long time.

The crux of the problem of productivity and its measurement in information contexts may lie in our failure to recognize information as a productive resource. To some extent this was briefly discussed in the last chapter. It is worth emphasizing here, however, that better control of the systems, people, and processes that produce and transfer information products and perform information services will provide a more solid base for measuring information productivity. Simply put, the profession needs a structure whereby it can isolate and intelligently discuss, if not measure, outputs that are comparable across time as well as across institutions and organizations. Despite our previous caveats, we need to be prepared to discuss outcomes—the result of information outputs on performance—as long as we separate the two.

INFORMATION OUTPUTS

The measurement, indeed the definition, of output in service industries (the information industry is usually included here in the national accounts) is difficult because, frequently, the outputs are highly intangible or qualitative in nature. Service industries have traditionally posed problems for economists and others concerned with questions of productivity measurements, for a variety of reasons:

1. the belief of some economists, notably Adam Smith, that only the primary and secondary sectors (agriculture and manufacturing) were "productive";
2. the difficulty of measuring service output;
3. the difficulty of obtaining data because of the heterogeneity of activities and of the small size of most firms in the service sector;
4. the difficulty of analyzing their (service firms) behavior. (Fuchs, 1969; 1–2)

Since the mid-1960s when V.R. Fuchs wrote these words, we have seen not only a significant rise in the service sector, but more specifically a marked increase in the information industries, and especially in our awareness of information and its provision. This is true not only of the separate industrial sectors, such as computers, telecommunications, data bases, and governments, but also of information operations internal to organizations, the quasi-firms discussed in Chapter Seven. As information activities become more pervasive, the problems of identifying, managing, and controlling the costs become critical. We tend to measure what is easily identifiable and available, where data can be collected easily, ignoring the aberrations. This works until these aberrations become significantly large and when they affect base measurements in rather gross ways. This is what is happening now. As long as information processes and their costs could be tucked away and made to disappear in various departmental budgets or absorbed as overhead, they were ignored. This can no longer be tolerated. Overhead costs have, in some cases, become larger than production costs: The costs are too apparent, too pervasive, and too big to be overlooked as mere aberration. The problem in organizations is that information costs cut across many departmental lines and might be generated both inside and outside the organization. Consequently both information professionals and cost accountants find it difficult to untangle the skein of threads.

We are not concerned in this chapter with national or macroeconomic measures of productivity or gross national product, except as they may reflect our concern with value-added processes. We concentrate at the organizational or firm level. In one sense, this chapter outlines an approach to making an audit of information resources based on output description. "Since outputs are produced by firms or organizations, when there are difficulties in conceptualizing and measuring outputs, it seems sensible to seek clarity at the firm level" (National Research Council, 1979; p. 255).

In order to maintain, indeed to establish the milieu and the means for managerial control over information productivity and information processes, we need to identify some significant questions on the road toward basic definitions.

- What can and what should be counted?
- How should it be counted?
- What variations in products and services exist and how can they be accounted for?
- How should special problems such as quality control and quality change over time be handled?

It does little good to say that it costs X dollars to produce an abstract of a scientific paper, to type a one-page letter, or to write Z lines of programming instructions. Beside some inherent difficulties in counting these things, such statements tell us very little unless we have some comparisons, either at some other time period, or in comparable output in some other operation. "Productivity measures exist largely to be compared—we are interested almost exclusively in productivity differences or productivity changes" (National Research Council, 1979; p. 22). Output then is understood as both external—something sold to clients outside the firm—and as internal products and services which may or may not be charged back to users within the firm. Examples of the latter are data- and word-processing centers, company libraries, and financial accounting systems.

Outputs of information systems are not only a necessary factor for the determination of productivity. When we look at total systems from input to processes to output *to use,* the concept of output becomes extremely important. Outputs become, in such a systemic view, a focal point where one can look backward into system processes, as well as forward to the client or customer or environment served. In the former case, looking backward into the system, output provides an approach to the analysis of system efficiencies. In the latter case, looking forward to the use of the information, output provides a base for the determination, quantitative or qualitative, of the usefulness of outputs—what effect that particular output has on the performance of a recipient or on an organization; outputs and outcomes.

In discussing outputs of information systems we need to remind ourselves constantly that an output is but a point, albeit an important one, in the flow of information in an organization. Identification of outputs is critical both for better control of information system costs, *and* for better awareness of system effectiveness.

Products and Services

Products and services are quite different, though the distinction may become blurred as information technologies intrude more into the information delivery process or as a service is provided with the commodity. Both are outputs. A product or a commodity is a tangible piece, and, in the case of an external product, may be bought and sold like any other commodity—breakfast cereals, automobiles, cosmetics, or gin. In information processes, such products are represented by things like a book, a software package, a computer display, a letter from a file, or a work order. Note that these examples are ordered from economic commodities that are frequently bought and sold on the open market (a book or a software package) to the information product within a system that acts principally as a trigger for action (a work order) or as input to a decision (a letter from a file). Regardless of context, however, they are all products of information systems.

Services, on the other hand, "are intangible, they are usually provided on demand, they are a performance rather than a product . . . they are nearly inseparable from their production" (Stankard, 1981; p. 5). Services generally use relatively little physical capital and are based principally on human interpreters or intervention between system and client. In the information areas these could range from low-level negotiations or queries in an online bibliographic retrieval system to the development of a new synthesis of information derived from already available data in response to a specific inquiry. The key element in services is the interposition of human expertise between client and system. The visions of highly automated office and information systems may be attractive and easy to predict, but such visions tend to oversimplify the complexity and variety of tasks performed in information systems and in offices. This complexity and variety require an active human component, and will for a long time.

Despite these reservations concerning indiscriminate use of technology, there is no doubt that information technologies have had, and will have, a profound effect on the form and delivery of information products and services. In some cases, they will alter or enhance a product through, for example, computer graphics, computer-aided design, word processing systems, and online handbooks and encyclopedias. At the same time, services can be enhanced by better backup processes providing, for example, diagnostic and laboratory data in hospitals, and similar support systems for information service providers. The unique attribute, however, of services is that they are basically dependent on human intervention. Ironically, these services in the information field have arisen, principally, because of the inability of the technology to filter, label, correlate, or to "deflect the system's garbage" (Heaton,

1977; p. x). Technology per se does nothing to make a better decision. Technology does nothing to alleviate information overload. In fact, it increases overload because it can produce more and can transmit faster. As long as these two capabilities—quantity and speed—are major characteristics of the technology we will have pressing need for information services with a human face. Not to understand this, not to factor this into system design, is an invitation to disaster.

Outputs then may be either products or services, or a combination of the two. The difference between them is based principally on the level of human intervention between client and system. In this context, outputs are artifacts of systems. Though there may be significant differences between products and services, the fact remains they should be perceived as outputs—in a traditional sense—of the system behind them, the backward look mentioned above.

Products and services, as discussed above, need to be differentiated but not separated. It is best to think of them as two opposite ends of a spectrum of outputs along which the following characteristics are controlling: (a) the degree of "rigidity" in output from fixed format "mass-produced" products to interactive output with dynamic negotiation and feedback potential; (b) the amount and type of value added by the process; (c) the level and quality of human interpretation in the interface between system and clientele. The differences between products and services are illustrated in Figure 9-1. It is worth noting that the service end of the spectrum tends to emphasize the client's needs more specifically, i.e., closeness to problem, than does the product end, and hence tends toward a higher level of direct human intervention.

Process Characteristics

An information output, be it product or service, must have several qualities or attributes if its designation as output is to be appropriate as a basis for auditing, that is, of potential use in the productivity equation.

1. *It should be an identifiable point in a process.* An information output may take a number of shapes. It may be an abstract or a collection of abstracts of scientific papers. It may be a regularly issued financial report from an internal management database. It may be a formal oral or written report specifically designed in response to one or several problems. It may be a computer program designed

PRODUCT	SERVICE
no variation	variable
static	dynamic
mass produced	on demand performance
economic commodity (can be replicated)	human intervention (unique)
tangible	intangible
low system cost	high system cost
high user cost	low user cost
general values added	custom values added

Figure 9-1. Attributes of Products and Services

to accomplish a specific applications task. Worth noting here is that the foregoing examples range in function from the unspecific potential usefulness of abstracts to the highly specific application of a computer program. This range of specificity of function may have implications for measurement. Some may complain that these outputs are too complex and too unpredictable for any formal productivity measures. At this stage of our ignorance our objective should be the level of measurement and control that is practical, recognizing that there may be some wide variations. As Richardson has pointed out:

> There are cases in which a work unit itself is almost impossible to reduce to a neat quantitative measure. This is particularly true in service areas both in and out of government. . . . Although we may not be able to come up with a nice neat measure of output, we should be able to make some judgements about what creates work for the people involved and to evaluate this. (Richardson, 1976; p. 93)

This is an important point—what creates work for the people involved. Information activities produce things called products and services, which seem to be useful (though we do not have good measures here), and which require labor to produce. Specifically there are several necessary requirements if an output is to be identified and isolated (Richardson, 1976; pp. 86–87).

(a) *It should be easy to count*. That is to say, though there be variability, such differences can be cited, understood, and contained. Thus, there can be but one unit of output. Complexity of task, variations in tools (e.g., different programming languages), and gross differences in the amount of time necessary to accomplish a task are examples of types of variations that may be encountered in identifying specific output types. In the context of services, for example, it might be possible to contain these problems by using specified time limits as boundaries for defining an output. For example, a reference operation in a busy library, for purposes of defining output, might classify any question response that takes more than 30 seconds and less than 5 minutes as one type of output; anything between 5 and 15 minutes as another; and so on. Though not completely satisfactory, once an arbitrary division of this sort has been made, then analysis can be made of the specific variations, such as complexity, subject matter, individual capabilities, access guides. But this cannot be done until some basic and definable boundaries have been set. The same is true of programming productivity. We can use lines of code generated per day. No doubt there are problems: language differences, complexity of task, error rate, maintenance costs, and so on (Parikh, 1981). Despite the problems, this is a base line measure.

(b) *A defined output should be consistent with existing information systems and, if possible, covered by historical data*. The purpose of this is to make certain that the defined output is not artificial, created only for measurement purposes. It should be a true output serving, if internal, some organizational function, or, if external, it should be specific and deliverable. The reference processes cited above, for example, are true outputs of an external nature, for the recipient has placed a demand on the system, has had that demand reacted to, and has walked away, presumably with something of value. This is true, even though the response may have informed the recipient that an answer to that demand is not available.

An historical context is desirable so that comparisons can be made over time. Comparable measurements are the heart of the productivity measurement process. If historical data do not exist then "data" must be defined and collected so that some kind of time series can be established for comparison. With systems such as conventional management information systems, meeting these criteria may be fairly easy. Reports (output) are well defined and may not have changed significantly for some time. Information technology may be changing these processes—the shape of the output—in certain qualitative ways. Fundamentally, however, the *intent* of the output, and hence its function, remains the same. That function is what can be used as the basis for isolating an output type. Libraries, for example, cataloged books before the advent of the Online Computer Library Center (OCLC). It would be relevant here to be able to measure the change in productivity in the cataloging process in an academic library as a result of the OCLC operation. For this particular operation, certainly output records (number of books cataloged) exist both for periods before and after OCLC. Whether full and appropriate input data are available is moot, for example, for investment in terminals and staff training. Where entirely new products or services are being created, obviously there can be no historical record. The real question is whether or not these *are* truly new products or services. If a new output, data will need to be defined and generated for any future productivity measures.

2. *The output should have a terminal quality.* The word "terminal" does not necessarily mean that it is the final product of a system. Rather, it implies that the output, though it may be part of a larger and longer process, can be isolated and identified because, at some particular point it changes function and status. It is here that it can be isolated and counted. This allows us to measure the productivity of parts of total systems. The product or service should be a unit which can account for most of the input of money and labor necessary for its production or performance. That is to say, we need to be able to count in dollars the cost of producing a particular type of output. This is an important attribute, for it focuses attention on both the goals of an information providing organization (the product or services) and on the costs necessary to achieve those specific goals, which we have labeled output. In organizational terms, this question begins to ask what a particular organization does with its capital and labor investment.

3. *The output should be the result of a process in which value is added.* Information systems are a series of processes by which the potential usefulness of a specific item—the message—being processed is enhanced. This is the primary reason for the existence of formal information systems. Recognition and acceptance of this value-added process is necessary for effective systems analysis and improvement. This means we look at output rather than process, at clients and users rather than only the technology. It begins the necessary change in system philosophy from technology-driven systems to user-driven systems.

4. *Output should be in a form useful in the future as input to other processes.*

This requirement has been hinted at several times in the foregoing paragraphs. Be it product or service, information is gathered, organized, stored, retrieved, analyzed, packaged, and transmitted for some purpose. It has an effect on some future act, decision, or knowledge change. Sometime soon, we will need to begin serious investigation of the impact of information on the performance and behavior of its recipients—managers, engineers, research scientists, legislators, decision makers, and the general public. This is one of the fundamental problems of the information field. It is a very complex problem, and though we may never solve it, a better understanding of its boundaries and ambiguities will allow us to describe better what it is we know and what we do not know.

User-Oriented Characteristics

The last quality mentioned above—input to other processes—is directly relevant to our concern with the analysis of the benefits and costs *(to users)* of information outputs. In this context, the following classes of characteristics for describing outputs become important: purpose and direction; scope of the output; type of output.

1. *The purpose and direction* of an output are basic for they establish the context for follow-through to the individual customer, to a class of users, or to an organization. An information output has direction: It goes to or is used by someone or some group. It has a purpose. That is to say, the intent of those who initiate and transmit the output is to have an effect on some future act, decision, or knowledge change. That we do not pay attention to these factors is a major cause of information overload. We have very little understanding of what might be called ''informational safety factors.'' This is the reason we have to have so many filters in the information process. Such filters, of course, raise the costs relative to the benefits of information. These costs might be costs to the system or costs to the user, dependent on where in the process we identify an output. Is output perceived only as being on the system side? Or do we identify output with its use? Who is to bear the costs—the system or the user? Cost here means (a) for the system, dollars expended for labor, rent, materials, and capital equipment; (b) for the user, not only dollars exchanged for the information (the price) but also the cost in time, energy, and lost opportunity. The attributes of products and services shown in Figure 9-1 suggest some of the influences on costs, and the trade-offs. There is a total cost for the use of an information output. The question then becomes: What is the division of that cost between system and user (Taylor, 1982b).

Within the context of this chapter, the function or purpose of an information output is a critical determinant in the productivity process. There are a number of purposes or functions that different products and services might meet or perform. These cluster in two ways: tangible and intangible. *Tangible functions* include such direct activities as triggers for action and responses to questions, where attributes such as time savings, clarity, and timeliness are critical. The *intangible functions* include the softer, less well-defined areas of service: informing, instructing, clarifying, and socializing. Far too many of our information products are designed to inform: selective dissemination of information, news capsules, "for your information" memos, newsletters, and so forth. Now the process of informing should be a very important function of information systems. Many decisions depend on soft information for their quality and accuracy. However, the explosion of information and the assumption of omnipotence of computable processes, coupled with indiscriminate notification processes left over from quieter times are direct causes of overload. We need to be able to target information. This must be done, of course, without sacrificing the potential of true serendipity, if indeed that is a quality required of a particular information output. Much decision failure by a particular information professional is tucked away in the name of serendipity: "You might be interested to know that. . . ." One may well wonder how frequently the recipient is "interested." The reduction of extraneous and redundant information cannot of course be an absolute. However, different products and services can be designed to fulfill different functions. We need to be able to state, more specifically than we do at present, what intangible functions a product or service performs.

There are, dependent on purpose and direction, many different ways information about a specific subject can be arranged, ordered, and filtered. Consider the following five scenarios concerning the need for information about a specific pharmaceutical compound XYZ (from Taylor, 1981):

> My child has just swallowed half a bottle of pills labelled XYZ and is lying on the floor unconscious but breathing. What do I do?
>
> I am designing a series of experiments on the relationship of XYZ toneurofibromatosis. I am especially concerned with disordered growth of Schwann cells. What is already known about this, and what experiments have been performed?
>
> How much *XYZ* is manufactured in the US and in Western Europe by major pharmaceutical firms? What is the reliability of these figures? I need to know by 5 P.M. Friday for licensing negotiations with European firms in London on Monday.
>
> What is the per-unit cost for XYZ production in our plant in Syracuse? What are comparable figures for a year ago, and projected costs for next year?
>
> I am a teacher. For my twelfth-grade biology class, I need illustrative material on XYZ: effects of various dosages on normal body functions, etc. Anything useful?

Each of these questions, though concerned with a common subject, XYZ, requires a different kind of output. Obvious. The answer to one question or problem would be deemed irrelevant by another. The differences, above all, are in the intent and context. There are also differences in immediacy of need, comparable time frame, comprehensiveness of coverage, reliability of data, and level of sophistication. In terms of responses to these needs, the productivity question asks (a) how well the question is answered (effectiveness), and (b) what level of resources were consumed in providing an answer (efficiency). With care and adjustment these could also be labelled output and input, or benefit and cost.

2. *The scope of the output* is concerned with several different aspects of an information product or service: subject matter, time frame, complexity, and reli-

ability. There could be many more such aspects or information traits of outputs, for example, hardness/softness of data; qualitative or quantitative spectrum; or theoretical/applied. These were reviewed in Chapter Three. For the purpose of beginning analysis of the impact of information on productivity, however, the four aspects noted above are probably sufficient.

The naming or identification of *subject matter*—what an information chunk is about—is a process about which certain segments of the information profession (librarians, indexers) are highly knowledgeable and capable. Subject analysis and the organization of information are concerned with the naming of information items and with their interrelationships.

The question of *inclusiveness* begins to answer several concerns, especially in terms of organizations. What does an output cover: individual, department, division, total organization? Such information has special implications for managers who must decide whether or not a particular information chunk is worth spending time on. Are the data in the item generalizable? Or are they specific to the organizational level noted? We hazard a guess that a great deal of time is wastefully spent deciding whether or not an item is useful, not in terms of subject matter, but, among other things, in terms of inclusiveness of data. Such descriptions are important in commercial, industrial, and managerial areas.

The element of *time* is important for describing an output. What is the time frame of the information in a product or service? Is it historical, and if so what span of time is included? Is it future oriented? Could it have an effect on forecasting future events or affecting future acts? Time may be of particular relevance in describing a service output, which, because of its person-to-person or customized nature, may have a conscious and planned impact on future acts, even though that impact may not be measurable in quantitative terms. The time frame becomes particularly important for comparability purposes. For example, we may be presented with aggregate figures for the first four months of the present year. Last year's figures were divided by quarters. Consequently, comparisons are not possible.

The question of *complexity* of information in a product or a service has something to say about the intended audience. The same information cannot be presented in the same way to audiences with varying levels of education or with varying levels of familiarity with the situation described. For these reasons messages about a specific subject will and should vary, dependent on the intended audience. This relates back directly to the earlier discussion of purpose and direction.

Finally, for purposes of effect on performance, the *reliability* of the information or data in the output is a necessary part of the description. This is true because the quality of performance or the productivity of the recipient may well be directly related to the validity of the input received and on which decisions are based. Most systems issue data as though the data were accurate and complete pictures of a situation, as though there were no qualifiers. We tend to want and to accept hard figures without qualification *because* they are quantified and therefore "closer to reality." Some attempt must be made to validate and to describe the reliability of the data in the product or service. We tend to overlook the qualifications and compromises that surround the collection of data, sometimes with disastrous effect on decisions or actions.

3. *The type of output* is important and has to do with its placement on the *product/service spectrum*. At the product end there may be simple low-cost mass-produced items; an unannotated bibliography, a computer-generated financial report, or unevaluated news notes. At the other, the service end, are such outputs as: a customised report with evaluative and qualitative judgments on the information contained; a consultant's oral report with comment, feedback, and discussion; a critically annotated bibliography arranged by perceived relevance to a problem at hand; a verbal response to the crisis cited above in which the child swallowed XYZ; a report outlining options for decision with potential advantages and disadvantages for each option. In the information field, we tend to think of outputs only as physical products of systems. These, in truth, are but a beginning. For effective information systems, we will need to go beyond this primitive form of thinking. If we take, for instance, the point of view of the user, the client, the customer, then the total process becomes important. From the user's side, the amount of energy or time that must be expended to get useful information will be an important determinant as to the utility—and therefore value—of that information. Generally it is the systems personnel who have decided how output will be defined. The value-added approach demands that we see systems as but one part of a larger process of providing information.

Though the following three characteristics pertain mostly to products, they shade into services, especially when we begin to ask about user costs: type of message; standardization and frequency; media and dissemination mode.

Type of message is related to scope of output, discussed above. However, this category is directed more toward the physical and logistical aspects of the message—the ways the message is organized. What is the usual level and amount of quantitative data? Does the message merely point to something, as in a bibliography or an online retrieval system? Or does it provide specific answers, perhaps with some evaluation? If the output is large are there access mechanisms such as tables of contents or indexes? Does the scope or coverage match the function or intent of the output? Does it require some (or much) interpretation of output?

Standardization and frequency are concerned with various kinds of routines that may, if well conceived, reduce both system costs *and* user costs. Is the format standardized so that repeated use and comparability can be routine? How much novelty is there in the structure of outputs of this class? What is the effect of formal rules, policies, and procedures on the output and on its standardization? Can a service be partially standardized? That is to say, can pieces of a service be routinized so that customized enhancements, perhaps at high system cost, can be kept relatively low in total cost. The Congressional Research Service of the Library of Congress does this to some extent in its *Issue Briefs,* in which the format is preestablished and modularized, but the content is periodically updated and changed as necessary to meet the needs of a specific time. What is the periodicity of the product, if any, and how is it established? What is the frequency of output per unit time? What is the demand for the product or service? The principal function of standardization is to save time for the recipient and to control systems costs. We need, however, to be careful that standardization is not so rigid as to destroy other attributes such as data qualification. Frequency assumes that data as collected and displayed have a certain time span which give them value because it is an accepted work span, for example, a day, a week, a year, which is also accepted by the user of the data as natural and useful.

The question of *media and dissemination modes* is concerned with the shape and dynamics of the interface between client and system. The difference in output between product and service becomes very apparent here. In what medium is a product disseminated: print, computer printout or CRT display, graphics, charts, film or similar animated medium? Are there particular attributes of the medium that will affect a product's function and utility? For example, is this a passive or an active output? Does it respond only when asked, as, for example, an online search system does? Does it periodically issue a report, for example, a monthly activity report or an SDI listing whether the respondent wants it or not? Does it provide an interactive interface, such as a dynamic decision support system? What are the technologies of delivery and how do they affect usefulness? Are formal messages of a particular type routed in the organization? How and why? Are they altered in the process?

Moving beyond products to the delivery of services, we need to ask about the nature of the human expertise required for this particular service? How much preliminary and ongoing negotiation takes place? How much evaluation, analysis, and interpretation of information occurs in the process *and* at the output end? What is the nature and amount of feedback in the process? How, in fact, is a service delivered to a client? How does the mode of delivery affect the value of the service to the user? For example: an oral presentation, possibly with feedback and clarifying discussion; a written product specifically designed to meet the needs of an individual customer; or an online display, such as computer-aided design, allowing a client to manipulate the data in order to facilitate choice of options. These are questions that need consideration in order to provide an early interpretation of the interface between system and client, whether that interface be a formalized product or a dynamic human negotiation.

Outputs—Recapitulation

The preceding parts of this chapter have presented an organized way of describing classes of output of information systems. For reference purposes these attributes and characteristics are outlined below.

A. *Process Characteristics*

1. An output should be an identifiable point in a process;
   - easy to count
   - consistent with existing information systems
   - covered by historical data, if possible

2. An output should have a terminal quality: It can account for most of the input of money and labor necessary for its production or performance.
3. An output should be the result of an identifiable value-added process.
4. An output should be in a form which can be analyzed in the future as input to other processes.

B. *User-oriented characteristics*

1. An output has a purpose and a direction:
   - What is it supposed to do?
   - Who gets it and why?
2. What is the scope of the output? How can it best be described?
   - What is it about (subject matter)?
   - What is the time frame of its content?
   - What is the level of complexity?
   - How reliable (consistent, valid) are the data and facts in the output?
3. Is the output a product or a service or a combination of both?
   - type of message
   - standardization and frequency
   - media and dissemination mode

The attributes and characteristics of outputs presented in this chapter may be seen as an extension and refinement of the first three of Horton's five-step approach to the management of information resources.

1. identify and inventory the organization's information assets, both external and internal, and their flows;
2. cost each major information line item;
3. value (i.e., price out) each major organizational information source, service, and system, in terms of how important each *really* is to results and bottom-line profits;
4. analyze information flows and holdings to detect duplication and gaps;
5. synthesize carefully restructured information system, records and files, and other information streams. (Horton, 1981; pp. iii–iv)

The emphasis in this chapter has been on the outputs of any information system, or resource in Horton's words. Our concern is with the first three steps. Horton's last two steps, analysis and synthesis, are of obvious importance to the management of information resources. The major difference in approach is that Horton emphasizes the identification of the resource (system). This may be the most feasible and politic approach at this time. The approach of this chapter has concentrated on the output of those resources as well as other sources of information outputs because it is felt that this provides a better way of identifying sources of information not included in the conventional resource. As we noted in the last chapter, the office itself and the knowledge center are both major producers of information, but they are seldom identified as information systems (resources). The major costs of information and its provision and use may not be incurred by conventional systems such as data processing and library/information services. These are easily identified. The major costs are those hidden in the maintenance of office filing systems (whether automated or not), in centers of expert knowledge or in the products of the ubiquitous copying machine. We feel that Horton's approach will not capture this information easily. Two approaches discussed below, output tracing and overhead value analysis, are possible ways of identifying these outputs. The problems of costing and assigning value (benefits) to information outputs, or flows in Horton's terms, are discussed below.

OUTCOMES: BENEFITS AND COSTS

Thus far in this chapter, concern has centered on the definition and description of information outputs in terms potentially useful for estimating the effect an output has on the performance of an individual or on some type of organization. In order to provide context for this approach and for these descriptive categories, it is useful to look at the environment of users and customers, and at the kinds of concerns they have when faced with information choices.

Decisions concerning the utility of an information system or resource and its outputs are benefit and cost decisions, made in the light of some specific criteria, whether those criteria are explicit or not. These decisions may range from "its just not worth the effort" to the analytic reports, the discussions, and consequent decisions resulting from a rigorous and time-consuming study on the cost-effectiveness of acquiring a major new computing system. Note the use of the phrase "cost-effectiveness" in the last sentence. There is a difference between "effectiveness" and "benefit," and the difference is crucial to the management of information resources in the value-added context. When we talk of system *effectiveness* we are essentially describing the attributes that can be controlled by the system, for example, speed, accuracy, quality, or relevance. It is basically system centered. On the other hand, *benefits* describe *consequences* of system performance, of system output. A benefit takes the form of cost savings, cost avoidance, improved operational performance, better allocation of resources, or better understanding of a particular situation (King and Schrems, 1978). That is to say, it promotes the well-being of an organization or enhances a particular activity. Benefits are centered on the users, the customers, the consumers, of the system outputs.

There are very real difficulties in measuring benefits, in assigning a dollar value to them. Measuring improved operational performance, for example, can only be partially accomplished by breaking such an intangible benefit into smaller concrete benefits: decrease in the rate of error, faster response, or measurably better understanding of a subject.

In a very few cases we may be able to link information directly to these specific benefits. We need to realize that benefit assessment will be subjective, because our focus is not just on the output of an information system, but on the consequences of that output—the outcomes. Generally this is not a comfortable place to be. We want numbers, simplicity, stability, and quick calculations. Unfortunately, for this attitude, the information environment is complex, unstable, and frequently unpredictable in any precise sense. Although we must live with subjective data, this does not mean there can be no rigor or standards. On the contrary, it calls for a qualitative type of rigor, and for means of dealing with subjective data on scalar terms. (See Packer, 1983, for an illuminating and cogent discussion of these problems.) This is something that will take time. The consideration of benefits of information products and services can be approached in several ways, three of which are considered here: information output tracing, overhead value analysis, and the critical success factors approach.

Information Output Tracing

Information output tracing follows the movements of individual products and services of an information system: To whom does it go? How is it used? How much effort goes into its use? What effect does it have on performance? For both products and services, there are many unique outputs. It is obvious that assessing the effect of all outputs would be a mammoth and, at least in the short term, probably an impossible task. The purpose here, however, is to suggest approaches.

For each *product* of an information resource or of an information process, it is necessary to know who the recipients are. This may be a department, in which case we need to know who in fact handles that particular output. Personnel in the information systems from which reports and other information products are issued tend to believe that all things emanating from that function have value to all those on the receiving end. This is not the case; and that fact is the reason for looking at those who receive the report. There are a number of reasons why people in organizations look at information products. They were discussed in Chapter Eight. They are listed here in brief form for convenience:

- fear of not being informed;
- status in receiving information;
- as a trigger for action;
- for one's own specific responsibilities;
- to make new package of information.

These will have an effect on the kind and quality of answers to the questions posed below. These questions, though they are directed principally at organizational concerns, can be adjusted to systems such as public libraries where purposes and objectives are more amorphous, audiences less well defined, and benefits even less apparent. Better definitions of classes of users and market fragmentation will gradually support a more sophisticated understanding of the characters of particular library publics. There are several classes of questions which need answering if the value of the product or service is to be assessed at any level.

What is done with the standard product, such as a report, of an information system?

- not looked at, discarded (probably a not uncommon case);

- not looked at, filed, but rarely used;
- filed and used later;
- trigger for immediate and direct action;
- read, filed, and used in future;
- extracted and integrated into new report;
- analyzed and combined with other reports.

The purpose of this question is to get some sense of the quality, intensity, and function of the use made of the product. In library terms, these might be translated into general uses such as instructional, research (i.e., curiosity generated), leisure, informing (or even more practical, as for example to prop up a table leg with a book or to solve a crossword puzzle).

How much time is spent on the information by the person or the department receiving it? Note that an information product may be received automatically and periodically. Such an estimate of time begins to indicate what level of effort, measured in time committed, that that person or group is willing to invest in this information product. Such effort, translated into dollar costs, is a measure of the value of that product to that recipient, at that time, and in that given situation. The assumption here of course is that the recipient of the report has a finite amount of time, and has made a conscious choice to invest some portion of that time into an activity directly related to the information product in question. What is being said here is that, because a person in a particular setting has certain kinds of problems, with certain kinds of criteria for resolving those problems, that person is the best judge of the value (and potential benefit) of that particular information product. Since we have no direct measures of value, this becomes a proxy measure of value, with all the hazards associated with such proxies.

In a situation where formal pricing is not a question, this then becomes the price that person is willing "to pay" for that information, what King Research Inc. has called the "apparent value" of information (King Research, Inc., 1982; p. 15). In a charge-back situation, the apparent value would be the price paid, plus the expenditure of effort and time by the customer translated into dollars. This approach, in a very gross way, has been used by King Research, Inc., in the report cited above, to estimate the value to researchers of the research data base generated, processed, and produced in the US Department of Energy. It is suggested here as an approach to the question of value on a much more specific level. This dollar value, estimated from the costs of time and effort invested, when associated with an answer to the first question (what is done with the product?) provides a rough quantitative measure, tempered by a qualitative assessment of how the report is used.

Is it possible to go further than this? That is to say, can we measure in any way the "consequential value" of information in, for example, a specific type of report, (the benefits to the department of using the information product)? It is possible to evaluate performance in various ways. However, as was pointed out before, it is difficult to assess cause and effect relationships between information and performance. It would be possible, by questionnaire and scaling, to obtain subjective estimates of those relationships (Packer, 1983). This may be the only way a quantitative estimate of benefits can be made. It can be handled in formal ways by established statistical techniques. How valid such approaches might be depends a great deal on the skill in deriving appropriate questions, utilizing appropriate statistical techniques, and in their interpretation and analysis.

Overhead Value Analysis

The approaches suggested thus far are, in a way, external approaches to the study of benefits and costs. That is to say, they perceive cost and benefits from outside the process, not as participants or active users. There are more direct approaches where the analysis is done by the participants themselves, and the costs of supplying information are weighted against the perceived benefits of receiving the information. Within this context one particular approach is worth comment, because it directly addresses the questions of benefits and costs as a result of participant negotiation. It is called *overhead value analysis* (Neuman, 1976). Since the production and performance of information products and services make up the major portion of what is called overhead, then this approach is pertinent to our discussion of information and productivity. Overhead value analysis differs from traditional value analysis by "making both the managers who incur the costs (suppliers) and those who benefit from them (receivers or demanders) responsible for identifying which costs to cut" (Neuman, 1976; p. 117).

What this approach basically does is to establish a set of procedures for (a) estimating costs of specific products and services; (b) creating lists of potential targets for reduction or elimination; (c) recommending options where cost savings outweigh adverse consequences; and (d) deciding actual cuts to be made, such decisions being made by top management. Neuman suggests a target of 40%. This may seem extremely high, but a truly challenging target may be the only way to spur exhaustive search and, in some cases, to generate fundamental rethinking of services. The initial step of identifying and costing each information output is a critical one. These outputs may range from reports and forms to analysis, advice, and decisions. Such a process could be exhausting; consequently, it is important to decide on critical levels and order of magnitude costing. The significant point is to identify information outputs, if possible, classes of outputs, from all departments—their purpose, direction, and cost. Challenge groups, "made up of suppliers and receivers of related sets of services" analyze and suggest options. Options include: elimination, deferment, reduction of quality, amount, or frequency, or substitution (Neuman, 1976; pp. 120–121).

The total process requires complete support of top management. Indeed top management should initiate the process in full cognizance of potential consequences: readiness, if necessary, to fire executives; commitment of some of the best managers to the project for several months; assurance of fairness in reviewing the options; making decisions despite a lack of hard data.

A successful operation of overhead value analysis, however, will not only contain and reduce costs, it will develop a sensitivity throughout the organization for the costs and the benefits of information and its provision. This and similar approaches may indeed be the beginning of rational control over the information process in organizations of any type.

Critical Success Factors

The Critical Success Factors approach (CSF), developed by John Rockart and others at the Massachusetts Institute of Technology, is a top-down approach (Rockart, 1979). It is a user-oriented approach. Critical success factors are defined as "the few key areas where "things must go right" for the business to flourish . . . areas of activity that should receive constant and careful attention from management" (Rockart, 1979; p. 85). The identification of CSFs "allows a clear definition of the amount of information that must be collected by the organization." The method "centers on information needs for management control where data is needed to monitor and to improve existing areas of business" (Rockart, 1979; p. 88).

The purpose of CSF is to ascertain, by intensive interviewing, those few key areas of activity in which favorable results are absolutely necessary for a particular manager to reach his or her goals within the organization. From this set of factors one can derive a picture of the kinds of information, both internally and externally derived, necessary to support and to facilitate good decisions in those areas of concern deemed critical.

This is a subjective approach (though it can be fairly rigorous) to the provision of information to management. It provides no particular measurement of value of information or of benefit. By implication, however, the customer has, after thorough analysis, decided what general classes of information (and something about its presentation) would be of most benefit because of his or her tasks, problems, time constraints, and responsibilities. Borbely, of what was once known as AT&T Long Lines, points out that CSF is not new. It does, however, highlight the need for a manager not only to pinpoint strategic concerns, but also to define the kinds of information needed to meet those concerns (Borbely, 1981). It provides an impetus for designing information outputs for users. As such, though less thorough, it bears some resemblance to overhead value analysis just discussed. The major difference is that CSF is concerned with benefits only. This approach, at this stage, may be more important than a quantitative calculation of benefits. The real payoff in productivity terms must be useful information when needed, *at minimum cost to both the information provider and the customer*. More than anything else, the CSF approach demands that users define their position, their tasks, and basic responsibilities in information terms. On the other side, it requires that the information systems reflect user requirements rather than system requirements alone. The weakness is that CSF seems to have been used only in the context of conventional management information systems—an unfortunate and unrealistic restriction, as has been discussed before.

There is an interesting and potentially fruitful extension of CSF that has not surfaced as yet. The CSF approach may provide a new way of defining a position: by the amount of information resources required. When a new position is created today, space and financial resources are formally committed, including necessary support personnel. The commitment of information resources to a position is also a cost, possibly even a large cost. Though defining such a commitment may be difficult, with foresight and practice this could be a significant step in a better understanding and consequent control of the costs and benefits of information and its provision.

COSTING

The process of costing information resources is a difficult but critical step in coming to grips with the whole productivity question. It might be tempting, after identifying a set of outputs, to stop because so many obvious and correctable problems may have surfaced. This desire, however natural, should be curbed, because the calculation of benefits and costs, rough as it may be, is a necessary piece in understanding the value-added approach. This chapter will not go into detail on the costing process. For reasons noted below it is a larger and more difficult task than is possible in a mere section of a chapter. The reader is referred to Horton's *Information Management Workbook* (1981), to the seminal article by Strassmann (1976) on the cost of information, and to the work of Neil Burk of the Auditor-General's Office of Canada (Burk, 1984).

Why Costing Is Important

The process may be illuminated by reviewing some of the managerial reasons why information costing is important. These are basic to the establishment of an information resources management function in organizations. The following is partially derived from Horton (1981; 3/1–26).

To determine the level of financial investment in information resources in the organization: We rather suspect that the magnitude of these resources, when a complete inventory is made, will come as a surprise. Indeed, the information resources may well be the largest financial investment by most organizations. This, of course, depends on what is included and how one counts. But with some degree of surety it can be said to represent a major investment. Indeed its explosive growth over the past two decades and the fact that its cost is frequently "hidden" in overhead accounts throughout the organization has made those costs difficult to unbundle and hence to control. The purpose of information resources managements is to begin the process of finding out where an organization is spending its information dollars.

To account for the costs of information resources by departments: Whether it be a public or private organization, all units regardless of level in the organization produce and use information resources in some form. These may take the form of a production schedule, an evaluation of a program, a marketing survey, an annual report, or a feasibility study for a new product or program. Each such information product requires an investment of money, time, and personnel. Accounting for the costs in such circumstances will require separate estimates of expenses in support of information activities, and those in support of noninformational activities: The two should add up to 100%. How this division is made can only be done after some trial and error and rough estimating.

To account for the costs of information resources by equipment and handling media and by specific information centers: These are rather obvious information systems: engineering drawings, cartographic services, mainframe computer centers, standalone and personal computers, mail services, telecommunication services, libraries and information centers, or printing services. Most of the costs of these should be fairly easy to ascertain, at least in total. However, the breaking out of expenditures related to types of information outputs may be somewhat more difficult.

To assist in "make-or buy" decisions for information products and services: Better accounting of the full costs of development, operation, and maintenance of information services and systems will allow for more rational decision than is presently the case, that is, whether to generate internally or to procure externally. We tend generally to underprice information products and services, resulting in frequent cost overruns and consequent uneasiness as to the efficacy of the decision process in these instances. A better handle on complete costs will provide better data for decision and hence more assurance in these cases.

To isolate information costs by purpose: What does it cost to provide a user or group of users with an information product or service? What does it cost those users to use the product or service? or not to use it? Costs developed here can eventually provide a base for chargeback pricing. Though chargeback may not be used now, it is one of the more effective ways of exercising control over information costs, for it forces the user to make decisions on benefits and costs. Some see a danger in chargeback processes as inhibiting the freedom of decisions or analytic processes and the serendipity factor. This reluctance is the result of our inability to understand the role of information in organizational processes and societal concerns.

To "shred out" hidden information costs from overhead accounts, as well as from direct accounts: Hidden costs tend to grow as the investment in information systems and services grows, hiding under such rubrics as "other services." The purpose is to make them visible by naming them, and therefore to make them more controllable.

To standardize unit costs for routine information processes: Standardized costs would provide a base for analyzing, for example, productivity in information processes (Strassmann, 1976; pp. 137–138). Standard costs are essential in making any estimates for pricing, chargeback, or make-or-buy decisions. Standard units costs may not always be possible because of the uniqueness of some of the information outputs. Many such benchmarks, however, can be made: cost per printed page; cost per line of instruction in COBOL; cost per computation; cost per periodical check-in; or cost per text edited page. Standardized costs should include not only labor costs, but also the costs of management overhead, employee benefits, and capital prorated expenditures. These must be part of the unit cost for any valid comparisons in deciding on, for example, office automation. There obviously must be some means of adjusting these over time.

Difficulties in Costing

These reasons for costing information resources, and by implication, the types of data required for the process, signal some very real difficulties.

First, information is pervasive throughout the organization—its production, its transmission, its use. It cuts across all activities, and its costs are hidden in many different types of accounts. Consequently, it may be necessary to set boundaries on the breadth and level of aggregation that can be dealt with on a manageable basis. Care must be taken not to take on more than can be handled. It must be a phased process.

Second, the bookkeeping, accounting, and financial management information systems, which grew over the past century, have generally not developed the means for handling information products and services. There is no form of information accounting, as there is, for example, for personnel, sales, or manufacturing. It may be possible, with some effort, to cost out completely an information product, such as a monthly departmental report. It is probably possible to ascertain the cost of transferring that report to those supposed to receive it, whether by messenger, mail, facsimile transmission, or computer to computer transmission. Ascertaining these costs would take effort, but it could be done. However, if we are truly concerned with the utility and value of information then we must be concerned with those people who receive the report. How much effort (time/cost) do customers put into reading the report, extracting from it, combining its data with data from other quarterly reports, analyzing and repackaging that combination, and filing it? These are significant costs. In fact, if they are not significant, then there is reason to question the existence of the report in the first place. In a paradoxical sense, if the benefit of a periodic report remains the same over time in the customer's judgment, but the time invested is less (because of better formatting) then the cost-benefit ratio becomes more favorable. We have no way of ascertaining the costs of utilizing these information outputs, except by the amount of time expended with them. Yet these are real costs associated with an information product. In fact, an information accounting approach may eventually provide a means of controlling those costs because it focuses attention on *the complete process from generation to process to production to use of information products and services*. This is not possible under present accounting systems. However, a good deal can be identified and costed at the production and transmitting level, and by sampling at the use stage. It will take time and understanding, and solid dialogue between an information resources management unit and the accounting department.

Another problem in costing is our tendency to look upon each information product and service as *unique*. To be sure there are differences, but we tend to exaggerate differences rather than emphasize the similarities. Eventually, we need to be able to group outputs into useful categories, probably based on the purposes they are intended to serve. At present, if we group at all, we group by specific resource or process—computer services, word processing center, statistical services, printing services. One of the reasons for the inventory, and especially for the emphasis on end use, is to begin to provide a new frame of reference that could help in the cost accounting process.

There are variations in cost accounting systems of different corporations and organizations. Some may follow a detailed "income and expense" approach. Others may build their cost accounting structures on a profit or cost center basis. Others may follow strict organizational lines. Whatever the approach may be, it will have an effect on the process of information costing.

Any audit effort should first be concentrated on the outputs of those organizations that are obviously "data handling" in character: computer centers; libraries and information analysis centers; mailrooms; telecommunication services. One exception should be made in any early audit: a major office of the organization should be analyzed and its information outputs traced and costed.

Costs for those *units that are data handling in character* might be broken into the following classes (Horton, 1981; 3/20–21). There is a tentativeness about this because much depends on how the corporate accounting system is structured.

- *Capital* investments: hardware, equipment, books.
- *Personnel* costs: compensation, benefits.
- *Operating* costs: supplies, equipment lease, space, system software.
- *Purchased services* (external): online services, leased telecommunication services, special studies made externally.
- *Shared services* (internal): computing systems, shared software, telecommunication services.
- Other costs: there may well be other divisions possible here. Without being familiar with the accounting system this is difficult to assess at a distance.

In addition it would be helpful to break out costs for different classes of outputs: production reports, financial reports, applications programming, and external online searches are examples of these outputs. This will require time estimates for personnel and equipment, that can be prorated into costs per output type.

At the *user- or customer-end of this process,* we would like to ascertain, at minimum, the time spent on particular information outputs which are generated by the units described above. That is to say, we wish to trace the costs throughout the life of the particular output. This would complete the cost cycle of a product or service from generation to process to production to use.

In costing the *information activities of the major office* mentioned above, it would be necessary to identify and to make rough cost estimates for

- information versus noninformational activities;
- major informational tasks, including identification of any information output from that office;
- major internal office information systems, such as files, data collections, and reports.

The *rough costing process* suggested here does several things. It focuses on information outputs—the cost of their production and of their use. It begins the process of separating information activities from noninformation activities. There is, by the way, no simple algorithm for dividing these two activities. That division rests on what is feasible and useful at the time. The costing process will provide useful input to the accounting department for the long range and necessary development of accounting procedures for information resources, their processes, and their outputs.

BEYOND PRODUCTIVITY

It is quite obvious that, as we move away from conventional measures of output, we have moved into an area that is more diffuse, harder to define, and less quantifiable. This move must take place, however, because conventional measures have become unimportant. Except for control of efficiency, they don't really tell us anything useful: lines of programming code generated; number of abstracts provided; number of reports generated. Note that none of these say anything about quality or utility, only about quantity. We measure and treasure efficiency, because it is easily measured; but efficiency is but one part of a larger equation. It may be that once we have developed measures for some activity, it is no longer important. That is to say, if you can measure something, it becomes unimportant.

This chapter has presented a beginning outline for isolating and defining outputs in terms better adapted to a society based on information flows and use. It has been argued here that attention must move from output as product of efficient systems and focus now on output as input to a variety of knowledge processes. Though the incongruity of "output as input" may confuse, it is so stated in order to emphasize information movement and utility. What we normally define and accept as outputs are but one step in the total information process. It might have been more appropriate to use the term "outcomes." Packer identifies this as one of the fundamental problems with classical productivity measures.

> Classical techniques focus on outputs—the immediate results of organizational activity—rather than outcomes—the ultimate impact of the organization on the outside world. . . . While outputs are usually easier to quantify than outcomes, we often care more about outcomes than outputs. This is particularly true in the case of knowledge work. . . . The distinction between output and outcome is mirrored in the twin concepts of efficiency and effectiveness. Efficiency refers to how well the enterprise converts its input resources into immediate outputs. . . . Effectiveness, on the other hand, relates to how well the enterprise uses its input resources to meet its ultimate goals and purposes. . . . Traditional formulas for measuring productivity stress efficiency and neglect effectiveness. (Packer, 1983; p. 33)

This approach requires examination of the variety of knowledge processes in order to determine what roles information plays in these processes. More importantly, we need to know what shape, size, and scope of information outputs are best suited to a particular process. These processes might range from problem solving to decision making, from question answering to orienting. More specifically it means focussing attention on typical environments from which problems are generated and for which information may be useful, and on the differences in information use behavior among, for example, scientists, legislative staff, consumers, managers, students, chemists, teachers, and real people coping with the real world. This has been stressed here because the real problems of the future will arise from information overload, meaning both glut and unfiltered information. Such analysis will provide important insights for the design of better outputs.

In addition, one could with good reason surmise that attention paid to clients and their requirements will have pervasive and long-term effects on the information environment, a sort of permanent Hawthorne effect. Simply put, the more awareness there is of the benefits and costs associated with the use of information, the more demanding information users will becoming in specifying their requirements with consequent impact on the design of information systems and their outputs.

Chapter Ten

SUMMARY AND IMPLICATIONS

This chapter begins with a very brief summary of the notions that have been presented and explored in the previous chapters. The book is an early sketch of the value-added model. The wording and the implications of the previous statement should be noted; it is correct. This is but a beginning, an early model of a significant set of processes in our society: those systems organized to provide information and knowledge to a large variety of publics with different kinds of problems in many different settings. They represent a large and complex set of operations. Nevertheless, the book has developed a structured image of processes and practices which already exist—libraries, management information systems, information analysis centers, abstracting and indexing services—and which, in fact, do a rather remarkable job. The point has been made, however, that present information systems and their technological- and content-derived models are no longer enough.

This book starts from the base of operating information systems, from the ordinary contexts of praxis. This is our reality. It has been and will be argued here that what we need now are rigorous definitions and descriptions of present practice, including the three elements of technology, content, and people. Systems design generally omit—or pay only lip service to—the third element, the users of information. This book has emphatically put them back in.

This chapter also examines some of the weaknesses of the value-added model. As an early picture, there are particular areas where the author feels the definitions are neither precise enough nor descriptive enough. On the other side, there are strengths in the model. Assuming the validity of the model, or something like it, we will also examine its implications for education in the field, for research, and for general information literacy.

THE VALUE-ADDED MODEL

The model should be looked upon as a means of describing a set of formal social practices called information systems. It is not a predictive model. The model is comprised of three basic elements:

- a *formal system* made up of specific processes which add value to items being processed;
- *user or sets of users,* who, because they sit in particular environments, have

certain problems which establish criteria for judging the utility of the system's output;
- *a negotiation space* between system and users, where the system displays its outputs and the values accumulated through the system to assist users in making choices.

We have not been, and do not intend to be, particularly concerned with a definition of information, except to say it is the "stuff" which is processed by information systems and comes in chunks ranging from a single datum to very large organized collections of data and/or knowledge. Information is sought for and/or received voluntarily by people because they think it will help them in various ways. The one caution made throughout the book is that we must distinguish between the information content or meaning of a message chunk and the services or resources that process, transmit, or contain the messages. We manage these services and resources in order to raise the probability that the system outputs will be useful to users. We do not intend to pursue the definition any further. It does not seem a fruitful direction at this time.

The model is user driven. That is to say, it adds the user perspective to present technology- and content-driven system design. Such an approach is by no means universally accepted, because the user environment is at present not amenable to easy structuring. Indeed it is messy and ill defined. The purpose of this book, however, is to point out ways through which better structure and definition might be imposed. The model does come closer to the reality of information systems as they exist. It is the argument of this book that, despite this messiness, the user and his environment are a critical and necessary ingredient for the understanding of systems and their improvement. This means that we must be able to describe those environments and to translate those descriptions into useful parameters for system design. The most important of these translations are (a) what we have called (after Brinberg) "intellectual technologies" as input to systems design, and (b) problem dimensions as a basis for understanding the interface between system and user.

As a summary, it is appropriate here to reiterate in brief some of the salient points of such concepts as system, value, value added, and information outputs, as they have been used here. The reader is referred to earlier chapters for more extensive discussion and illustration.

Information systems are formal sets of organized activities that add value to messages being processed. Systems may be machine based or human based, or more likely a combination of the two. The value adding activities performed on and to information take several general forms; their importance will vary in different types of systems:

- selecting input;
- storing and organizing for physical access;
- describing and labeling for retrieval;
- analyzing, evaluating, and comparing for quality;
- combining and interpreting;
- responding and adapting to specific user problems.

The merit of an information system is determined by its success (a) in signalling the potential for value of messages; (b) in combining, interpreting, and reexpressing information content in addressing or clarifying particular problems; and/or (c) through system flexibility, in allowing users to develop routines adapted to their individual needs and styles.

If certain system activities, other than maintenance, do not add value to these contexts then there is good reason to suspect that they may not be performing any useful function. Maintenance poses a particular and critical problem, especially in computer systems, because it has grown to alarming proportions. This is partly because in the past we have not understood very well what systems were intended to do other than collect and organize chunks of information. Nor have we comprehended the effect that the extraordinarily rapid rate of change, caused by the application of the computer and associated technologies, has had on information systems and on the proliferation of data and information. This inability to comprehend or to accept the magnitude of the cost of maintaining information systems is the result of injudicious application, inappropriate design, lack of standards, and lack of quality control at input. A large portion of operating budgets are being consumed by maintenance costs. We may indeed have to live with this situation for another 50 or 100 years, until we learn better how to manage the information resource. In the meantime, the need for human interpreters and filters at the output side of our information systems will grow rapidly.

The *value of information* cannot be measured in precise terms prior to its use. Value is not inherent in, nor is it carried by, an information message. A message has value only in context. It is given value by its users. Consequently, a message has potential for value. This means that the better we understand the environment in which the output of a system will be used, the better we will be able to estimate the potential value of those outputs, and to design systems accordingly. A posteriori, the value of information might be measured by its apparent value—the sum of dollars expended by the user, plus time and energy dollars costs, and the opportunity costs lost in not doing something else. *Value-added activities* in information systems are those processes that produce, enhance, or otherwise strengthen the potential utility of messages in the system. The values that result from these activities—23 of them—are classified in six categories: ease of use, noise reduction, quality, adaptability, time savings, and cost savings. These added values may be either tangible (e.g., formatting or physical accessibility) or intangible (e.g., reliability or closeness to problem). The reader should refer to Figure 4-1 and Table 4-1, as well as to the discussion of these criteria and values in Chapter Four.

The description of *system outputs* is important for several reasons. First, this is the side the system turns toward the user or client. It represents the message, of whatever dimension, that is or is not given value by a user. Second, the output comes in two forms: product or service. The dichotomy provides additional ways of interpreting use value and message formation. Third, the vantage point of system output provides an opportunity in linear terms for looking backward into the system and evaluating its efficiencies in producing the output, and for looking forward toward the user and estimating the effectiveness of the output on performance.

The principal strength of the value-added model lies in its stress on the user and on the needs and dimensions of the information environment as a major element in the design and evaluation of systems. It is important to emphasize here, as was done in Chapter Three, that the model goes beyond the content and technology. The analysis of the environment takes cognizance of critical dimensions of problems which have a significant effect on information need and choice in that environment. These problem dimensions are not included in the usual content-driven models which are limited to the naming of subjects. This requires that information systems be perceived as more than question-answering systems. This is not to say that we are insisting on problem-solving systems—a foolish attempt at best—but rather on problem addressing, problem clarifying, or (after Lindblom and Cohen) problem-attacking systems. This implies that we consider any human intermediary—searcher, analyst, evaluator, synthesizer, or interpreter—as part of the system. By concentrating on the true end-user of an information system *and* on the ultimate use of the information, we place emphasis on the real functions and purposes of systems. Some readers may feel uncomfortable with the use of the word "system" in this context, rather than, say "process." The term "system" has been used because it is felt that all the activities from generation to point of use constitute a coherent and systematic set of steps or operations, hence a system. With the stress on specialization and the separation of function, our culture tends to emphasize differences rather than similarities, static activity rather than dynamic process. This base of specialization reinforces the idea of separate systems (plural) which are perceived to be dissimilar. One of the arguments of this book has been that by stepping back and gaining perspective, we can begin to see the similarities and allow experience with one type of system to inform another.

This is a critical point, for it asserts that the system elements that supply the added values are not bounded or limited by whatever technologies are available at that time. The value-added model is not dependent on the efficiency of a particular technology, but rather on how effective the combination of technology and human expertise is in providing information where it is needed and where it will be used. This does not mean that costs and efficiencies are not important, rather the model poses a different set of questions: what is the *total cost* of getting appropriate information into the hands of those who need it at the time they need it; and how is that cost to be shared between system and user. Under present conditions, if the true costs of this process were analyzed and totaled, we daresay that we would be shocked by these real costs of information provision, and by the resultant low benefits. As King and Kraemer (1981; p. 112) remark: Whoever heard of "runaway benefits" or "benefit overruns"?

As a consequence, the value-added model has several advantages which recommend it over the traditional models—conscious or unconscious—that presently hold. It has an applicability, a permanence, and a validity for all types of information-use environments. It is a valid approach, regardless of medium, subject matter, technology, or level of human contribution. The model only insists that the function, purpose, and hypothetical user of the system be defined. The model assumes a human user, but it could also pertain to machine-to-machine information transfer, though this would not be very interesting. The added values defined here (or something like them) are permanent features of any information system or service. Paying attention to those values, despite system and process changes, will provide long-term evaluation and costing measures.

Thus, within limits, the value-added model appears to be generalizable. It has, however, no particular predictive power at this stage. Its principal purpose now is to organize a way of thinking about effective means of moving information through organized sets of processes. In a conventional sense, information systems are not usually perceived as comparable. That is to say, management information systems (MIS) are not perceived as similar to libraries, scientific data analysis centers with decision-support systems. There appear to be several reasons for this. The perceived variety of content and organization, for example, between thermophysical properties and newspaper clippings, between medical patient records and educational research, between laboratory notebooks and corporate financial statements, between the literature of chemistry and consumer price data, tends to emphasize differences rather than similarities. The handling processes and contexts strengthen this assumed disparity. The use of coputer systems and the use of hard data, which is more easily manipulated than soft data in the computer, creates a halo effect which exaggerates the view of uncomparability. Different training, background, and traditions strengthen feelings of territoriality and thus differences. These forces foster divergence. One of the major assets of the value-added model is that it provides a focus for convergence of systems thinking and systems planning. By emphasizing usefulness (use value) of a system, the focus is on effectiveness and benefit, rather than technologies, efficiencies, and costs. It is not that the latter are overlooked, but rather that a new context has been established against which costs can be equated. This provides the means to explore and to evaluate the best ways of delivering or providing information of different types to a set of clients in a particular environment with particular problems. In this sense we think the model is not only generalizable, but possesses considerable merit by emphasizing similarities rather than differences among systems. It allows for better total planning.

We have brought up the idea of facilitating choice of messages as the defining purpose of information systems. This was derived principally in the context of abstraction and indexing (A&I) systems and similar organizing processes. Choice of message, however, may not be a major purpose of other systems. In order to meet the requirements of information systems beyond the basic organizing processes of document-based processes, we need to enlarge our definition of system purpose. Information systems then are sets of activities that add value to the items being processed in order

- to make choice easier, by attaching labels to information chunks and by providing the means for reducing noise;
- to clarify a situation by providing a new structure to information thereby allowing users to make better sense of situations than they would have otherwise;

- to raise the probability of a better decision by providing better quality, better formatted, and more precise information which is better adapted to the problem or situation.

Management information systems, for example, are basically algorithmic and transactional. The question of choice does not seem to be present in the output at all. The question of choice of output may arise in the early design of MIS outputs, if indeed it is present at all; certainly such choices are not presented to clients at the time of delivery. In decision support systems (DSS), the idea of choice may play a role in that the client is offered ranges of options for manipulating data; and potential or estimated advantages and disadvantages of certain courses of action may be presented. It is significant and worthy of note that, in DSS, "the managers' opinions and understanding of the decision situation are a major input to the design process" (Keen & Morton, 1978; p. 185). However, both MIS and DSS are technology driven, bound by the constraints of the data processing and computing devices they have espoused as their systems environment. Therein may rest the seeds for their eventual failure as true information systems.

The major perspective, in the value-added sense, of DSS design seems to be the clarification of what we have called the negotiating space, or, where system and problem meet. Clarification here is seen as the presentation of means to allow a client to play with, that is, to manipulate, different variables in order to see what might happen under varying conditions. Such play, if controlled, has the function of structuring the problems a client has in more useful ways (clarifying). In value terms, *flexibility* would be the value added by the system. Clarification may indeed be the purpose of such systems. Decision support systems, however, could be a much more powerful organizing concept if attention were paid to the human extensions of the system in the analysis, interpretation, and transfer of information.

The question of what purpose an information system serves and what the target environment is will in large part determine the kinds of values that should be added by the system. For example, the value *validity* was not added in the abstracting and indexing process, and there were very few adapting activities. Yet these seem to be significant values for decision support, engineering design information, and information analysis systems. Different information systems add different sets of values. The question here is whether or not the 23 values which have been defined are sufficient to cover information system variety. We think they are; but this cannot be said with any certainty until a variety of system types have been analyzed in the value-added context.

There are problems with the definitions. As they have been stated and defined in Chapter Four, they may be too oriented toward document-based processes. They may need to be made more general, so as to better cover system variety and to look across systems at comparable processes.

There is concern with those values grouped under "Adaptability": closeness to problem, flexibility, simplicity, stimulatory. The criterion of adaptability is a critical one for the model. Whether it has been described as well as it should be is moot.

It, more than any other criterion, asks what the system does to understand and to help clarify the problems that its clientele have. This is not meant, by the way, to imply that information is a universal panacea.

> The mere fact of having access to information does not create the disposition to act appropriately. Information is not a substitute for human experience. . . . Information is necessary for rational decision making and conflict resolution, but it is certainly not sufficient. (Mowshowitz, 1976; pp. 164–65)

Adaptability implies, on the part of the user, a desire that, whatever face the system turns toward him, it will fit its output to his real needs. The value we have labeled "Closeness to Problem" is critical in this context. It implies an awareness and empathy on the system side that only a human being can provide. This is not the same as closeness to decision. Only the decision maker can be at that point. Only he or she can decide whether or not to use the information. Only he or she is fully aware of the constraints and opportunities of the situation. How sensitive the system is to that situation is a measure of its value.

The concept of "Use" of information is a hazy one. It has been briefly discussed in various parts of the book, without fully coming to grips with all its variations in our contexts. The word has been employed in a very pragmatic sense. It is not the intent of this book to pursue this further, except to stress the need for fundamental analysis and definition of the forms and attributes of information use—definitions and structures which have utility in the practice-based model we have derived and presented. Wilson (1978) in his succinct essay on some of the fundamental concepts of information retrieval, has briefly explored the implications of the attempts to define "use." Paisley (1980) in his paper on information and work has begun to sketch out some of the problem. The Rouses have also begun to codify some of the approaches in this area (Rouse & Rouse, 1984). This incipient structuring is one of the necessary early steps to the long-range development and utility of the value-added model.

One can easily argue with the value *stimulatory,* the term used to encompass those activities that may not be directly supportive of the specific system mission but which tend to enhance the system's overall objectives in information provision. Managing seminars, editing speeches and papers, consulting on equipment, providing space for meetings are a few of the activities included under this rubric. The principal reason for its inclusion is to be able to account for as much of the total costs of providing information as possible. There is a danger, of course, that inappropriate activities and their associated costs will be pushed into this category so that overhead costs will not appear to be too large. Each installation will need to describe what does fit into the stimulatory category, or if indeed it is a useful classification.

In examining the processes of information analysis, the idea of filtering kept surfacing. *Filtering* seemed to be an important activity in support of several classes of value. It is worth exploring some of this for the light it may shed both on some of the practices that add value and on the difficulty of defining and limiting a particular value. It might be noted that, at first consideration, filtering was thought of as a value within the criterion adaptability. It gradually became apparent that filtering was not a value itself, but rather was a pervasive activity throughout the value spectrum. As a verb it is used in the sense of "passing through some medium in order to purify or to separate or both." In the context of information, the process can exist at input to reduce the quantity of data and/or to raise the quality of data coming into the system. It can be used throughout the process to "separate the wheat from the chaff." It can be used at output so that the user will be better served. At various stages it enhances such values as precision, selectivity, validity, closeness to problem, and simplicity. The noun form implies that, before we can perform the act of filtering, we need to have defined a set of standards or criteria; the size and shape of the mesh so to speak, which determines what does or does not enter the system, move to the next stage, or pass on to the client or user. At various stages and through diverse ways, the process of filtering reduces noise, raises quality, and adapts information to different needs.

This question of filtering and filters has been explored here because it represents a primary process and value-added activity that future information systems must be concerned with. As with all significant activities, it also bears seeds of danger. The act of filtering may also deny important and valuable information. In a democratic society the solution to this dilemma has been, ideally, to maintain open channels and access to all information. Security systems have found it necessary to measure and present their requirements against this ideal. This should not be tampered with. It is absolutely necessary for an open society. In the context of specific information systems, however, witholding information (without prejudice) is a critical and necessary protection against information overload. It is happening anyway, but in a highly haphazard way. Consequently, the definition of a filter and its implementation become of paramount importance.

The brief review of some of the problems with the value-added model illustrates the difficulties of coming to grips with a process—information transfer—still in the throes of defining itself. As was said earlier in the chapter, part of the dilemma seems to be with disparate vocabularies, a diversity of preconceptions, and differing attitudes and assumptions concerning the role of technology in the information process. A primary concern at this time may be linguistic and definitional, developing a means whereby we in the information and data processing professions, the management sciences, and the information sciences can talk to each other, stressing similarities rather than differences.

IMPLICATIONS FOR EDUCATION

For reasons that should be apparent by now, the approach of this book has been practice driven. That is to say we have started from operating systems rather than from intellectual structures. Though there may be parallels in the disciplinary context, the two approaches are quite different. As a matter of fact, as Anna Harrison points out,[1] there may be three traditions of knowledge and practice we are dealing with: science, engineering, and technology. We are hampered in discussing these three traditions by a vocabulary that is not adapted to a technical age, let alone to the age of information. To distinguish the three very briefly, at some loss of precision and intent, we will say that

- *science* deals with explanations, with the production of new knowledge;
- *engineering* deals with the design of systems and with their improvement;
- *technology* deals with the processes of production and delivery of goods and services.

All three are necessary approaches for the development of a discipline, whether it be pure, applied, or operational. We believe, however, that the three approaches will merge as a result of perceptions of similarities of operating systems rather than through the intellectual constructions of information processes imposed on information systems. The coalescence of the field will come about *because* there are operating information systems and services which are successful in providing information and knowledge to people called users, clients, or customers. These successful systems need to be explained. Like the steam engine, in the eighteenth century, they work, whether we can describe them or not. Our need at this time, therefore, is to describe as precisely and concretely as we can

- what these systems do;
- how they do what they do;
- how well they perform;
- what their dynamics are in operating terms.

This will require the development of new vocabularies, so that we can talk about similarities across systems, about the provision of information to different types of users, and about the benefits and costs of these systems. When we have learned how to describe these systems well, only then will we begin to be able to develop useful theoretical constructions.

The essential key to this is that we are dealing with a human calling. Human beings are the benefactors of information systems. It is their needs that are served. Human information needs are difficult to describe, and difficult to measure. We have tended, as Boulding has pointed out, "to substitute unimportant questions which can be answered for important questions which cannot" (Boulding, 1961; p. 164). We do not therefore quite agree with the introductory statement to a symposium on the Empirical Foundations of Information and Software Science held at the Georgia Institute of Technology in November 1982:

> Spectacular advances of information processing technology notwithstanding, there is a growing consensus of the scientific and technical community that further progress

---

[1] From Anna J. Harrison. (1984). Editorial—Science, engineering, and technology. *Science, 223;* 543.

> in the effective application of that technology depends on advances in the underlying sciences of which the information and software sciences are the focal ones. (Davis & Zunde, 1984; p. 1)

Our disagreement may stem less from the dichotomy between science and practice, than from the fact that the symposum almost completely omits consideration of information in human settings and the realities of those systems. Pranas Zunde, of the host school and one of the guest editors of the proceedings, defines the two principal concerns:

> Information science is a science that deals primarily with the composition, structure, and properties of *informative texts* and of the transformations they undergo. On the other hand, software science deals primarily with the composition, structure and properties of *prescriptive texts* and of their transformations. (Davis & Zunde, 1984; p. 5)

Now these can in part be related to what we have called the content-driven approach (information science) and the technology-driven approach (software science). It is our argument that these are not enough. The user-driven approach must be included. One does not build a stool with two legs.

It is easier to measure, to describe, and to teach formal systems, for example, without consideration of the human equation. Such an approach has had a profound and deleterious effect on professional education and on the approach to the problems that a profession is trained to deal with. Andrew Hacker, in a critique of professional schools, writes:

> Our top professional schools have ascended to such heights that they are out of touch with the ordinary conditions of our national life. To begin with mathematical models and biochemical research, or even ''legal reasoning,'' obscures the basic fact that any professional practice is a very human calling. We are turning out professionals who tend to look upon people as something of a bother. (Hacker, 1981; p. 28)

In discussing the medical profession, Lewis Thomas writes:

> If I were a medical student or an intern, just getting ready to begin, I would be more worried about this aspect of my future than anything else. I would be apprehensive that my real job, caring for sick people, might soon be taken away, leaving me with the quite different occupation of looking after machines. I would be trying to figure out ways to keep this from happening.[2]

The concern in this section is less to define an intellectual field as it is to provide a preliminary outline for professional education, in the belief that the underlying (we'd rather say parallel) sciences (see Machlup & Mansfield, 1983) will come because we describe our practices well. The user-driven approach discussed in Chapter Three is the basic touchstone. This does not mean that content and technology are neglected; it merely says that these have meaning only within the framework of human users. The value-added model is a means for describing

---

[2] From Lewis Thomas (1983). *The youngest science* (p. 60). New York: The Viking Press.

systems and their benefits and costs in human contexts. In the suggested professional program the approach is practice driven, with an emphasis on the function, design, and operation of information systems and services as they exist now and as they can be predicted to be in the near future.

Generally, the program is perceived as at the graduate professional level, built upon a solid liberal arts background emphasizing strength in both the humanities and the sciences, with solid skill in writing and logical analysis, and beginning knowledge of and skill in using computers. From this outline, certain research areas will begin to emerge and define themselves. We reiterate, however, that the primary need now is to analyze and to define what information systems of all descriptions and levels do. This approach will define and inform both education needs and research. This is not as constraining as it sounds. The six areas outlined below, with one or two exceptions, have no common names nor do the terms used, familiar as they may sound, encompass quite the same territory. As was said in the Introduction, our vocabulary is limited. We can only use what seem to be appropriate terms from the English language, fully cognizant that these terms may carry meanings that do not quite match our intent. There is no other choice except to coin new words, a path this author is reluctant to take. The six areas are:

1. Information use environments
2. Intellectual technologies
3. Availability of data, information, and knowledge
4. Information systems and services
5. Information technologies
6. The economics of information provision and use

These are in no particular order, except that they generally follow the diagram of the user-driven model of Figure 3-1. A most important part of the model is omitted—the negotiating space, the system–user interface. This omission is based on the belief that this interface can and should be threaded through several of the concerns, specifically use environments, systems and services, and economics. The six rubrics do not represent courses, but rather areas from which courses should be developed. They represent knowledges that information professionals should be cognizant of and where, if appropriate, skills should be developed. They require what today appears like a very diverse set of subject knowledges in those who teach the subject matter. This is part of the eclecticism espoused in this book. Tomorrow we hope—and expect—that the apparent diversity and variety will no longer seem strange and infrequent: that there will indeed be a new profession and a new discipline of information. In the meantime we need to describe, analyze, and develop new syntheses useful in research, educational, and operating contexts.

Information Use Environments (see Chapter Three)

The student should have an understanding of the contexts from which the need for information arises and of the various ways of perceiving and describing those environments. It is expected that as a result of courses under this rubric, the student will have developed skills in analyzing the environments within which he or she will be working. Our knowledge is admittedly primitive at this time and methodology in a practical sense rather crude. Organizing what we do know for a course is one rather effective way of discovering the structure and lacunae of a subject.

- types of environments: geographical, social and cultural, intellectual, organizational.
- information use patterns in various identifiable groups: scientists, doctors, lawyers, engineers, health professionals, managers, teachers, students, accountants, scholars, educated lay persons, the information poor.
- organizations as information processors; differences between public agencies and private for-profit organizations; knowledge as a corporate resource; organizational memories; differences among organizations in information terms, that is, research and development operations, educational institutions, testing and diagnostic laboratories, offices in different settings, legislatures.
- problem dimensions; relationship to information use environments and potential effect on system design.
- methods of describing (possibly measuring) information use environments in terms useful to systems design.

Intellectual Technologies

These are the methods used to organize information for storage, retrieval, *and* for communication in textual form, graphic structure, and visual image. These technologies are content driven, tempered and informed by the ways that users (a) structure their information environments and (b) make use of information. These will range from the design of a data base management system to the design of a form used to record an order, from the grammar of a statistical table or chart (Clark, 1983) to the structure of an indexing system, from the presentation of displays of data or images to the design of computer software for portfolio management, from the structure of accounting systems to the design of library classifications. These all require a type of organization—a structuring of the information content, whether the purpose is for storage or for communication. Their purpose, however, will affect the end design.

Part of the assumptions of this book is that the user-driven approach informs and structures all of these technologies. That is to say, there is a basic set of questions, despite the seemingly disparate nature of the forms and systems noted above, which will cause us as information professionals to consider what is best for a particular setting regardless of the origin of the intellectual technology. The following outline is in the form of questions rather than statements because the nature of our integrating knowledge here is so slight.

- Will different information environments require different types of these organizing technologies?
- Conversely, are certain intellectual technologies inherently better adapted to particular patterns of information needs?
- How do constraints of storage and communication affect the patterns of infor-

mation use and hence the application of a particular intellectual technology?

- What are the strengths and weaknesses of different intellectual technologies? under what conditions?
- How have different intellectual technologies developed historically and what effect does that development have on their utility in computer and telecommunication systems?
- What are the comparative benefits and costs of different intellectual technologies? How can they be evaluated?

Availability of Data, Information, and Knowledge

This area is concerned principally with understanding the variety of agencies which generate, store, analyze, publish, transmit, and market data, information, and knowledge; and how these processes may be affected by current and potential information technologies.

The kinds of considerations which structure and inform this particular concern can be seen in the following groups of questions.

1. What is the structure and role of *information industries* in generating and providing information? What is the role of *governments and international agencies* in generating and distributing data? What is the role of *information analysis centers* and specialized *consultants* in processing, evaluating, and providing scientific, technical, economic, and social data and advice? What means presently exist to inform us of the existence, product, and reliability of these industries, agencies, centers,and consultants?

2. Historically what has been the role of traditional publishing? In primary publication? in secondary publication? What are likely short- and long-term effects of computers and telecommunication technologies on the publishing industry and on the availability and forms of information and knowledge?

3. How are different types of *numerical data* created and produced? How are they made available? How reliable are they, how accurate or valid? What are the means for assuring reliability? What are the problems of longitudinal comparability?

4. *Within organizations,* what types of internal information and data are generated? For what purposes (e.g., financial control, production, sales, planning)? How are these data made available? How are such data presently accessed? What security problems are there?

5. What are *constraints* on the availability of information and data? technological? national security? privacy? proprietary? legal (copyright, patents, transborder data flow)? What effect does the Freedom of Information Act have on the availability of information?

6. What are the potential roles for *expert systems* in these processes? Will they give new meaning to the idea of availability by providing linkages, software for data manipulation, and filtering mechanisms not available now?

Information Systems and Services

This book has delineated several specific types of information systems: document based, information analysis, management information, decision support. Under this rubric, however, we are more concerned with analytic questions.

- What is a system?
- What does any particular system do?
- How is a system designed?
- How can a system be analyzed?
- How can a system be evaluated?

Present courses and instructional approaches to systems analysis cover these questions rather well in traditional ways. That is to say, system analyses and evaluation is usually concerned with the efficient and effective operation of systems, *as perceived from the systems' point of view*. The value-added approach, however, suggests that the user or presumed beneficiary be brought into the analytic process. Consequently, a different set of questions has been asked about systems than is usual: What do specific system activities, or subprocesses, do for the hypothetical user? This has been discussed at some length in the section on systems in Chapter Three, in Chapter Six in the context of A & I services, and in Chapter Nine on productivity.

If, as has been argued, an information system is a formal set of value-adding processes, then we should be able to teach students how to analyze a system in this context, and to ask, if a subprocess does not seem to add value, what its purpose is and why it is there in the first place. These are not easy questions to ask or to answer because generally we have not thought in these terms. Additionally, information processes and information costs are difficult to break out of larger organizational processes, such as office systems.

In a certain sense, by using the value-added approach in the analysis of systems, we have integrated evaluation with analysis. The approach demands that each subprocess be examined for its contribution to user well-being. It is too easy and convenient to dismiss this approach as impractical at this time. Students being trained now will be designing, managing, and evaluating information systems well into the twenty-first century, by which time user-based criteria to systems concerns will become primary inputs to analysis. They need to be prepared not only to participate but also to provide an informed basis for such user-oriented system design.

Information Technologies

Knowledge of the technologies of information storage and transfer should be one of the primary forms of expertise of the information professional. In our context, such knowledge includes at least the following types of systems:

- publishing, printing, and duplicating;
- computers, together with associated input and output devices;
- nonprint media;
- television and radio;
- micrographic;
- telecommunication.

We do not yet have courses that look upon all of these technologies as an integrated whole. It has been a piecemeal approach, because each technology has attracted a particular disciplinary interest: departments of computer science or computer engineering or book publishing or telecommunications or instructional media or radio and television. As the need grows for the rational costing and control of information resources and their associated technologies, an integrated approach becomes critical. The emerging information professionals and the curricula that support their education are perhaps the only place in academia where this integration can take place. It is in this context that the technologies can be evaluated for system compatibility and utility, and combined into cost-effective total systems.

Because of the centrality of the computer in some form in all of these technologies, knowledge of computer hardware and software is basic. However, this should not stop here as is usually the case today. For each technology, a student should know

- general engineering design;
- function in information systems;
- performance characteristics;
- present hardware and structure of the market, including manufacturing and services;
- information sources for data, specifications, and, if possible, reliability and test information;
- the economics of the technology; original costs, maintenance, operating costs;
- potential directions of development of hardware and software;
- compatibility and interfacing with other hardware and technologies;
- potential role in value-adding systems;
- need for special staff expertise.

It is obviously impossible for a student to know all these things about all types of hardware and software. It is important to know the general engineering design and operational characteristics, present and potential hardware and function, compatibility with other system elements, and sources of data and information. The purposes of this knowledge is only useful if it teaches one to ask the right questions and to know when one gets good answers. The purpose of the previous section on systems and services was the design and analysis of information systems. The objective of this section on information technologies is the design of information systems using the most appropriate technology for the job to be done. This means that the student should have the opportunity to design mixed systems in specific contexts.

The Economics of Information Provision and Use

The reader will notice that words—provision and use—have been added to the usual phrase. This has been done purposely in order to maintain our focus on the practice and use of information. It implies systems that are formally designed and managed to generate, acquire, organize, store, retrieve, and transmit information. Information is not a by-product. On the other side, it implies people who actively search for, are the willing recipients of, and frequently may even make use of information. Generally we perceive economics in this context, as the study of how people and organizations chose to use and to distribute information resources in order (a) to generate new information; (b) to produce other commodities or services; (c) to provide the basis for governance and management; and (d) to improve the quality of life. We are interested in the analysis of benefits and costs of information choice and with the ways of improving that benefit/cost ratio at several levels. Threaded throughout all of these concerns are the two facets of value-added central to this book: the economist's view of added value—the creation of wealth—the difference between the input costs and the output costs of a particular product or service; and the information consumer's view of added value, who asks "What am I getting from an information system for my expenditure of time, energy, and dollars?" The professional needs to distinguish between the two approaches and to consider how they complement each other.

1. At the *societal level,* it is necessary to know how the economy (especially the American economy) has changed over the past century from an agricultural to an industrial to an information economy. From the seminal works of Machlup (1962; 1984) and Porat (1977), a student should begin to see how this new economy has grown, what investments are made by various sectors, and how the structure of that economy might be mapped (McLaughlin, 1980). This is a necessary setting for any professional in the field.

2. At the *organizational level,* a student should be aware of the processes of allocation, both open and hidden, of resources used to support, maintain, and use information processes. The major problem at this level, as discussed in Chapters Eight and Nine, is the identification and costing of information processes that are concealed in overhead accounts. This is a difficult process because accounting systems and other organizational structures are not attuned to these processes. A student needs to be sensitive to these difficulties and to the organizational climates that surround and reinforce these problems. At the same time, the student needs to be sufficiently aware of the principles of cost accounting and methods of information resource auditing so that he or she is prepared to analyze and to cost out information processes when the need and opportunity arise. The student should be prepared—though how one trains for this is questionable—to analyze the effects of information on organizational performance (benefit) and the costs of providing and using that information. At minimum a student should be prepared to think in terms of benefits and costs.

3. At the *group or individual level,* the student needs to know the processes and attributes of trade-offs that are necessary in seeking and using information. This is necessary for two reasons. First, the student will be called upon to design and to implement, possibly to manage, small information systems or services designed for a specific task. This requires negotiation and an articulate understanding of the reasons for the need, the options open, and the costs involved. This may range from applications programming to information provision in support of a research

effort, from an analytic report on information equipment to the development of ongoing data on productivity in a dataprocessing operation. The second reason is that one of the hallmarks of the profession will be to raise the level of information literacy in an organization, that is, to inculcate a sensitivity to the benefits and costs of information use. This is the subject of further remarks in the last section of this chapter.

4. At the *system level,* the student should be aware of some of the methods, albeit crude at this time, of deriving rough cost and benefit figures for information provision and information use. An example of this for a broad and widely scattered user audience may be seen in the methods and estimates of value (in dollars) of the energy data base of the US Department of Energy's Technical Information Center (King Research Inc., 1982). Griffiths (1982) has summarized current approaches. This author suspects that many such studies have been made internally in organizations but have never been published.

These concerns will give a student both a theoretical and applied base for understanding the economics of information provision and use.

Underlying all six of these subject areas or any pedagogic division of the information field at the professional level is the need for intelligent and informed use of research and its results. Katzer, Cook, and Crouch in their book on evaluating information, point out that most research courses in information studies programs are "taught from a researcher's point of view." Professionals, however, will not be deeply concerned with designing experiments or performing research. Therefore, "what these students need is a research course with a consumer's point of view" (Katzer, Cook, & Crouch, 1982; p. v). We need to nurture an informed skepticism among professionals about the research data they see reported. In addition, because we suggest in the next section a sort of experimenting community of professionals, we need to educate for a capability in field observation, data collection, and precise description, so that we can begin to structure praxis: systems, content, users. This may require a separate course on evaluating information.[3] More importantly, the attitude of intelligent consumption (and limited generation) of research data should affect and inform all professional education.

RESEARCH

It is not the intent here to summarize present research or to discuss future research in the field. Rather, we wish to suggest a few areas, derived from the assumptions and ideas expressed in this book, where research might have special import. There are three particular points of view which have been argued in this book and which are relevant to the discussion here.

---

[3] Just such a course (IST 551) has been offered for the last decade or more at the School of Information Studies, Syracuse University. The book by Katzer, Cook, and Crouch (1982) grew out of the experience and needs of that course.

1. This is a practice-driven field. That is to say, we have systems (sets of practices) that work (generate, organize, retrieve, and transmit information to people who can make use of that information). We need to know how and why these systems work.

2. We have described a user-driven model as a necessary addition to the present content- and technology-driven models. This approach, in contrast to the other two, reinforces the perception of similarities among systems, and hence comparability of system and praxis, despite seemingly disparate content and technologies. It is, if you will, an ecumenical approach.

3. The value-added approach emphasizes the need to look at user benefits and costs. It focuses on the output of systems, be it product or service, and allows us to look backward at the system and its efficiencies and forward to the user's choices and performance.

If we accept the notion that science is "observation organized," then there are some very basic needs for the field of information. It has been argued here that, at this time, the basic needs of the information field are rigor in definition and systematic typologies of the entities and processes we deal with. We need to learn how to observe, how to organize those observations, how to apply the insights gained to operating systems, and how those observations can inform theoretical constructs. For example, though we have gained some knowledge in the work of the past 25 years on relevance, recall, and precision, we have not been able to transfer that knowledge to real information systems.

There are very real difficulties in transferring to operating systems the knowledge resulting from these experiments. This is at least partially so because of the highly artificial and constrained conditions necessary for the experiments. This author does not intend to discuss the questions of epistemology implied here. This is a problem at the heart of research and knowledge transfer in the information field. The approach espoused in this book, however, argues that, at this time, instead of controlled experiments, the field needs controlled and rigorous ways of explicating and evaluating praxis that are acceptable to the information community.

In a way, we in the field, and especially those who have design and operating responsibilities, need to become an experimenting community (Campbell, 1982; Dunn, 1982). We need to go far beyond the usual "how we do it good in our shop" kinds of reports that clutter up meetings and journals. We need ways of recording observations of practice so that the data derived from such observations can be compared, first across similar systems, and then across all information systems. We need methods of perturbing operating systems in controlled ways, and of developing useful and generalizable data from these attempts. We need ways of learning from doing. Elting Morison, writing of "building things in early America" and especially of the canals in the eighteenth century, points out that "little bits of hard-won knowledge, fragments of partial understanding were strewn in disorder around the country at the sites of smaller, often half-finished projects" (Morison, 1974; p. 38). These fragments could not come to fruition until they came together in a large project. That project was the construction of the Erie Canal in Upstate

New York, a 363-mile-long structure that opened up the middle of the North American continent. As Morison so eloquently writes: "they opened the first—and quite possibly the best—school of general engineering in this country . . . scores of untutored men learned how to think and to work their way through unfamiliar problems . . . taken all together, they were the principal agency in the accumulation, codification, and consolidation of the information that gave to our engineering its first sustaining body of knowledge" (Morison, 1974; pp. 44–45).

We are in a somewhat similar plight, except that our "fragments of partial understanding" are buried in tons of trivial and inconsequential information, the effluent of our civilization. The fragments do exist, however, in our professional know-how, scattered in operating systems across the country and the world. This author, after working with the knowledgeable professionals in the A&I services (see Chapter Six), is convinced that there is much knowledge in praxis that needs to be codified. We have not yet found the structure for codification. Nor do we know quite the right questions to ask. The value-added approach (or some refinement of it) may provide that structure.

To this end there is a need for a practical and useful typology of formal information systems, hospitable to all the types of systems discussed in this book, and their variations. Such a typology should include at minimum

- purpose of the system, that is, what it is intended to do;
- kinds of information/data input;
- general system processes and their possible contributions in adding value;
- types of outputs, including services provided;
- total system costs, including staffing and level of expertise required;
- types of clientele and their contexts.

Each of these six categories requires, in turn, their own typologies and definitions. For valuable insight on the taxonomy and evaluation of information systems see Arnovick and Gee (1978). Such a process would allow the development and testing of value-added processes across systems and would begin to provide similar ways of talking about information systems of varying types.

Related to this, in fact based on the typology just discussed, is the need to develop system analysis protocols within the value-added frame of reference, together with cost accounting procedures. Such protocols must be acceptable and applicable across all system types. Though such an approach may seem incongruous—even banal—in the setting of children's services in a large public library, nevertheless, the process if carefully thought through can contribute to an understanding of that particular process. The same rigor in the analysis protocol should be applied to a business information control system (Kerner, 1982). When we can truly compare such seemingly disparate systems, we will have a solid beginning toward a science of information systems. We rather suspect that the operation of a children's room will be more systematic than thought to be at first glance, and the business information system far less amenable to systematization than its proponents assert. Rigor in analysis, by the way, does not necessarily need quantification. In fact, quantification at this time may tend to mask a lack of thorough analysis.

In order to provide the kinds of data and information for the system we have described, there is a need to develop a taxonomic and systematic approach to information use environments. We need to understand this process at two levels.

1. At the level of the environment, it is necessary to be able to describe the contours and dynamics in information terms. Such description can vary, depending on the variables under scrutiny, from quite precise in the case of a factory production line or the financial office of a school system to highly qualitative in the case of a general manager (Kotter, 1982) or an inner-city neighborhood. Present forms of describing these contexts have been determined by the kind of system assumed to be relevant to that particular environment. This is going at things backward. Though it may be a difficult and slow process, we need to start at the end of the potential user. Some of the descriptive parameters of information use environments were discussed in Chapter Three. We now need as complete a list of possible variables as can be identified and defined. This can provide not only a structure for current description of context, but, more importantly, a base for empirical studies over the next several decades.

2. We need to develop acceptable and tested ways of translating these descriptions into terms useful for system design. Such a transformation would be informed and affected in three ways (see Figure 3-1):

- by the available intellectual technologies;
- by the data and information available to the particular context;
- by the capabilities of technology current at the time.

Obviously this process is a compromise between the ideal response to the needs of a particular environment and the constraints of equipment, time, money, and level of systems expertise.

Intellectual technologies have been mentioned several times as a collective rubric for the structures we impose upon data and information in formal systems. The intent of such structures are both to organize content and to assist users in making choices or in clarifying a problem. Sometimes these two objectives are not compatible: content description versus user need. The value-added approach, especially as related to the criteria of adaptability and of noise reduction, provides a means of bridging this dichotomy between the storage and descriptive requirements of the system content and the information needs of the client.

For the past quarter of a century, starting with the Cranfield experiments in the late 1950s, the work on recall, relevance, precision, and associated terms, has helped to clarify these concepts and to cast light on the intellectual technologies involved, specifically subject indexing (Cooper, 1978). We now need to transfer that knowledge into operational concepts. There are several caveats, however, about the transfer of the knowledge gained. First, almost all of the research was done in very restricted environments, that is, science and technology, which make up but a very small segment of the information spectrum. If the field is to have meaning across system variety, then the scope needs to be enlarged. Second, there are several difficulties of measuring the relevance of information chunks in artificially constrained experimental situations. The simplifying assumptions, however necessary, tend to remove the results from real systems. This is a fundamental question of course in the natural sciences, and even more so in the behavioral sciences. Third, the retrieval measures have been entirely based on subject-oriented access systems. As was discussed in Chapter Three, there are many other factors beside subject matter upon which users base their choice of information packages: problem dimensions, information traits, time constraints, and level of sophistication. (Rouse & Rouse, 1984). We need to examine the utility of filters based on approaches other than subject matter. Such approaches would be valid not only in present document-based systems but will become even more necessary in the text-searching and paperless systems of the future in order to alleviate overload. Users must be given opportunities other than subject matter, not only to narrow their searches, but more critically to be able to match the information clues they are presented with to the problems they have. Reflecting the approach we have taken, we need better descriptions, definitions, and, when appropriate, empirical testing of these nonsubject variables. The ASK approach (anomalous states of knowledge) is a significant first step in this direction (Belkin, Oddy, & Brooks, 1982).

Another area of research concern to be mentioned is that of the value-added approach itself. Despite the discussions in Chapters Two and Four, the fundamental question of information value has been skirted. We may never have an unambiguous definition of value of information. It is, however, as the Rouses point out, "the central theoretical issue. Significant progress in modeling human information seeking, developing design frameworks, and devising evaluation methodologies depend on progress in dealing with the issue of value of information" (Rouse & Rouse, 1984; p. 135). As may be surmised by now, the approach of this book has been to start from a different departure point—from the practice of successful information system operation. "Successful" here means that systems provide information products and services to their clientele with some degree of usefulness, unmeasured perhaps, but nonetheless of value. In this process the system assists users in making choices and in clarifying puzzling situations by adding certain attributes or signals to and performing certain operations on information being processed. These attributes and operations have been called value adding. Though starting from the other end—that of practice—this is one way of responding to the Rouses' expression of concern. The value-added approach will begin to clarify why people make use of (or do not make use of) information systems in the first place, and thereby shed some light on how they view the benefits anticipated vis-à-vis the costs incurred. These are questions of value. Though an act of faith, we believe the theoretical and the practical will inform and illuminate each other.

In this context it is necessary to examine the values that have been isolated and defined. Are they sufficient to cover all the practices of information systems? Many more such values could have been added to the list. It is felt, however, that the ones noted are sufficiently general—yet capable of differentiation one from the other—to include all the enhancements that information systems do add. This is an assumption that should be examined and tested. There is a need to look at a single value or a cluster of values across systems to assess applicability. For example, Access I, II, and III which are locating, tagging, and summarizing values, need to be looked at for their relevance to all types of systems? Our hunch is that they, or some variation of them, do perform an enhancing function in other systems. The whole criterion of adaptability and its associated values need examination and controlled observation in operating situations. This is a particularly important set of values, especially within the problem context discussed in this book.

A final area of research concern to be mentioned is based on the paucity of verified and accepted data in the field. The field desperately needs a data analysis program of its own to collect, analyze, evaluate, compare, discard, and synthesize data already available. As anyone knows who reads the literature of management information systems, office automation, and document-based systems, we are bombarded by data which if valid (and accepted by the profession) would have a profound effect on the design of information systems. Unfortunately, much of such data is less than useful because of poor definition or methodology, or it is inapplicable because of local or special constraints in derivation. These data float freely in our milieu. We pick out those pieces which match our needs at the time. As have most people in the field, this author has participated in this game, using these data for illustration or emphasis in the classroom, as arguments in a paper, or as support in negotiating a budget or a new piece of equipment. It is hoped that appropriate qualifiers were attached to the data. Such is not always the case because qualifiers would weaken the argument, and data are data and, therefore, except for ranges, cannot be qualified.

These remarks are not meant to imply that there are no good data or no careful analyses being made. It is rather that such studies tend to get buried in the mass of information in the field. An example of what appear to be useful data are those emanating from the work of Kantor and others at Tantulus, Inc. in Cleveland. Through econometric studies of academic and medical libraries they are developing ways of deriving unit costs of circulation and reference in relation to in-house use of materials. This is a beginning toward the necessary analyses implied in the value-added model—how a library allocates its resources in relation to the user or client. The importance of these studies at this time, however, is less in the data derived, but in the methodology presented and tested, which "focuses on objectively measurable parameters describing the interface between the information storage and retrieval system and the individuals who use it" (Kantor, 1983; p. 297). Other such carefully designed studies of systems in user contexts are beginning to be made. It is important that these data and methods begin to inform the profession to see how comparable and applicable they might be in different kinds of information systems.

Without prejudice, nor with any attempt to criticize the data cited below, the following excerpts and summaries are indicative of the variety of data which, if only slightly valid, have something critical to say about system design. It should be noted that the quotations are out of context for brevity sake, and therefore may not carry the necessary qualifiers.

> It has been estimated by office consulting services that some 35 percent of the material in business files is never retrieved and that 90% could be discarded after being retained one year.[4]
>
> Human beings (as opposed to documentary or physical sources) provide 67% of all important information acquired by the executives whose information practices were studied.[5]
>
> In sending a message over a network, a typical service price is $1, and a typical user time cost for message preparation, reception, and filing is $5. Similarly, in time-shared computing, a $5 per hour figure is a typical price, and perhaps three to five times this figure is a typical user time cost.[6]
>
> A user of an academic research library will have immediate access to only about 50 percent of the materials which he wants and which the catalog informs him are in the collection; the remainder are lost, in circulation, misshelved, at bindery, or otherwise inaccessible.[7]
>
> In studies of a medical journal collection, an Air Force research library, two university libraries and a public library, approximately 80 percent of the requests were satisfied with about 20 percent of the materials held, and 99 percent of the requests were filled with 50 percent of the holdings.[8]

These have been cited to illustrate some of the problems and benefits associated with data in the field. Because of inflationary trends and the transformation of the field by information technologies, dollar figures, as in the third item cited, may only be valid for a short time. It is the method of derivation and the ratios (in this case, service price to user costs) which are of importance. Detailed description of the methods of defining, deriving, and manipulating the data in question is necessary, especially in dealing with cost and price data. Though these methods might be deemed imperfect, even "quick and dirty," we need to be able to see them and to review them in the larger context of data derivation and utility. They may represent the only figures we can get, but we need to know the circumstances and assumptions of their derivation. Only by doing this can we (a) make informed use (or nonuse) of the data already available, and (b) develop or refine methods for

---

[4] Quoted by R.H. Miller in Mason and Creps (1981, p. 184) from Stanford Research Institute, Business Intelligence Program, Guidelines No. 1001: "Office of the Future" Stanford, CA.

[5] From W.J. Keegan (1968). Acquisition of global information. *Columbia Journal of World Business, 3*(2); 36.

[6] From D.A. Dunn & A.C. Fronistas in Goldberg & Lorin (1982). Vol. 1, p. 141.

[7] The reader will have to take the author on faith here. This is a well-known truism in academic library circles.

[8] From Trueswell (1969), who also points out that the 80/20 ratio seems to be common in many types of systems, such as in business inventories.

deriving and analyzing new data. A second point to be made is that there is a great deal of available data floating unattached, as it were. By acquiring and organizing those data, weak as they may seem, we will begin to structure a data base. We learn by doing. The user-driven approach is a possible framework within which data can be placed. That structure appears to be hospitable to data on most of the concerns of praxis and use.

- user environments, that is, characteristics of different types of users and settings;
- availability of data and information, that is, data on the sources and suppliers of information and data;
- the intellectual technologies, including evaluative tests;
- the information technologies, especially performance test data;
- system design, including cost-efficiency and productivity data; for example, programmer productivity;
- system outputs, for example, data on different types of outputs and on specific value-added processes;
- the negotiation space, cost-benefit data;
- outcomes, effects of information on performance.

The foregoing is only a very crude sketch of a possible structure for the organization of data in the field. It should be limited to quantitative data, with appropriate qualifying descriptions. This is obviously a very large task, but, after initial exploration and testing for hospitality, the operation could inform the field by providing (a) rough clusters of data; (b) beginning comparisons among data; (c) early approaches to evaluation of data collection and analysis; and (d) identification of lacunae where new or better data would strengthen the field. Building such a data base is an important task for the field and one that will have to be performed before the field can "stand on the shoulders of others," or, be cumulative. It is critical if we are to know what we are presently doing, and necessary if we are to develop intelligent and cost-effective information systems in the future.

INFORMATION LITERACY

We are beginning, in the United States, to see an explosive growth of computer literacy. This implies a high skill in using the computer through a terminal and, in many cases, skill in designing and writing new software. This is beginning to permeate the school systems down to the elementary level. The terminal and/or the personal computer is becoming a ubiquitous artifact on the university campus. Its effect on certain segments of American society during the next decade will be profound. Computer literacy, however, is not enough and never will be enough for intelligent survival. It is unfortunate that many schoolchildren will receive this impression. They will develop into a new group of illiterates. We need to remind ourselves constantly that the computer is but a technology for the storage, provision, and manipulation of data. True, it will do many things we could not do before. It allows us to explore combinations and problems we have not been able to undertake before. It has certain magical qualities, confirming Arthur Clarke's Third Law that any sufficiently advanced technology is indistinguishable from magic.[9]

There is an unfortunate tendency to equate computers and information, and hence to mistake computer literacy for information literacy. This is a dangerous myth, for it assumes that information is only that which is storable and manipulable in a computer. This has been discussed in several places throughout this book and will not be pursued further here, except again to stress that computer literacy is but a small part of the new form of literacy necessary to survive in an age of information. True information literacy is made up of a number of knowledges and skills. It is important to remember here that we are not discussing the education of information professionals, who by definition are information literate, but rather the kinds of knowledge and capabilities that any educated person will need to operate effectively in an information-rich technological society.

1. Knowledge of the gross availability of information resources: human, print, computer.
2. Capability to utilize these resources:
   - skill in extracting or obtaining information from other people
   - print literacy
   - computer literacy.
3. Skill in evaluating from surface clues the probable reliability and validity of data and information.
   - What or who is the source?
   - Is the source biased?
   - If so, does it affect the data?
   - What does the data measure?
4. Skill in identifying problems, especially those that one can do something about.
5. Capability to recognize the level and scope of information necessary to address or to clarify a particular problem.
6. Skill in applying information to the problem at hand.
7. Skill in articulating, organizing, and communicating information to others in ways appropriate to the situation.

Information literacy is not just one of these capabilities. It is not a facility in writing programs for an Apple Computer, nor is it a good working knowledge of online retrieval systems. It is not just the knowledge of where information will be found nor is it the design knowledge of decision support systems. Information literacy is the effective combination of the knowledge and skills outlined above. That combination and the concomitant awareness of its implications makes an individual (or a group or an organization) sensitive to the benefits and costs inherent in the provision and use of information. He or she is information literate. Whether or not we are able to hang dollar figures on these benfits and costs or deal with them in precise fashion is immaterial. An individual does not, in most cases, carefully

[9] From Arthur C. Clarke (19 January 1968) letter, *Science, 159,* 255.

calculate ahead of time the costs of lost opportunity nor does one carefully consider whether or not to use the terminal in the next office to access data of possible interest. It does mean, however, that, *because he or she is information literate,* the information user thinks of his or her problems in information terms.

- How important is the problem and its resolution to me?
- How much time and energy do I have and want to invest in this problem?
- What information is needed to address the problem?
- Where do I get the information, and how useful is it likely to be?

These are benefit and cost questions. Decisions based on answers to at least the first two questions are made continually by all of us all the time. The significant and critical concern here is whether individuals make these choices consciously and rationally and whether they are sensitive to the last two questions on the provenance and relevance of information to the situation. Now most people, if they can identify a problem at all, will stop after the first two questions, "I just don't have the time for this," hoping it will go away, which of course it sometimes does. Without getting into the psychology of problem avoidance, people will base their behavior in these situations on previous experience and learning.

This means that the information professionals, as well as the programs that educate them, have a role to play in developing a climate hospitable to the growth of information literacy. Such a climate change will not happen overnight; it will take time, patience, and commitment. The professionals in an organization can do this by careful analysis of those portions of the information resources, structure, and flows for which they have some degree of responsibility. From such analysis they can begin to derive rough estimates of benefits and costs, and gradually introduce these into reports, discussions, and conversations. The word "gradually" is used purposely because there is no doubt but that there will be incomprehension, even hostility, because good data on benefits and costs may affect many sacred cows and threaten the integrity of many territories. Specialization has made all of us conscious of the need to protect our turf. This is the reason for the rise of the information resources manager (IRM), in the best sense a generalist who can begin to effectively relate one to another, the specialties of computing, printing, libraries, mail service, telecommunications, and information analysis. Unfortunately, because of the mistaken notion that equates computers with information, the IRM function may be going by default into the hands of computer literates who in many cases have a limited conception of the information problems. The value-added approach, by the way, has a significant role to play here, for it insists that the user, the client, the receiver of information be brought into the equation. When that step is made, then user benefits and costs must be considered and the question asked: What is the best way to get the most appropriate information to the persons who need it when they need it? The means of delivery—the computer, the human being, and the printed page—become possibilities to be considered, not determinants of an answer.

In this context the schools and programs that educate information professionals should not only be concerned with the education of those professionals. By their insistence that information—its provision and use—is a fundamental characteristic of our emerging society, the schools have the opportunity to affect education in general in very positive ways. Undergraduate courses built around the seven knowledges and skills outlined above would be especially appropriate. This may require joint teaching with another department in order to wrap these skills around a subject matter and its application. This author believes, however, that information, its attributes, its processes, its disciplines (Machlup & Mansfield, 1982) and its uses represent a sufficient, but still undefined, structure for courses of high use to any undergraduate student. That student is growing up in a world where information and its effective use will be basic skills, perhaps even the hallmark of an educated person. Getting the student to think about these concerns in gross benefit and cost terms will help.

This process toward information literacy is a gradual one. When our society recovers from its present technological kick, its love affair with the computer, there will be a real need for the information generalist/professional. They are, in Boulding's words, "intellectual traders . . . somewhat despised both in economics and in the intellectual world" but "absolutely essential to the development of large and complex organizations" (Boulding, 1968; p. B651). These are those persons who, because they are technologically sophisticated *and* information literate, can begin to combine the technologies, the human intermediaries, the information content, and the delivery systems into systems of high utility to the users. Their task will be made easier by a population that is information literate, and therefore hospitable to the kinds of questions the professional will have to ask.

References

Ackoff, R. L. (1967). Management misinformation systems. *Management Science, 14* (4), BB147–BB156.

Allen, T. (1977). *Managing the flow of technology*. Cambridge, MA: MIT Press.

Anthony, R. (1965). *Planning and control systems: A framework for analysis*. Boston, MA: Harvard University, Graduate School of Business Administration.

Arnovick, G. & Gee, L. G. (1978). Design and evaluation of information systems. *Information Processing and Management, 14*, 369–380.

Aspnes, G. (1980). A philosophy of special librarianship. In E. B. Jackson (Ed.), *Special librarianship: A new reader*. (pp. 3–13). Metuchen, NJ: Scarecrow Press.

Belkin, N., Oddy, R., & Brooks, H. (1982). ASK for information retrieval. *Journal of Documentation, 38*, 61–71, 145–164.

Bernier, C. L. (1970). Terse literatures: I. Terse conclusions. *Journal of the American Society for Information Science, 21*, 316–319.

Berry, J. F. & Cook, C. H. (1976). *Managing knowledge as a corporate resource*. Washington, DC: Department of Defense. (NTIS AD–029891).

Black, S. H. & Marchand, D. A. (1980). *Assessing the value of information in organizations: A challenge for the Eighties*. Columbia, SC: University of South Carolina, Bureau of Governmental Research and Service. (Also in *The Information Society, 1* (3); 191–225, 1982.)

Borbely, J. (1981). The critical success factors method: Its application in a special libraries environment. *Special Libraries, 72* (3), 201-208.

Boulding, K. E. (1961). *The Image*. Ann Arbor, MI: University of Michigan Press.

Boulding, K. E. (1968). The specialist with a universal mind. *Management Science, 14*, B647–B653.

Bourne, C. P. (1979, October). *The economics of providing online services*. Paper presented at the Annual Meeting of the American Society for Information Science, Minneapolis, MN.

Bourne, C. P. (1980). On-line systems: History, technology, and economics. *Journal of the American Society for Information Science, 31*, 155–160.

Braunstein, Y. M. (1979). Costs and benefits of library information: The user point of view. *Library Trends, 28*, 79–87.

Braunstein, Y. M. (1982). The functioning of information markets. *Information Reports and Bibliographies, 11* (1), 3–20.

Brinberg, H. R. (1980, August). *The contribution of information to economic growth and development*. Paper presented at the 40th Congress of the International Federation for Documentation, Copenhagen.

Buckland, M. K. (1983). *Library services in theory and context*. New York: Pergamon Press.

Burk, C. F., Jr. (1984). *Auditing the management of information resources*. [Ottawa, Canada], Office of the Auditor General. (Discussion Paper No. 39).

Campbell, D. T. (1982). Experiments as arguments. *Knowledge: Creation, Diffusion, Utilization, 3,* 327–337.

Carroll, B. & Maskewitz, B. K. (1980). Information analysis centers. In M. E. Williams (Ed.), *Annual review of information science and technology,* (vol. 15, 147–189). White Plains, NY: Knowledge Industry Publications.

Childers, T. (1983). *Information and referral: Public libraries.* Norwood, NJ: Ablex.

Churchman, C. W. (1975). What is information for policy making? In M. Kochen (Ed.), *Information for action: From knowledge to wisdom* (pp. 33–40). New York: Academic Press.

Clark, N. (1983, August). *Statistical presentation—Of what, to whom, and for which purpose.* Paper presented at the Joint Statistical Meetings, Toronto.

Cochrane, P. A. (1981, April). *Tasks performed by online searchers in presearch interview.* A report of the Presearch Interview Project (NLM Grant No. 1 Rol LM03074). Syracuse, NY: Syracuse University, School of Information Studies.

Cooper, W. S. (1978). A perspective on the measurement of retrieval effectiveness. *Drexel Library Quarterly, 14* (2), 25–39.

Cronenberger, R., Jr., & Luck, C. (1976). Defining information and referral service. In P. G. Schuman (Ed.), *Social responsibilities and libraries* (pp. 194–199). New York: Bowker.

Crouch, W. W. (1979). *The information interview: A comprehensive bibliography and an analysis of the literature.* Syracuse, NY: Syracuse University, ERIC Clearinghouse on Information Resources.

Davis, J. S. (1984). Chunks: A basis for complexity measurement. *Information Processing and Management, 20*(1–2), 119–127.

Davis, J. S. & Zunde, P. (Eds.). (1984). Empirical foundations of information and software science. Proceedings of First Symposium held at Georgia Institute of Technology in Atlanta, Georgia on 3–5 November 1982. *Information Processing and management, 20*(1–2), 1–337.

De Grolier, E. (1979). *The organization of information systems for government and public administration.* Paris: UNESCO.

Dervin, B. (1975, April). *Strategies for dealing with the information needs of urban residents: information or communication.* Paper presented at the International Communication Association Meeting, Chicago.

Dervin, B. (1976, November). *Information for sense-making.* Paper presented at the Symposium of the Committee on Public Information in the Prevention of Occupational Cancer, Assembly of Life Sciences, National Academy of Sciences.

Dolby, J. L. (1983, May). *Meaning from data: Implications for data analysis and database management systems.* Paper presented at the Meeting of the American Association for the Advancement of Science, Detroit, MI.

Dolby, J. L. & Clark, N. (1982). *The language of data.* Draft, Prepared under a grant from the System Development Foundation.

Dosa, M. L. (1983). The consultant as information intermediary. *Information Services & Use, 3,* 301–318.

Drucker. P. F. (1974). *Management: Tasks, responsibilities, practices.* New York: Harper & Row.

Dubos, R. (1973). The despairing optimist. *American Scholar, 42,* 378–382.

Dunn, E. S. (1974). *Social information processing and statistical systems—Change and reform.* New York: Wiley.

Dunn, W. N. (1982). Reforms as arguments. *Knowledge: Creation, Diffusion, Utilization, 3*, 293–326.

Eisenhart, C. (1968). Expression of the uncertainties of final results. *Science, 160*, 1201–1204.

Eisenstein, E. L. (1979). *The printing press as an agent of change: Communications and cultural transformations in early-modern Europe* (2 vol.). New York, Cambridge University Press.

Elias, A. W. (1979, October). *The economics of online data base creation*. Paper presented at the Annual Meeting of the American Society for Information Science, Minneapolis, MN.

Fabisoff, S. G. & Ely, D. P. (1974). *Information and Information Needs*. Syracuse, NY: Syracuse University, Center for the Study of Information and Education.

Fabisoff, S. G. & Hurych, J. (1981). Is there a future for the end user in online bibliographic searching. *Special Libraries, 72*, 347–355.

Fallon, C. (1971). *Value analysis to improve productivity*. New York: Wiley-Interscience.

Farid, M. A. (1982). Time allocation in students' bibliographical decisions: An economic and time budget approach. Doctoral dissertation, University of California, Berkeley.

Feldman, M. S. & March, J. G. (1981). Information in organizations as signal and symbol. *Administrative Science Quarterly, 26*, 171–186.

Fenichel, C. H. (1981). Online searching: Measures that discriminate among users with different types of experience. *Journal of the American Society for Information Science, 32*, 23–32.

Frischmuth, D. S. & Allen, T. J. (1969). A model for the description and evaluation of technical problem solving. *IEEE Transactions Engineering Management, EM–16*, 58–63.

Frondizi, R. (1971). *What is value? An introduction to axiology*. (2d ed.). La Salle, IL: Open Court Publishing.

Fuchs, V. R. (Ed.). (1969). *Production and productivity in the service industries*. New York: National Bureau of Economic Research, (Studies in Income and Wealth, vol. 34.)

Gerstenberger, P. G. & Allen, T. J. (1968). Criteria used in the selection of information channels by R&D engineers. *Journal of Applied Psychology, 52*, 272–279.

Getz, M. (1979). *An economic view of public libraries*. Cambridge, MA: National Bureau of Economic Research.

Gevarter, W. B. (1983). Expert systems: Limited but powerful. *IEEE Spectrum, 20*(8), 39–45.

Gibbs, M. N. & Laszlo, G. A. (1980). Document ordering through Lockheed's DIALOG and SDC's ORBIT—A user's guide. *Online,4*(4), 31–37.

Giuliano, V. E. (1979). *Productivity in the information society: The United States as a case example*. (Multilithed.)

Goldberg, R. & Lorin, H. (1982). *The economics of information processing* (Vols. 1,2). New York: Wiley.

Goldfield, R. J. (1980). The automated office in the 1980's. *Dun's Review, 115*(3), 129–155.

Goodrum, C. & Dalrymple, H. W. (1982). *The Library of Congress*. Boulder, CO: Westview Press.

Griffiths, J-M. (1982). The value of information and related systems, products, and services. In M. W. Williams (Ed.), *Annual review of information science and technology*, (Vol. 17, 269–284). White Plains, NY: Knowledge Industry Publications.

Hacker, A. (1981, October). The shame of professional schools. *Harpers, 263,* 22–28.

Hall, H. (1982). *Services for the analysis and evaluation of information.* Final Report (NSF/DIST—Grant 78-16628). New Brunswick, NJ: Rutgers University, Graduate School of Library and Information Studies.

Hall, K. (1981). The economic nature of information. *The Information Society, 1,* 143–166.

Hammond, L. W. (1982). Management considerations for an information center. *IBM Systems Journal, 21*(2), 131–161.

Hanson, J. V., McKell, L. J. & Heitger, L. E. (1977). Decision-oriented frameworks for management information systems design. *Information Processing and Management, 13,* 215–225.

Heaton, H. (1977). *Productivity in service organizations: Organizing for people.* New York: McGraw-Hill.

Hilts, P. (1980, December). The clock within. *Science 80, 1*(10), 61–67.

Ho, C. Y. & Touloukian, Y. S. (1977). Methodology in the generation of critically evaluated, analyzed, and synthesized thermal, electrical, and optical properties data for solid materials. In *Proceedings, 5th Biennial International CODATA Conference.* Boulder, CO, 615–627.

Horton, F. W., Jr. (1981). *The information management workbook.* Washington, DC: Information Management Press.

Huber, G. P. (1980). *Managerial decision making.* Glenview, IL: Scott, Foresman.

Huber, G. P. (1981). *Organizational informational systems: Determinants of their performance and behavior.* (Wisconsin Working Paper 4-81-7.) Madison: University of Wisconsin, Graduate School of Business.

Hutchinson, T. W. (1979). *Knowledge and ignorance in economics.* Chicago: University of Chicago Press.

Innis, H. A. (1951). *The bias of communication.* Toronto: University of Toronto Press.

Jackson, E. B. (Ed.). (1980). *Special librarianship: A new reader.* Metuchen, NJ: Scarecrow Press.

Janis, I. L. & Mann, L. (1977). *Decision making: A psychological analysis of conflict, choice, and commitment.* New York: Free Press.

Johnston, R. & Gibbons, M. (1975). Characteristics of information usage in technological innovation. *IEEE Transactions on Engineering Management, EM–22*(1), 27–34.

Kahneman, D. & Tversky, A. (1979). Prospect theory: An analysis of decision under risk. *Econometrica, 47,* 263–291.

Kantor, P. B. (1983). Cost and productivity in library operations. In *Proceedings of the 46th ASIS Annual Meeting* (Vol. 20, pp. 297–300). White Plains, NY: Knowledge Industry Publications.

Katzer, J., Cook, K. H. & Crouch, W. W. (1982). *Evaluating information: A guide for users of social science research.* (2nd ed.). Reading, MA: Addison-Wesley.

Keen, P. G. W. (1981). Information systems and organizational change. *Association for Computing Machinery, Communications, 24*(1), 24–33.

Keen, P. G. W. & Morton, M. S. (1978). *Decision support systems: An organizational perspective.* Reading, MA: Addison-Wesley.

Kerner, D. V. (1982). Business information control study methodology. In R. Goldberg & H. Lorin, (Eds.), *The economics of information processing* (pp. 71–83). New York: Wiley.

Kertesz, F. (1980). The information center concept. In E. B. Jackson (Ed.), *Special librarianship: A new reader* (pp. 714–727). Metuchen, NJ: Scarecrow Press.

King, J. L. & Kraemer, K. L. (1981). Cost as a social impact of information technology. In N. L. Moss (Ed.), *Telecommunications and productivity* (pp. 93–130). Reading, MA: Addison-Wesley.

King, J. L. & Schrems, E. L. (1978). Cost-benefit analysis in information systems development and operation. *Computing Surveys, 10,* 19–34.

King Research, Inc. (1982). *Value of the energy data base*. Work performed under Contract No. A105–800R11232. Submitted to Technical Information Center, US Department of Energy, Oak Ridge, TN.

Knight, K. E. & McDaniel, Jr., R. R. (1979). *Organizations: An information systems perspective*. Belmont, CA: Wadsworth.

Kotter, J. P. (1982). What effective general managers really do. *Harvard Business Review, 60,* 156–167.

Laudon, K. C. (1980). Problems of accountability in large federal databanks. In M. M. Henderson & M. J. MacNaughton (Eds.), *Electronic communication: Technology and impacts*. AAAS Selected Symposium 52 (pp. 123–139). Boulder, CO: Westview Press.

Levitan, K. B. (1980). Applying a holistic framework to synthesize information science research. In B. Dervin & M. J. Voigt (Eds.), *Progress in Communication Sciences* (Vol. 2, pp. 241–273). Norwood, NJ: Ablex.

Lide, D. R., Jr. (1981). Critical data for critical needs. *Science, 212,* 1343–1349.

Lindblom, C. E. (1959). The science of muddling through. *Public Administration Review, 19,* 79–99.

Lindblom, C. E. & Cohen, D. K. (1979). *Usable Knowledge: Social science and social problem solving*. New Haven, CT: Yale University Press.

Lindley, J. A. (1984). *The Congressional Research Service*. July 25, 1980, updated January 3, 1984. (The Library of Congress, Congressional Research Service, Report No. 84–1D, JF 522)

Loasby, B. J. (1976). *Choice, complexity and ignorance: An inquiry into economic theory and the practice of decision making*. New York: Cambridge University Press.

Lundberg, S. O. (1981). A Delphi study of public library goals, innovations, and performance measurements. *Library Research, 3,* 67–90.

McClure, C. R. (1978). The information rich employee and information for decision making: Review and comments. *Information Processing and Management, 14,* 381–394.

McDonough, A. (1963). *Information economics and management systems*. New York: McGraw-Hill.

McHale, J. (1976). *The changing information environment*. Boulder, CO: Westview Press.

McLaughlin, J. F. (1980). *Mapping the information business*. Cambridge, MA: Harvard University, Program on Information Resources Policy. (Publication No. P-80-5).

MacMullin, S. E. & Taylor, R. S. (1984). Problem dimensions and information traits. *The Information Society,* 3(1), 91–111.

Machlup, F. (1962). *The production and distribution of knowledge in the United States*. Princeton, NJ: Princeton University Press.

Machlup, F. (1979). Uses, value, and benefits of information. *Knowledge: Creation, Diffusion, Utilization, 1,* 62–81.

Machlup, F. (1984). *The economics of information and human capital*. Princeton, NJ: Princeton University Press.

Machlup, F. & Mansfield, U. (Eds.). (1983). *The study of information: Interdisciplinary messages*. New York, Wiley.

Manzer, B. M. (1977). *The abstract journal, 1790–1920: Origin, development, and diffusion*. Metuchen, NJ: Scarecrow Press.

Martin, J. (1981). *An end-user's guide to data base*. Englewood Cliffs, NJ: Prentice-Hall.

Martin, L. A. (1974). *Adults and the Pratt Library: A question of the quality of life*. Baltimore, MD: Enoch Pratt Free Library.

Mason, R. M. (1977). *Development of cost benefit methodology for scientific and technical information communication and application to information analysis centers*. (Final Report National Science Foundation Grant No. SIS75-12741). Atlanta, GA: METRICS. (PB 278566)

Mason, R. M. (1979). *A study of the perceived benefits of information analysis center services*. (Final Report National Science Foundation Contract No. DSI-7718035). Atlanta, GA: METRICS.

Mason, R. M. & Creps, J. E., Jr. (Eds.). (1981). *Information services: Economics, management, and technology*. Boulder, CO: Westview Press.

Meadow, C. T. (1981). Matching users and user languages in information retrieval. *Online Review, 5,* 313–322.

Meadow, C. T. & Cochrane, P. A. (1981). *Basics of online searching*. New York: Wiley.

Meindell, J. (1982). The abundance of solutions: Some thoughts for theoretical and practical solution seekers. *Administrative Science Quarterly, 27,* 670–685.

Mick, C. K., Lindsey, G. N., & Callahan, D. (1980). Toward usable user studies. *Journal of the American Society for Information Science, 31,* 347–356.

Mintzberg, H. (1975). The manager's job: Folklore and fact. *Harvard Business Review, 53*(4), 49–61.

Mintzberg, H. (1979). *The structuring of organizations*. Englewood Cliffs, NJ: Prentice-Hall.

Mintzberg, H., Raisinghani, D. & Theoret, A. (1976). The structure of "unstructured" decision processes. *Administrative Science Quarterly, 21,* 246–275.

Mooers, C. N. (1960). Mooers' Law, or, why some retrieval systems are used and others are not. *American Documentation, 11*(3), ii.

Moore, G. (1981). *Organizational structure and the politics of MIS*. Paper for IST 684. Syracuse, NY: Syracuse University, School of Information Studies.

Morison, E. E. (1974). *From know-how to nowhere: The development of American technology*. New York: Basic Books.

Mowshowitz, A. (1976). *The conquest of will: Information processing in human affairs*. Reading, MA: Addison-Wesley.

National Academy of Sciences. (1969). *Scientific and technical communication: A pressing national problem and recommendations for its solution*. Washington, DC: Author.

National Federation of Abstracting and Information Services. (1982). *Member services statistics*. Philadelphia: Author.

National Federation of Science Abstracting and Indexing Services. (1963). *A guide to the world's abstracting and indexing services in science and technology* (Report No. 102). Washington, DC: Author.

National Research Council. Panel to Review Productivity Statistics. (1979). *Measurement and interpretation of productivity*. Washington, DC: National Academy of Sciences.

Naylor, T. H. (1980). *Strategic planning management*. Oxford, OH: Planning Executives Institute.

Neelameghan, A. (1980). Information-for-action systems: Challenge to classification and indexing. In P. J. Taylor (Ed.), *New trends in documentation and information* (pp.

203–213). Proceedings of the 39th FID Congress, University of Edinburgh, 25–28 December 1978. London: Aslib/FID.

Neufeld, M. L. & Cornog, M. (1983). Secondary information systems and services: Current issues and trends. In M. E. Williams (Ed.), *Annual review of information science and technology* (Vol. 18, pp. 151–183). White Plains, NY: Knowledge Industry Publications.

Neuman, J. L. (1976). Make overhead cuts that last. *Harvard Business Review, 54*(3), 116–126.

Newell, A. & Simon, H. (1972). *Human problem solving*. Englewood Cliffs, NJ: Prentice-Hall.

Packer, M. B. (1981). Measuring the intangible in productivity. *Technology Review, 86*(2), 48–57.

Paisley, W. J. (1980). Information and work. In B. Dervin & M. J. Voigt (Eds.), *Progress in communication sciences* (Vol. 2, pp. 113–165). Norwood, NJ: Ablex.

Paisley, W. J. & Butler, M. (1977). *Computer assistance in information work.* (Report, National Science Foundation Contract No C76–05489). Palo Alto, CA: Applied Communication Research.

Parikh, G. (1981). How to measure programmer productivity. *Computerworld, 15*(14), 55–59.

Pelz, D. C. & Andrews, F. M. (1966). *Scientists in organizations: productive climates for research and development*. New York: Wiley.

Pfeiffer, J. E. (1977). *The emergence of society: A prehistory of the establishment*. New York: McGraw-Hill.

Pollet, D. & Haskell, P. C. (Eds.). (1979). *Sign systems for libraries*. New York: Bowker.

Porat, M. (1977). *The information economy: Definition and measurement* (9 vols). Washington, DC: US Department of Commerce, Office of Telecommunications.

Powell, R. W. & Touloukian, Y. F. (1973). Thermal conductivity of the elements. *Science, 181,* 999–1008.

Powers, T. M. (1980). *The economic value of the quality of life*. Boulder, CO: Westview Press.

Price, D. (1965). Is technology historically independent of science? A study in statistical historiography. *Technology and Culture, 6,* 553–568.

Ramsey, H. R. & Grimes, J. D. (1983). Human factors in interactive computer dialog. In M. E. Williams (Ed.), *Annual review of information science and technology* (Vol. 18, pp. 29–59). White Plains, NY: Knowledge Industry Publications.

Richardson, W. J. (1976). *Cost improvement, work sampling, and short interval scheduling*. Reston, VA: Reston Publishing.

Rockart, J. (1979). Chief executives define their own data needs. *Harvard Business Review, 57,* 81–93.

Rosenberg, V. (1966). *The application of psychometric techniques to determine the attitudes of individuals toward information seeking*. Unpublished master's thesis, Lehigh University, Center for the Information Sciences, Bethlehem, PA.

Rouse, W. B. & Rouse, S. H. (1984). Human information seeking and design of information systems. *Information Processing and Management, 20*(1–2), 129–138.

Roussel, P. A. (1983). Cutting down the guesswork in R & D. *Harvard Business Review, 61*(5), 154–160.

Sabatier, P. (1978). The acquisition and utilization of technical information by administrative agencies. *Administrative Science Quarterly, 23,* 396–417.

Saracevic, T. (1970). The concept of "relevance" in information science: A historical review. In T. Saracevic (Ed.). *Introduction to information science* (pp. 111–151). New York: Bowker.

Saracevic, T. (1971). Selected results from an inquiry into testing of information retrieval systems. *Journal of the American Society for Information Science, 22,* 126–139.

Schmittroth, J., Jr. (Ed.). (1982). *Abstracting and indexing services directory*. Detroit, MI: Gale.

Schuchman, H. L. (1981). *Information transfer in engineering*. Glastonbury, CT: The Futures Group.

Simon, H. A. (1969). *The sciences of the artificial.* Cambridge, MA: MIT Press.

Simon, H. A. (1970). The new science of management decision. In L. A. Welsch & R. M. Cyert (Eds.), *Management decision making* (pp. 13–29). Baltimore, MD: Penguin.

Simon, H. A. (1971). Designing organization for an information-rich world. In M. Greenberger (Ed.), *Computers, communications, and the public interest* (pp. 38–52). Baltimore, MD: Johns Hopkins Press.

Simon, H. A. (1976). *Administrative behavior: A study of decision-making processes in administrative organization* (3rd ed.). New York: Free Press.

Simon, H. A. (1977). *The new science of management decision*. Englewood Cliffs, NJ: Prentice-Hall.

Simpson, G. S., Jr. (1962). Scientific information centers in the United States. *American Documentation, 13,* 43–57.

Slamecka, V. (1970). Methods and research for design of information networks. *Library Trends,* 18, 551–568.

Smith, C. S. (1981). *A search for structure: Selected essays on science, art, and history*. Cambridge, MA: MIT Press.

Sowell, T. (1980). *Knowledge and decisions*. New York: Basic Books.

Spence, A. M. (1974). An economist's view of information. In C. Cuadra (Ed.), *Annual review of information science and technology* (Vol. 9, pp. 57–78). Washington, DC: American Society for Information Science.

Stankard, M. F. (1981). *Successful management of large clerical operations*. New York: McGraw-Hill.

Starr, M. K. (1971). *Management: A modern approach*. New York: Harcourt Brace Jovanovitch.

Strassmann, P. A. (1976). Managing the costs of information. *Harvard Business Review, 54*(5), 133–142.

Strassmann, P. A. (1977). Organizational productivity—The role of information technology. In B. Gilchrist (Ed.), *IFIP Congress Proceedings* (Vol. 77, pp. 503–508). Amsterdam: North-Holland.

Strassmann, P. A. (1980). The office of the future: Information management for the new age. *Technology Review,* 82(3), 54–65.

Sutherland, J. W. (1977). *Administrative decision-making: Extending the bounds of rationality*. New York: Van Nostrand Reinhold.

Swanson, R. W. (1975). Performing evaluation studies in information science. *Journal of the American Society for Information Science, 26,* 140–156.

Swanson, R. W. (1982). An assessment of online instruction methodologies. *Online, 6*(1), 38–53.

Syracuse University. School of Information Studies. (1982, June). *A study of the impact of representations in information retrieval systems,* Final Report, (NSF/DIST 79–21468)

J. Katzer, Principal Investigator.

Taylor, R. S. (1962). The process of asking questions. *American Documentation, 13,* 391–396.

Taylor, R. S. (1968). Question negotiation and information seeking in libraries, *College & Research Libraries, 29,* 178–194.

Taylor, R. S. (1975). Patterns toward a user-centered academic library. In E. J. Josey (Ed.), *New dimensions for academic library service* (pp. 298–304). Metuchen, NJ: Scarecrow Press.

Taylor, R. S. (1980). Information and productivity: Definition and relationships. In: *Proceedings of the 43rd ASIS Annual Meeting* (Vol. 17, pp. 236–238). White Plains, NY: Knowledge Industry Publications.

Taylor, R. S. (1981). On defining organizational information environments. In *Proceedings of the 44th ASIS Annual Meeting* (Vol. 18, pp. 129–131). White Plains, NY: Knowledge Industry Publications.

Taylor, R. S. (1982a). Benefits and costs of information use. In *Proceedings of the 45th ASIS Annual Meeting* (Vol. 19, pp. 296–297). White Plains, NY: Knowledge Industry Publications.

Taylor, R. S. (1982b). Organizational information environments. *Proceedings of the International Conference on Information and the Transformation of Society,* Dublin, Eire, June 1982 (pp. 309–322). Amsterdam: North-Holland.

Taylor, R. S. (1982c). Value-added processes in the information life-cycle. *Journal of the American Society for Information Science, 33,* 341–346.

Taylor, R. S. (1982d). Information and productivity: On defining information output (I). *Social Science Information Studies, 2,* 131–138.

Taylor, R. S. (1983). *Value-added processes in the information life cycle.* Final Report (National Science Foundation Grant No. IST-81-06080). Syracuse, NY: Syracuse University, School of Information Studies.

Taylor, R. S. (1984a). Information and productivity: On defining information output (II). *Social Science Information Studies, 4,* 31–41.

Taylor, R. S. (1984b). Value-added processes in document-based systems: Abstracting and indexing services. *Information Services and Use, 4*(3), 127–146.

Taylor, R. S. (1984c). Value-added processes in information analysis. *Proceedings of the 46th ASIS Annual Meeting* (Vol. 20, pp. 7–9). White Plains, NY: Knowledge Industry Publications.

Toffler, A. (1980). *The third wave.* New York: William Morrow.

Trueswell, R. L. (1969). Some behavioral patterns of library users: The 80/20 rule. *Wilson Library Bulletin, 43,* 458–461.

Tukey, J. W. (1977). *Exploratory data analysis.* Reading, MA: Addison-Wesley.

Tversky, A. & Kahneman, D. (1981). The framing of decisions and the psychology of choice. *Science,* 221, 453–458.

U. S. Comptroller General. (1980). *Report to the Congress—The value-added tax in the European Economic Community.* Washington, DC: General Accounting Office.

Van de Ven, A. H. & Ferry, D. L. (1980). *Measuring and assessing organizations.* New York: Wiley.

Waldrop, M. M. (1984). The necessity of knowledge. *Science, 223,* 1279–1282.

Wallin, C. C. (1982, March). *Information Analysis—The elusive imperative.* Paper presented to Chemical Information Division of the American Chemical Society, Las Vegas, NV.

Warner, E. S., Murray, A. D. & Palmour, V. E. (1973). *Information needs of urban residents*. Final Report from Regional Planning Council of Baltimore and Westat, Inc., Rockville, MD., to the US Department of Health, Education, and Welfare, Office of Education, under Contract No. OEC–0–71–455.

Weisman, H. M. (1972). *Information systems, services, and centers*. New York: Becker & Hayes.

Westbrook, J. H. (1981a). *EMPIS: A materials data program*. (General Electric Company, Corporate Research and Development, Technical Information Series Class 1, Report No. 80 CRD297, Feb. 1981.) Also available in *Proceedings*, Eighth International CODATA Conference, Kyoto, Japan, 1980. New York: Pergamon. 1981.

Westbrook, J. H. (1981b). Material standards and specifications. In *Kirk-Othmer: Encyclopedia of chemical technology*, vol. 15, Third ed. New York: Wiley.

Westbrook, J. H. (1983a). Extraction and compilation of numerical and factual data. Paris: North Atlantic Treaty Organization, Advisory Group for Aerospace Research & Development. Lecture Series No. 130, *Development and use of numerical and factual data bases*, 4–1—4–15.

Westbrook, J. H. (1983b). Progress toward a coordinated system of databases covering the engineering properties of materials. Paris: North Atlantic Treaty Organization, Advisory Group for Aerospace Research & Development. Lecture Series No. 130, *Development and use of numerical and factual data bases*, 9–1—9–9.

Williams, M. E., Lannom, L. and Robins, C. (Compilers). 1982. *Computer-readable databases: A directory and data sourcebook*. White Plains, NY: Knowledge Industry Publications.

Wilson, P. (1978). Some fundamental concepts of information retrieval. *Drexel Library Quarterly, 14*(2), 10–23.

Wood, E. G. (1978). *Added value*. London, Business Books.

Yellott, L. (1982). Onondaga County Public Library and the Consumer Health Information Consortium (CHIC) Syracuse. In A. M. Rees, (Ed.), *Developing consumer health information services* (pp. 51–79). New York: Bowker.

Zand, D. E. (1981). *Information, organization, and power*. New York: McGraw-Hill.

Zweizig, D. & Rodger, E. J. (1982). *Output measures for public libraries*. Chicago: American Library Association.

APPENDIX A

INTERVIEW GUIDE

Note: This guide was used in connection with the NSF Project to develop data on value-added processes in abstracting and indexing services described in Chapter Six.

1.0 *User Interface*. (Describe for different products if needed)
1.1 *Description of User and Use*
1.1.1 How is the "user" defined?
1.1.2 What are criteria for defining the user?
1.1.3 Who decides who the user is?
1.1.4 Who actually uses the service?
1.1.5 How is it used? (probe–open-ended)
1.1.6 What kinds of user problems is the service (product) designed to respond to?
1.2 *Market/Marketing Research* (Describe for different products if needed)
1.2.1 How is 'potential user' (desired customer) defined?
1.2.2 Is 'potential user' of the market concept different from the actual user?
1.2.3 What is being 'sold'? For what purpose? (product, service, information, bibliography, access)
1.3 *User Education*
1.3.1 How is user education conducted? (For whom? How often? How publicized? Free? Fee?)
1.3.2 Who performs user education?
1.3.3 How are user education programs designed? (What inputs? Users? User patterns? Competition?)
1.3.4 What are the objectives of the user education program?
1.3.5 How are costs determined for user education programs?
1.3.6 Who designs user education programs? Who makes final decisions?

2.0 *Management Information Systems*. (Note that the managers of the agency or service are the users in this context.)
2.1 What are the procedures and systems for monitoring your internal systems?
2.2 How are data defined (within context of MIS)?
2.3 How are data collected? Frequency? Kinds?
2.4 What reports are issued regularly?
2.4.1 Are these reports used? By whom?
2.4.2 How are they used?
2.5 How do these data and reports aid you in operational decision making, managerial decision making, quality control, long-range planning, etc.?
2.5.1 What kinds of information do you as a manager require to fulfill your regular responsibilities?

2.5.2 Are you getting those kinds of information?
2.5.3 How much would you be willing to 'pay' to get those kinds of information? (e.g., What are the costs and benefits of getting the kinds of information you need?)
2.6 What policies govern data collection and reports for managerial control and decision making? What is rationale behind these policies?

3.0 Input
3.1 Selection of All Forms of Input (serials/items/etc.)
3.1.1 How are serials (items) selected for inclusion in the service? (Note differences in services.)
3.1.2 What are sources of candidate serials (items, etc.)?
3.1.3 What criteria are used for selection? How are they applied? (Note this may vary from full coverage to selective coverage, also possibly other arrangements.)
3.1.4 How are these criteria developed? Modified?
3.1.5 Who develops the selection criteria?
3.3 Acquisition
3.3.1 How are items acquired? (purchase, exchange, gift? jobber, direct publisher contact? Other?)
3.3.2 How is an item, for purposes of acquisition, defined? (an abstract? or, if abstracting is farmed out, the abstractors may be a form of input to the system)
3.4 Serials/Item Control
3.4.1 How are serials/items checked in on arrival?
3.4.2 How are items tracked as they progress through the system?
3.4.3 Who does the tracking? In other words, Who has responsibility to see that production and 'speed' are maintained?
3.4.4 How are items claimed if they are not received in reasonable time?
3.4.5 Who makes decisions concerning serials/item control policies and procedures?
(Note: Here we shift attention to the entire input process.)
3.5 Input Summary (e.g., selection, claiming, control)
3.5.1 Are there other ways of handling input activities than those you presently use?
3.5.2 Do you have formal or semiformal guidelines, or even written standards or policies for input activities? (Note: These may have already been remarked on under the separate sections. If so, summarize only.)
3.5.3 How do you relate your decisions on input activities specifically to user benefits? i.e., How does the user (however defined) benefit from the decisions and policies you make?
3.6 Costing (Note: we may not want to pursue this too deeply at this point, saving it for the end. However, we do wish to keep an awareness of this throughout the interview because it is key. Emphasize costing processes, not costs.)
3.6.1 Methods of costing the *total* input activity?
3.6.2 Is it possible to break down costing by discrete types of activities? (e.g., selecting, claiming, etc.)
3.6.3 Is it possible to derive incremental costs (e.g., for single selection, single claiming, etc.)
3.6.4 Are regular reports generated relative to costing the input process, or any part of it? How often?
3.6.5 Are special costing studies made?
3.6.6 How do these reports (regular and special) and data aid in operational decision making, managerial decision making, quality control, long-range planning, etc.?

4.0 *Processing*
4.1 *Citation Development*
4.1.1 How are citations picked up (source)?
4.1.2 How are citations modified or augmented? (e.g., title, author, address, etc.)
4.1.3 What data elements are selected? Why?
4.1.4 How is citation formatted and recorded? (e.g., keyed directly, coding, or data sheet?)
4.1.5 Who develops and records the citations?
4.1.6 How is data entered in system and who does it?
4.1.7 What editing and verification procedures are performed, and who does them?
4.1.8 Are translations made? From what languages? Who does translating?
4.1.9 Who makes decisions regarding citation development standards and procedures?
4.2 *Indexing*
4.2.1 How are index terms chosen? (e.g., thesaurus; keyword from title/abstract/document; subject heading list)
4.2.2 How are new index terms derived or chosen?
4.2.3 How many terms are typically chosen per item? What is range?
4.2.4 At what level of specificity (how deep) is the indexing?
4.2.5 What types of indexes are produced? (Note: We may wish to ask here how users may benefit from these different kinds of indexes.)
4.2.6 How are index terms formatted and recorded?
4.2.7 Who chooses and records the index terms?
4.2.8 How are data entered into system and who does it?
4.2.9 What are the editing/verification procedures and who performs these functions?
4.2.10 Who makes decisions regarding indexing standards and procedures?
4.3 *Vocabulary Creation/Maintenance* (Note: Portions of this may already have been covered in the Indexing section, 4.2)
4.3.1 What are procedures for creating/maintaining vocabulary?
4.3.2 What are the sources of new terms?
4.3.3 How frequently is vocabulary updated?
4.3.4 Who creates and maintains vocabulary?
4.3.5 What standards/criteria are used to maintain consistency?
4.3.6 What kinds of statistics are kept on the vocabulary?
4.3.7 How is the process of vocabulary creation/maintenance costed?
4.3.8 Who makes decisions regarding these processes and standards?
4.4 *Abstracting*
4.4.1 What are procedures for using (or modifying) an existing abstract?
4.4.2 What are procedures for creating a new abstract? (Type: indicative, informative, etc.) Length?
4.4.3 How is abstract formatted and recorded?
4.4.4 Who creates/modifies abstracts?
4.4.5 How is data entered and who does the entering?
4.4.6 What are the procedures for editing/verification, and who does it?
4.4.7 Are translations made? From what languages? Who does translating?
4.4.8 Who makes decisions concerning abstracting standards and procedures?
(Note: Here we shift to entire Processing activities.)
4.5 *Processing Summary* (e.g. citation development, indexing, vocabulary creation/maintenance, abstracting)

4.5.1 Are there other ways of handling processing activities than those you presently use?

4.5.2 Do you have formal or semiformal guidelines/even written standards or policies for processing activities? (Note: These may have already been covered in the separate sections above. If so, summarize only.)

4.5.3 How do you relate your decisions on processing specifically to user benefits: How does user benefit from the policies you make?

4.6 *Costing* (Note: We may not wish to pursue this too deeply at this point, saving it for the end. However, we do wish to keep an awareness of this throughout the interview. Emphasize costing, not costs.)

4.6.1 Methods of costing the total processing activity.

4.6.2 Is it possible to break down costing by discrete types of activities? (e.g., indexing, abstracting, etc.)

4.6.3 Is it possible to derive incremental costs? (e.g., for modifying abstract, augmenting title, etc.)

4.6.4 Are regular reports generated relative to costing processing activities? Or any parts of them? How often?

4.6.5 Are special costing studies made?

4.6.6 How do these reports (regular and special) and data aid in operational decision making, quality control, long-range planning, etc.?

5.0 *Output and Dissemination*

5.1 What are the major products? (or families of products?) (Note: This should be covered fairly well ahead of time by project personnel. Major interest here is to explore market segmentation, special design for particular types of users, and how user benefits are perceived.)

5.2 Differences in coverage (including size, shape, format) between similar products (e.g., between print and online).

5.3 How do these differences affect use and users?

5.4 How are products disseminated/sold? (e.g., Product *X* is an SDI service disseminated bimonthly and sold on a subscription basis.) Do the processes of dissemination have an effect on use and user?

5.5 Are there other ways of handling output activities?

5.6 Since these activities are directly related to users, how do you perceive them as benefiting the user? Examples?

5.7 Is it possible to cost the total output activity?

5.8 Is it possible to break down costing by discrete types of activity, especially as it might relate to user benefits? (e.g., speed of delivery?)

6.0 *Planning/Product Design*

6.1 How are new products developed?

6.2 How are old products changed? What constitutes a change?

6.3 What inputs are used for product design or change? (Users? Use patterns? Competition? New technologies? Costs? etc.)

6.4 How are product changes perceived as affecting use?

6.5 Who participates in planning and product design?

6.6 Who makes final decisions on product changes or new products?

6.7 Is it possible to cost out the design and development of a new product? Of a major product change?

6.8 Can this costing process be related to benefit for the potential user or client group?

7.0 *Systems* (In this context, a system is a sequential set of processes designed to fulfill some specific function. A system may range from completely manual to completely automated, or any combination in between. For our purposes here, it is a convenient way of looking at the total operation, picking up some loose ends, and summarizing.)

7.1 *System Development*

7.1.1 Why is a system developed or changed? (e.g., new product; new equipment; personnel reorganization; productivity improvement, etc.)

7.1.2 How is a new system developed? Who has responsibility?

7.1.3 How are managerial controls built into the system? (e.g., data generation and reporting.) Probe here particularly what it is a manager needs to know from a new system in order to judge its effectiveness and efficiency.

7.1.4 How is system development related to user benefit?

7.1.5 How are costs for system development determined? How are they charged? Overhead? Chargeback?

7.2 *Standards*

7.2.1 Is there a unified approach to system standards (not covered in previous questions)? Describe.

7.2.2 To what extent do standards follow industry-wide norms?

7.2.3 What effect do the standards have on use? On users?

7.2.4 What effect do the standards have on costs? Can this indeed be costed?

7.3 *Staff Training*

7.3.1 What are the objectives of staff training?

7.3.2 How is staff training conducted? (Who is trained? For how long?) Who does the training?

7.3.3 Who has input to the design of training programs?

7.3.4 How does staff training benefit users or clients?

7.4 *System Documentation*

7.4.1 How are systems and processes documented?

7.4.2 How is documentation maintained and who has responsibility?

8.0 *Summary*

"Walk" quickly through total system again, summarizing processes or decision points where a value has been identified and added. Clarify and expand these particular activities, especially in relation to user benefits and system costing.

APPENDIX B

ABSTRACTING AND INDEXING PROCESSES/VALUES ADDED

The following table is organized by the processes illustrated in Figure 6-1. The table is formatted by major process, then by a sampling of specific activities in that process where value is added. On the right side of the table are those values added by that specific activity, as judged by the project staff. The phrase for the activities where value is added is a greatly reduced description from the original interview, edited for clarity and simplicity. Equivalent phrases may have occurred in several different interviews. Such repetitions are not shown.

SELECTION AND ACQUISITION

	Value-added Activities	Values Added
1.	Revision of record if a more complete version of an already selected item arrives	Reliability
2.	Consistency of input taken into account during the selection process	Reliability
3.	Upgrade quality in selection (due to budget cuts)	Selectivity
4.	Little knowledge about projected quantity and quality of input	Minus reliability
5.	Use formal printed criteria for selection	Reliability
6.	Hold regular meetings to redefine selection criteria	Selectivity, reliability
7.	Set coverage policy at high corporate level	Reliability
8.	Include marginal items because "one person's common knowledge or junk lit is another's find-of-the-year"	Comprehensiveness, minus selectivity
9.	Budget and costs govern coverage/selection	Selectivity
10.	Retain broader coverage because it serves more users	Comprehensiveness
11.	Cover original material only, not translations or reprints	Selectivity
12.	Cover principal sci–tech languages	Comprehensiveness
13.	Cover research, not popular materials	Selectivity

Value-Added Activities	Values Added
14. Negotiating to cover USSR and East German patents	Comprehensiveness
15. Online covers some items not covered in print version	Minus reliability (for print), comprehensiveness
16. Use relevance to subject as major criteria for selection, not quality	Selectivity, minus validity
17. Change coverage as research emphasis in the field changes	Reliability, selectivity
18. Cover core area comprehensively: peripheral areas, more limited	Comprehensiveness, selectivity, reliability
19. Currently doing a study to identify "strong" areas of coverage	Selectivity
20. Provide coverage which overlaps with other services	Comprehensiveness
21. Use advisory groups, staff, and users to select journals	Selectivity
22. Have one department whose sole function is to select new journals	Reliability
23. Monitor journal coverage of other organizations	Selectivity
24. Selection from publishers' brochures	Selectivity
25. Select from recommendations of consultants and outsiders	Selectivity
26. Use circulation figures to evaluate journals for selection	Selectivity
27. Use citation rates to evaluate journals for selection	Selectivity
28. Use input from users and customers in journal selection	Selectivity
29. Editorial board helps select journals	Selectivity
30. Outside peer review group evaluates journals for selection	Reliability, selectivity
31. Designate staff members whose only job is to select items	Reliability
32. Select *all* items from core journals, selectively from others	Reliability, comprehensiveness, selectivity
33. Select conference proceedings papers individually	Selectivity
34. Editor checks selection	Reliability
35. Establish average percent "yield" for journals	Selectivity
36. Obtain material in machine-readable form	Cost savings

CONTROL/CLAIMING

Value-Added Activities	**Values Added**
1. Claim missing journal issues	Currency, reliability
2. Borrow missing journal issues, index before claim comes through	Currency, reliability

3. Do not cover item if it arrives very late (keep data base current)	Currency, minus reliability, minus comprehensiveness
4. Claim item four times	Reliability
5. Twenty-four hour processing cycle for one data base (overnight input)	Currency
6. Use automatic journal control/claim system	Currency, reliability
7. Have three subscriptions to each journal, each delivered a different way, so that one comes in promptly	Currency, reliability, Response speed
8. No method for claiming	Minus comprehensiveness, minus currency; minus reliability

CITATION DEVELOPMENT

Value-added Activities	**Values Added**
1. Standardize citation format	Reliability, accuracy, formating
2. Use MARC standard for citation	Reliability, accuracy, formating
3. Standardize one or more data elements in citation	Accuracy, reliability
4. List all authors	Access I
5. Give full name of author(s)	Access I
6. Provide subtitle as well as title	Access I

CITATION AUGMENTATION

Value-added Activities	**Values Added**
1. Translate citation (title and/or journal name)	Selectivity
2. Provide document location	Physical accessibility, Access I
3. Provide CODEN	Ordering, Access II
4. Give language of document	Access I
5. Give molecular formula	Access II, Access III, ordering
6. Give Chemical Abstracts Registry System name	Linkage

INDEXING

Value-added Activities	**Values Added**
1. Provide an inventory index to patents	Access II
2. Indexing done by generalists, reviewed by subject specialists	Access II, accuracy, reliability
3. Conduct lengthy, in-house training for staff (key input, indexing, abstracting, editing)	Accuracy, reliability
4. Require that indexers go to an online training session for the data base	Reliability
5. Test regularly interindexing consistency	Accuracy

6. Assign subject categories (as well as index terms)	Ordering
7. Cross-reference subject categories	Access II, ordering
8. Use a controlled vocabulary for indexing	Precision, reliability
9. Update controlled vocabulary yearly/regularly	Currency
10. Choose new terms through advisory groups, other organizations, documents and subject experts	Precision, reliability
11. Assign large number of index terms per document (range from 5–6 up to 40–55)	Access II, precision
12. Up-post automatically within hierarchical vocabulary	Browsing, Access II
13. Segment some compound words to produce additional access points	Access II
14. Index separate chapters in a book (analytics)	Access II
15. Use identifiers/keywords for indexing	Access II
16. Use *both* controlled vocabulary and identifiers for indexing	Access II
17. Augmenting title with terms suitable for indexing	Access II
18. Use references as index terms	Browsing, linkage
19. Hire indexers with both subject *and* language expertise	Reliability
20. Use large staff of revisers for indexing	Accuracy
21. Provide an index guide (publication) to assist user	Interfacing II
22. Indicate cluster of related fields	Browsing, Ordering
23. Pointer to/from another database	Linkage

ABSTRACTING

Value-added Activities	**Values Added**
1. Use subject specialist as abstractors	Access III
2. Provide in-house training for abstractors	Accuracy, reliability
3. Use author abstracts	Cost savings
4. Send request to journal editors that abstracts printed in journals be improved	Reliability
5. Prepare informative abstracts	Interfacing I
6. Prepare indicative abstracts for conference proceedings	Access III
7. Slant abstracts to users	Precision
8. Use standardized format for abstracts	Reliability, formating
9. Have two-week quality control cycle: editing, proofing	Accuracy, response speed
10. Have abstracts available online (in-house processing)	Physical accessibility, accuracy

EDITING AND KEYING

Value-added Activities	Values Added
1. Have editing and proofing procedures	Accuracy
2. Have online editing system with error-correcting software	Accuracy
3. Require double keying of all information	Accuracy
4. Have "keysave" software which lowers keystrokes and reduces cost	Accuracy, Cost savings
5. Employ data entry personnel who can translate Cyrillic into English at the terminal	Cost savings

FORMATING

Value-added Activities	Values Added
1. Provide alphabetical sequence for items	Ordering
2. Provide subject groupings for items	Ordering
3. Group items by journal of origin	Ordering
4. Make "citation cycling" possible	Browsing, flexibility
5. Reformat new products from same database	Physical accessibility, formating

DISSEMINATION

Value-added Activities	Values Added
1. Scan input search by code number (for 1,800 different searches)	Ordering
2. Provide personal copy of product to keep or throw away	Physical accessibility
3. User-friendly hardware	Physical accessibility
4. User-friendly software	Interfacing II
5. Producer handles system maintenance	Physical accessibility
6. Provide rapid response time	Response speed
7. Use airmail for European delivery	Currency
8. Can change SDI profiles (on request) immediately	Precision, flexibility, currency
9. Provide document delivery	Physical accessibility, response speed
10. Provide access to outside data bases through terminals	Linkage, physical accessibility
11. Allow downloading	Flexibility, physical accessibility

AUTHOR INDEX

SUBJECT INDEX